Joint Workshop on Exploiting Synergies Between Information Retrieval and Machine Translation (ESIRMT) and Hybrid Approaches to Machine Translation (HyTra) 2012

Held at the 13th Conference of the European Chapter of the Association for Computational Linguistics (EACL 2012)

Avignon, France
23-24 April 2012

ISBN: 978-1-62276-470-9

Printed from e-media with permission by:

Curran Associates, Inc.
57 Morehouse Lane
Red Hook, NY 12571

Printed by Curran Associates, Inc. (2013)

Association for Computational Linguistics
209 N. Eighth Street
Stroudsburg, Pennsylvania 18360

Phone: 1-570-476-8006
Fax: 1-570-476-0860

acl@aclweb.org

Additional copies of this publication are available from:

Curran Associates, Inc.
57 Morehouse Lane
Red Hook, NY 12571 USA
Phone: 845-758-0400
Fax: 845-758-2634
Email: curran@proceedings.com
Web: www.proceedings.com

Introduction

Welcome to the Joint EACL Workshop on Exploiting Synergies between Information Retrieval and Machine Translation (ESIRMT) and Hybrid Approaches to Machine Translation (HyTra). This two-day workshop addresses two specific but related research problems in computational linguistics.

The ESIRMT event (1st day) aims at reducing the gap, both theoretical and practical, between information retrieval and machine translation research and applications. Although both fields have been already contributing to each other instrumentally, there is still too much work to be done in relation to solidly framing these two fields into a common ground of knowledge from both the procedural and paradigmatic perspectives.

The HyTra event (2nd day) aims at sharing ideas among researchers developing and applying statistical, example-based, or rule-based machine translation systems and who wish to enhance their systems with elements from the other approaches.

The joint workshop provides participants with the opportunity of discussing research related to technology integration and system combination strategies at both the general level of cross-language information access and the specific level of machine translation technologies.

This workshop has been supported by the Seventh Framework Programme of the European Comission through the T4ME (METANET) contract (grant agreement no.: 249119), through the TTC contract (grant agreement no.: 248005), through the Marie Curie HyghTra contract and by the Spanish Ministry of Economy and Competivity through the BUCEADOR project (TEC2009-14094-C04-01) and the Juan de la Cierva fellowship program.

We would like to thank all people who in one way or another helped in making this workshop a success. Our special thanks go to our plenary speakers, to the speakers of our invited project session, to our sponsors, to the participants of the panel discussion, to the members of the program committee who did an excellent job in reviewing the submitted papers, and to the EACL organizers, in particular the workshop general chairs Kristiina Jokinen and Alessandro Moschitti. Last but not least we would like to thank our authors and the participants of the workshop.

The Organizers
Avignon, France, April 2012

Organizers ESIRMT:

Marta R. Costa-jussà (Barcelona Media Innovation Center)
Patrik Lambert (University of Le Mans)
Rafael E. Banchs (Institute for Infocomm Research)

Organizers HyTra:

Reinhard Rapp (Universities of Mainz and Leeds)
Bogdan Babych (University of Leeds)
Kurt Eberle (Lingenio GmbH)
Tony Hartley (Toyohashi University of Technology and University of Leeds)
Serge Sharoff (University of Leeds)
Martin Thomas (University of Leeds)

Program Committee:

Jordi Atserias, Yahoo! Research , Barcelona, Spain
Sivaji Bandyopadhyay, Jadavpur University, Kolkata, India
Núria Bel, Universitat Pompeu Fabra, Barcelona, Spain
Pierrette Bouillon, ISSCO/TIM/ETI, University of Geneva, Switzerland
Chris Callison-Burch, Johns Hopkins University, Baltimore, USA
Michael Carl, Copenhagen Business School, Denmark
Oliver Culo, ICSI, University of California, Berkeley, USA
Andreas Eisele, Directorate-General for Translation, European Commission, Luxembourg
Marcello Federico, Fondazione Bruno Kessler, Trento, Italy
José A. R. Fonollosa, Universitat Politècnica de Catalunya, Barcelona, Spain
Mikel Forcada, University of Alicante, Spain
Alexander Fraser, Institute for Natural Language Processing (IMS), Stuttgart, Germany
Johanna Geiß, Lingenio GmbH, Heidelberg, Germany
Mireia Ginesti-Rosell, Lingenio GmbH, Heidelberg, Germany
Silvia Hansen-Schirra, FTSK, University of Mainz, Germany
Gareth Jones, Dublin City University, Ireland
Min-Yen Kan, National University of Singapore
Udo Kruschwitz, University of Essex, UK
Yanjun Ma, Baidu Inc. Beijing, China
Maite Melero, Barcelona Media Innovation Center, Barcelona, Spain
Haizhou Li, Institute for Infocomm Research, Singapore
Paul Schmidt, Institut for Applied Information Science, Saarbrücken, Germany
Uta Seewald-Heeg, Anhalt University of Applied Sciences, Köthen, Germany
Nasredine Semmar, CEA LIST, Fontenay-aux-Roses, France
Wade Shen, Massachusetts Institute of Technology, Cambridge, USA
Fabrizio Silvestri, Instituto de Scienza e Tecnologia del'Informazione, Pisa, Italy
Harold Somers, CNGL, Dublin City University, Ireland
Anders Søgaard, University of Copenhagen, Denmark
Jörg Tiedemann, University of Uppsala, Sweden
Zygmunt Vetulani, University of Poznan, Poland

Invited Speakers:

Christof Monz (University of Amsterdam)
Philipp Koehn (University of Edinburgh)

Speakers of the Invited Project Session:

Cristina Vertan
George Tambouratzis, Marina Vassiliou and Sokratis Sofianopoulos John Tinsley, Alexandru Ceausu and Jian Zhang
Svetla Koeva

Table of Contents

ESIRMT-HyTra Workshop Program

Monday 23rd

(9:00-9:30) Workshop Presentation

(9:30-10:30) Invited Talk Christof Monz

(10:30-11:00) Coffee break

(11:00-11:30) ESIRMT Morning Session

Semantic Web based Machine Translation
Bettina Harriehausen-Mühlbauer and Timm Heuss

(11:30-12:00)

Measuring Comparability of Documents in Non-Parallel Corpora for Efficient Extraction of (Semi-)Parallel Translation Equivalents
Fangzhong Su and Bogdan Babych

(12:00-12:30)

Full Machine Translation for Factoid Question Answering
Cristina España-Bonet and Pere R. Comas

(12:30-13:00)

An Empirical Evaluation of Stop Word Removal in Statistical Machine Translation
Tze Yuang Chong, Rafael Banchs and Eng Siong Chng

Monday 23rd (continued)

(13:00-15:00) Lunch break

(15:00-15:30) ESIRMT Afternoon Session

Natural Language Descriptions of Visual Scenes Corpus Generation and Analysis
Muhammad Usman Ghani Khan, Rao Muhammad Adeel Nawab and Yoshihiko Gotoh

(15:30-16:00)

Combining EBMT, SMT, TM and IR Technologies for Quality and Scale
Sandipan Dandapat, Sara Morrissey, Andy Way and Josef van Genabith

(16:00-16:30) Coffee break

(16:30-17:00) Project session

Two approaches for integrating translation and retrieval in real applications
Cristina Vertan

(17:00-17:30)

PRESEMT: Pattern Recognition-based Statistically Enhanced MT
George Tambouratzis, Marina Vassiliou and Sokratis Sofianopoulos

(17:30-18:00)

PLUTO: Automated Solutions for Patent Translation
John Tinsley, Alexandru Ceausu and Jian Zhang

Monday 23rd (continued)

(18:00-18:30)

ATLAS - Human Language Technologies integrated within a Multilingual Web Content Management System
Svetla Koeva

Tuesday 24th

(9:00-9:30) HyTRA 1st Morning Session

(9:30-10:00)

Tree-based Hybrid Machine Translation
Andreas Søeborg Kirkedal

(10:00-10:30) Coffee break

(10:30-11:30) Invited Talk Philipp Koehn

(11:30-12:00) HyTRA 2nd Morning Session

Were the clocks striking or surprising? Using WSD to improve MT performance
Špela Vintar, Darja Fišer and Aljoša Vrščaj

(12:00-12:30)

Bootstrapping Method for Chunk Alignment in Phrase Based SMT
Santanu Pal and Sivaji Bandyopadhyay

Tuesday 24th (continued)

(12:30-13:00)

Design of a hybrid high quality machine translation system
Bogdan Babych, Kurt Eberle, Johanna Geiß, Mireia Ginestí-Rosell, Anthony Hartley, Reinhard Rapp, Serge Sharoff and Martin Thomas

(13:00-15:00) Lunch break

(15:00-15:30) Hytra Afternoon Session

Can Machine Learning Algorithms Improve Phrase Selection in Hybrid Machine Translation?
Christian Federmann

(15:30-16:00)

Linguistically-Augmented Bulgarian-to-English Statistical Machine Translation Model
Rui Wang, Petya Osenova and Kiril Simov

(16:30-17:00)

Using Sense-labeled Discourse Connectives for Statistical Machine Translation
Thomas Meyer and Andrei Popescu-Belis

(17:00-17:30) Coffee break

(17:30-18:30) Panel discussion

Semantic Web based Machine Translation

Bettina Harriehausen-Mühlbauer
University of Applied Sciences
Darmstadt, Germany
bettina.harriehausen@h-da.de

Timm Heuss
University of Applied Sciences
Darmstadt, Germany
Timm.Heuss@web.de

Abstract

This paper describes the experimental combination of traditional Natural Language Processing (NLP) technology with the Semantic Web building stack in order to extend the expert knowledge required for a Machine Translation (MT) task. Therefore, we first give a short introduction in the state of the art of MT and the Semantic Web and discuss the problem of disambiguation being one of the common challenges in MT which can only be solved using world knowledge during the disambiguation process. In the following, we construct a sample sentence which demonstrates the need for world knowledge and design a prototypical program as a successful solution for the outlined translation problem. We conclude with a critical view on the developed approach.

1 Introduction

Over the past decades, Machine Translation (MT) has undergone various changes with regard to the underlying technology. Starting in the middle of the last century with rule-based MT, a first logical step was taken towards the end of the century, when statistical methods in Natural Language Processing (NLP) gained overall importance, as the growing number of online available texts could be used as a basis for statistical computations performed on these texts and translations, which resulted in an enhancement of existing rules, statistics and thus results. The new field of Statistical Machine Translation (SMT) was born and MT systems became increasingly better as more and more texts and translations were available. In parallel to the developments in MT, the Web has significantly grown and gained importance, especially in the recently defined field of the Semantic Web. After having accepted statistical methods as a promising change in MT, we believe that a next logical step will combine MT with Semantic Web technology, resulting in a new focus which can be called Semantic Web Machine Translation (SWMT).

In this paper, we will develop our ideas step by step and will demonstrate on a sample sentence including a lexical ambiguity that our approach does not involve a costly disambiguation process on the basis of parsing online-dictionaries. Instead, we believe that modern Information Technology (IT) is aligned and committed to information and its markup, as the W3C Semantic Web technology stack[1] demonstrates, and that we can use the contained knowledge in our disambiguation process without additional MT rules or statistics being applied.

2 Development and change of focus in MT : from the rule-based past to the web-based future of MT

Traditionally, most MT systems were rule-based systems built on electronic analysis and generation grammars as well as a language-pair-dependent transfer component . These Rule-based Machine Translation (RBMT) systems always involved a careful and time-consuming development of grammatical rules.

More recent development in MT has started to use the vast amount of texts and knowledge that is available online for translations based on statistics

[1] `http://semanticweb.org/wiki/Main_Page` (URL last access 2011-12-18).

Proceedings of the 13th Conference of the European Chapter of the Association for Computational Linguistics, pages 1–9,
Avignon, France, April 23 - 27 2012. ©2012 Association for Computational Linguistics

and probabilities, leading to a separate focus in MT, namely SMT.

With the growing size of texts available in the web, it is a logical next step to consider using the available knowledge in these texts to enhance NLP applications, including MT, leading to a yet new focus, which we call SWMT.

In this chapter we will develop our idea by starting with a look at how MT has developed over the past decades, how it has made use of the expanding Web in recent years and where we see further potential in using existing knowledge for MT technology.

2.1 Statistical Machine Translation

The dream of automatically translating documents from foreign languages into English, or between any two languages, is one of the oldest pursuits of NLP, being a subfield of artificial intelligence research. Traditional MT systems computed translations primarily on the basis of analysis and generation phrase-structure-rules, which had to be manually coded in a costly fashion.

One of the leading users of SMT is Google and Google Translate engineer Anton Andryeyev, who explains SMT's essence as follows:

"SMT generates translations based on patterns found in large amounts of text. [...] Instead of trying to teach the machine all the rules of a language, SMT effectively lets computers discover the rules for themselves. It works by analysing millions of documents that have already been translated by humans [...].

[...] Key to SMT are the translation dictionaries, patterns and rules that the program develops. It does this by creating many different possible rules based on the previously translated documents and then ranking them probabilistically. Google admits this approach to translation inevitably depends on the amount of texts available in particular languages [...]." (Boothroyd 2011)

Therefore, with the change of available resources and the growing number of natural language that is available in machine-readable format as well as the growing number of users inputting corrections to machine translations manually, thus allowing a direct and correct match between source and target texts, we have entered this subfield of MT which focuses on a statistical analysis of texts, in which documents are translated according to a probability distribution $p(e|f)$ which states that a string e in the target language is the translation of a string f in the source language.

Philipp Koehn, being among the most popular SMT researchers and developers, also highlights today's quality of SMT and the relevance of the vast amounts of texts in the web, which provide the basis for SMT translations, by stating "Now, armed with vast amounts of example translations and powerful computers, we can witness significant progress toward achieving that dream." (Koehn et al. 2012)

The research field of statistical machine translation is a rather new field. In his commented bibliography[2] Koehn includes statistics about the distribution of publications in the SMT field across the years 1953 until 2008. It is clearly shown that only a few publications appeared before the millennium change and that SMT clearly became an issue of growing interest in the new millennium, with a peak in 2006. Scientists working in the MT field suddenly became aware of the relevance and potential provided by statistics in machine translation and computational linguistics in general. Still in 2003, Knight & Koehn stated, that "the currently best performing statistical machine translation systems are still crawling at the bottom", (Knight & Koehn 2004, p. 10), implying that most of the approaches hadn't gone beyond simple word to word translations yet and hadn't included more advanced stages of NLP, like syntax or even semantics. Among those who made essential contributions to the field of SMT was Kevin Knight who stated in 1999 that "We want to automatically analyse existing human sentence translations, with an eye toward building general translation rules we will use these rules to translate new texts automatically." (Knight 1999)

The previous statements all point at the vast knowledge included in the just as vast amounts of texts available in digital form in the internet, partly in the form of human sentence translations.

At the same time that MT started clearly moving into using the Web to search for machine-readable texts and translations that could be used in the expanding SMT field, Tim Berners-Lee (Berners-Lee & Hendler 2001) defined the knowledge, that is included in the Web content, to ex-

[2] `http://www.statmt.org/book/bibliography/` (URL last access 2012-01-30).

pand the traditional WWW to become a Semantic Web

As we are looking at an expanded view of how to use the Web, and specifically the Semantic Web, for our approach of MT, we would like to draw parallels between what has been said so far about MT and the innovative possibilities that the Semantic Web provides for MT research.

2.2 W3C Semantic Web

The World Wide Web (WWW) was once designed to be as simple, as decentralized and as interoperable as possible (Berners-Lee 1999, 36f.). The Web evolved and became a huge success, however, information was limited to humans. In order to make information available to machines, an extending and complementary set of technologies was introduced in the new millennium by the W3C, the Semantic Web[3] (Berners-Lee & Hendler 2001).

The base technology of the Semantic Web is the data format Resource Description Framework (RDF). Aligned to the so called AAA slogan that "Anyone can say Anything about Any topic" (Allemang & Hendler 2008, p. 35), it defines a structure that is meant to "be a natural way to describe the vast majority of the data processed by machines" (Berners-Lee & Hendler 2001). In addition to the AAA slogan, a basic construction paradigms of the Semantic Web is the Open World Assumption - the fact that there is always more knowledge than we currently know; new knowledge can always be added later.

RDF expresses meaning by encoding it in sets of triples (Berners-Lee & Hendler 2001), composed of subject, predicate and object, which are, in the N3-notation format[4], likewise written down as triples:

```
:subject :predicate :object
```

We see strong connections between MT and the W3C Semantic Web.

A lot of ideas exist on how to augment the Resource Description Framework (RDF) - the base format of the Semantic Web - with natural language. Since the beginning, RDF itself provided capacities for a "human-readable version of a resource's name" (Guha 2004), `rdfs:label`, with an optional language notation following RFC-3066[5] (Klyne & Carroll 2004). In addition to that, the Simple Knowledge Organization System (SKOS) ontology features a small selection of unicode labels for "creating human-readable representations of a knowledge organization system", `skos:prefLabel`, `skos:altLabel` and `skos:hiddenLabel` - but also remarks that it "does not necessarily indicate best practice for the provision of labels with different language tags" (Miles 2008).

Some alternatives developed to the approches above, to address limitations especially of `rdfs:label` and to represent natural language within semantic knowledge in a more sophisticated way, like the SKOS eXtension for Labels (SKOS-XL)[6], Lemon[7] and LexInfo[8].

And even in the area of wordnets, which might be considered as a more traditional NLP domain, W3C Semantic Web technology plays a role, as approaches were developed to bridge the gap between natural language representations within these wordnets and the design principles of the Semantic Web (Graves & Gutierrez 2005). The conversion of Princeton WordNet[9], for example, to RDF/OWL is covered by a W3C Working Draft (van Assem et al. 2006) or the GermaNet wordnet[10] equivalent approach (Kunze & Lüngen 2007), adapting the ideas of the Princeton WordNet conversation.

We decided to give a brief overview of the state-of-the-art of SMT and the Semantic Web, as both areas of research are not only very new developments but they share using information in the Web for their applications and they both offer promising enhancements to traditional, rule-based MT technology. Nevertheless, SMT and Semantic Web Technologies have fundamental differ-

[3] `http://www.w3.org/standards/semanticweb/` (URL last access 2012-01-25).

[4] `http://www.w3.org/DesignIssues/Notation3.html` (URL last access 2012-01-29).

[5] `http://www.ietf.org/rfc/rfc3066.txt` (URL last access 2012-01-25).

[6] `http://www.w3.org/TR/skos-reference/skos-xl.html` (URL last access 2012-01-26).

[7] `http://www.w3.org/International/multilingualweb/madrid/slides/declerck.pdf` (URL last access 2012-01-31).

[8] `http://lexinfo.net/` (URL last access 2012-01-31).

[9] `http://wordnet.princeton.edu/` (URL last access 2012-01-26).

[10] `http://www.sfs.uni-tuebingen.de/lsd/` (URL last access 2012-01-26).

ences in that SMT, with systems like Moses[11], Babel Fish or Google compute their translations on a pure probability count of n-grams of different length in order to find the best translation by picking the one that gives the highest probability. As these systems have access to a growing text corpus, which is, as in the case of Moses, directly enhanced by collecting manual corrections given by users after the system has computed an inadequate translation, they become better with time. But exactly these statistically based computations are neither possible nor allowed in the Semantic Web because of the Open World Assumption.

3 New idea: Enhancing NLP with Semantic Web technology

With our new approach, we suggest to base MT on a newly defined set of rules, which differ both from rules known from earlier MT approaches but also from any rules that are applied in SMT. Our rules follow Tim Berners-Lees vision, in that knowledge, once defined and formalized, is accessible in arbitrary ways. As mentioned earlier, we believe that modern IT follows the commitment of information and it's markup, and the Semantic Web technology stack is a perfect implementation of that paradigm.

To demonstrate our approach, we selected a common and well known issue: The problem in many areas of NLP is the ambiguity of natural language on various levels, from word level to sentence level. In many cases, strings can only be disambiguated on the basis of world or expert knowledge. How else would a machine decide on whether the prepositional phase is modifying the verb or the preceding noun in "He eats fish with a fork." vs. "He eats fish with bones."? Especially with translations, it is often crucial to understand the source text correctly, as otherwise ambiguities may result in incomprehensible target language translations, as the examples below will demonstrate.

The state of the art technology of the World Wide Web to express information, facts and relations for both humans and machines is RDF. So it is not unlikely that nowadays expert knowledge is encoded in that format, too.

Taking care of lacking expert knowledge with Semantic Web technology and thus extending existing MT technology seems to be a promising research area. Instead of just combining RBMT with SMT, we suggest to add the power of the Semantic Web to these existing technologies, as the previous approaches were not able to extract and use knowledge from the Web in their translation algorithms and thus leave ambiguities unsolved.

The previously quoted statements made it clear that MT can only be enhanced on the basis of a growing size of text. We claim that the next logical step is to use this growing size of text not only statistically, but in a well-defined way which is offered by Semantic Web technology. The power of our idea is the combination of a strong, proven technology with a popular, open, machine-readable data format.

In order to demonstrate how our approach will enhance existing MT systems, we chose to use a variety of MT systems, some rule-based (e.g. PT[12]), other statistic-based (e.g. Babel Fish, Google, and Moses) to compare their context-free translation results against our approach. We use those context-free translation results as a starting point for further processing with Semantic Web technology. Traditional MT technology should therefore not be replaced, but enhanced with semantics, to benefit from the advantages provided by the Web.

In our sample scenario, the required world knowledge for the sample sentence `Pages by Apple is better than Word by MS.` is modelled as RDF instances. We selected a simple file-based storage, with the actual translations being stored as `rdfs:labels`[13] which are localized as defined in Best Common Practice 47[14] (BCP47). To take advantage of the powerful Semantic Web tool set, parts of the world knowledge are not directly defined, but can be inferenced by Web Ontology Language (OWL) capacities. The goal is to produce a semantically good translation for the given sentence.

[11] Moses is a statistical machine translation system developed by the Statistical MT Research group of University of Edinburgh, `http://www.statmt.org/moses/`.

[12] Personal Translator 14 distributed by Linguatec.

[13] `http://www.w3.org/TR/rdf-schema/##ch_label` (URL last access 2011-12-19).

[14] `http://www.rfc-editor.org/rfc/bcp/bcp47.txt` (URL last access 2011-12-19).

3.1 A sample scenario

The first step is the construction of an expressive sample scenario where world knowledge is critical for the MT. We looked at the results a number of different translation tools computed for our sample sentence: Google Translator[15], Bing Translator[16], an online demo of Philipp Koehn's Moses[17], Linguatec Personal Translator PT 14[18] (rule-based) and the reference translation in this paper, Yahoo! Babel Fish[19].

Research concluded with the following sentence, requiring the "expert knowledge" that a vendor called `Apple` produced a product named `Pages` and a vendor called `MS` (very popular shortform of `Microsoft`) a product named `Word`:

```
Pages by Apple is better
than Word by MS.
```

One important measure to stress the translation service is to use "indirect" product names (`Pages by Apple` and **not** `Apple Pages`) to prevent them from deriving product names from possible dictionary entries. Another "trap" was to abbreviate `Microsoft` with `MS` to irritate possible n-gram-statistics.

The resulting German translations of the sample sentence were the following:

Google Translator:

```
Pages von Apple ist besser
als Word MS.
```

Bing Translator:

```
Seiten von Apple ist besser
als MS Word.
```

Babel Fish:

```
Seiten durch Apple ist besser
als Wort durch Frau.
```

Moses Machine Translation Demo:

```
Seiten von Apple ist besser
als Word von MS behandelt.
```

[15] `http://translate.google.de/` (URL last access 2011-12-18).

[16] `http://www.microsofttranslator.com/` (URL last access 2011-12-18).

[17] `http://demo.statmt.org/index.php` (URL last access 2012-01-29).

[18] `http://www.linguatec.net/products/tr/pt` (URL last access 2012-01-29).

[19] `http://de.babelfish.yahoo.com/` (URL last access 2011-12-18).

Personal Translator PT 14

```
Paginiert von Apple ist
besser als durch MS
auszudrücken.
```

All translations failed, because they did not take semantic relations into consideration. This is a systematic issue in MT, demonstrating the necessity of including world knowledge in the computation of the target translation.

4 More examples

As ambiguities are a common MT problem, there are various examples where MT can be enhanced by world knowledge.

Consider, for example, popular persons that have ambiguous last names - like the politicians George W. Bush, Helmut Kohl[20], Joschka Fischer[21] to name a few. MT systems are likely to translate those names if they are not included in dedicated expert dictionaries. But thanks to projects like DBpedia[22], we already have the knowledge available in a Semantic Web accessible format and could just use it.

Another area that might benefit from a Semantic Web Machine Translation is the internationalization of technical documents or handbooks, which usual deal with several termini technici. Once modelled in RDF, the required expert knowledge is universally present and could aid the translation process as well.

5 Analysis

World knowledge is the crucial point for the translation quality of the selected sample sentences. It becomes obvious that in situations like this, with missing expert dictionaries, rule sets or lacking statistical tooling like N-grams, the translation quality is relatively low. And this is not an unrealistic scenario: There will always be uncovered areas in expert dictionaries or missing statistics in a certain domain.

In the given example, if we are looking at the Babel Fish translation, the translation engine was totally mousetrapped as it translated the `Apple` product `Pages` with the obviously context free,

[20] The proper name Kohl is also the German word for cabbage.

[21] Fischer means fisherman in German.

[22] `http://dbpedia.org/` (URL last access 2012-03-12).

German translation Seiten. Furthermore, it interpreted MS as salutation and Word as the German Wort - all mistakes made caused by lexical ambiguities because of the lack of context knowledge.

6 Implementation

In order to prove our idea, we have developed a prototypical application implementing a Semantic Web enhanced SMT. One principal design goal was to keep the program simple, but to apply state-of-the-art Semantic Web technology like RDF and the query language SPARQL, which are both W3C recommendations.

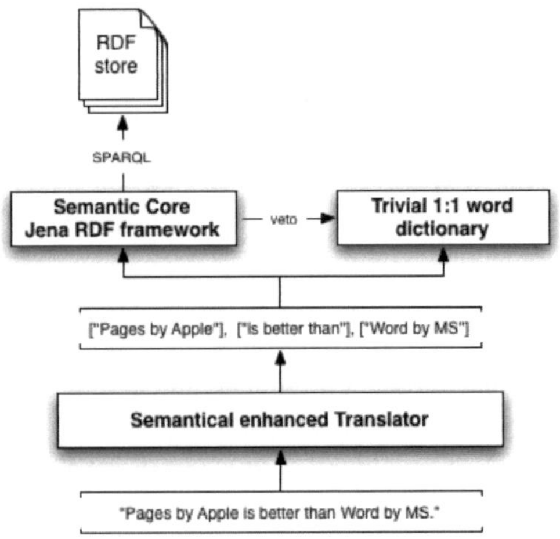

Figure 1: Architectural overview of the involved components and exchanged tokens.

And because of the powerful but easy to use Jena Semantic Web Framework[23], a prototype implementation is written in the Java programming language. The involved MT-components are:

Trivial word dictionary Performs a one-by-one word translation. Entries are designed to reflect the translation results of Babel Fish.

Semantic Core Reads a file based RDF triple store, executes SPARQL-queries and performs reasoning to inference new knowledge. Resulting text phrases may override certain results derived by dictionary entries.

The following sections give more details about the concrete implementation of those components and the overall execution logic.

[23]http://jena.sourceforge.net/ (URL last access 2011-12-19).

6.1 Trivial word dictionary

To fake Babel Fishs translation logic, a very simplified dictionary is defined with the content aligned at its online pendant. As figure 2 shows, the context free translation is reproduced with word-by-word translations.

English	German
Apple	Apfel
Pages	Seiten
Word	Wort
better	besser
...	...

Figure 2: Simplified dictionary to reproduce Babel Fishs simple and context free translation results.

6.2 Semantic Core

The much more interesting part is modelling the world knowledge with Semantic Web technologies. Thereby, a simple file based RDF store is used. The notation format is consistently N3[24], because of its very good human-readability.

As mentioned in previous sections, world knowledge about Apple and Microsoft is crucial in this translation task. So the first statements within the RDF store are about both vendors and the products they produce[25]:

```
:apple a :vendor, :trigger;
  rdfs:label "Apple";
  :produces :numbers , :pages ,
      :iphone .
```

In this case, the instance :apple is defined to be of the types :vendor and :trigger. While the former type has no special meaning in this context, the latter is especially important: :trigger-instances mark significant keywords, indicating that additional world knowledge should be loaded when they occur in a sentence. So in this example occurrence of the word Apple (rdfs:label of :apple) in the source text triggers loading and parsing of the :apple instance and all uses of it within the store.

Furthermore, some products are defined to be produced by :apple.

[24]http://en.wikipedia.org/wiki/Notation3 (URL last access 2011-12-19).

[25]For the sake of simplicity, all statements are aligned in the default namespace http://www.example.org/##.

The property `:produces` as well as its opposite `:producedBy` are defined as follows:

```
:produces rdfs:label "produces"@en-
    US, "produziert"@de-DE .
:producedby rdfs:label "by"@en-US, "
    von"@de-DE .
```

Note that both properties have dual-language-labels. This allows the program express the world knowledge `:apple :produces :iphone` in simple but natural English language as well as in German.

In the next step, both properties are semantically connected as `owl:inverseOf` each other:

```
:produces owl:inverseOf :producedby
```

This few statements already allow *inferencing* - reasoning about information that is given implicitly. So it is not only a fact that `:apple :produces :iphone`, but also after OWL-inferencing the fact that `:iphone :producedBy :apple` - without having to state that directly.

Finally, the products get their proper names assigned:

```
:numbers rdfs:label "Numbers" .
:word rdfs:label "Word" .
:windows rdfs:label "Windows" .
:pages rdfs:label "Pages" .
```

This few lines form the knowledge base which is, thanks to inferencing, sufficient to solve the translation task. The following dictionary entries can directly be read out of the RDF knowledge base:

```
Microsoft produces Windows
MS        produces Windows
Microsoft produces Word
MS        produces Word
Apple produces Pages
Apple produces Numbers
```

By evaluating the predicates `:produces` and inferencing the `:producedBy` statements, the knowledge base in addition contains the inverted entries:

```
Word by MS
Word by Microsoft
Word produced by MS
Word produced by Microsoft
Windows by MS
Windows by Microsoft
Windows produced by MS
Windows produced by Microsoft
```

6.3 Wiring it together

As mentioned before, the Semantic World Knowledge should enhance traditional MT translations. Therefore, the program produces technically two translations of the sentence `Pages by Apple is better than Word by MS.`: The first translation is done by the trivial dictionary, simply by string-replacing English with German words according to figure 2. The second translation first tries to find a better translation by checking trigger keywords, querying the RDF store for a knowledge, inferencing relationships and resolving labels for the right language, before it continues with the same word-by-word-replacing mechanism like in the fist translation.

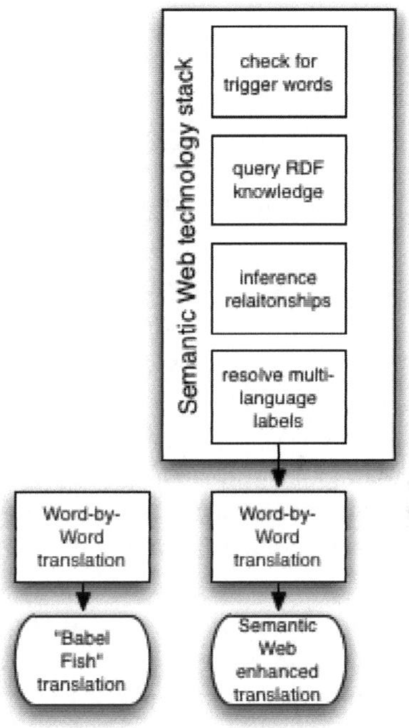

Figure 3: The two translations produced by the program and their technological foundation.

6.4 Program execution

Our prototype simply executes both described translations and print the result out.

```
Source sentence:
    Pages by Apple is better than
    Word by MS.

Semantic Web enhanced translation:
    Pages von Apple ist besser als
    Word von MS.
```

These simple lines, specially the "Semantic Web enhanced translation", involve a lot of processing in the background which is not visible to the user - except for his waiting time. However, a semantically correct translation solution was found.

7 Critical view on the solution

We feel we created something notable here. However, we stand at the very beginning of our research and have encountered corresponding issues.

Surprisingly, implementation of the program logic - especially the query mechanism - turned out to be quite complicated, even for a simple scenario like in this case with a very limited corpus. As a result, the stepwise refinement of a translation (trigger word, query of knowledge, inference relationships and multi-language-label resolution) consists of a lot SPARQL queries. These queries require some processing time and power, which is both already notable in this tiny example. This finally leads to the conclusion that performance might be a major withdraw of our approach, at least for the current implementation.

Another issue was connected to data format: the translation environment, especially the usage of RDF triples consisting of subject, predicate and object, might be regarded to be too much aligned at the very special and constructed problematic of only a number of realtime problems. Sentences have to be somehow split into triples, which is quite an artificial border - not to say a technical limitation - of RDF. Real world NLP surely does not fit into the tripartite simplifications of RDF, and the question is then how often real world problems would benefit from this solution.

Another issue is the Open World Assumption, built into each Semantic Web component: There is no golden standard truth in the Semantic Web and therefore we will never be able to find the "best" translation for a given sentence within SPARQL-queries or inferencing results. Probably, our approach does not hold for providing complete translation solutions, but for giving very qualified suggestions. Some SMT tools, like Moses, actually do work with suggestions.

However, some of this issues might be solved by applying more sophisticated NLP / MT technology, like n-grams. Besides these issues, the program works as expected and Semantic Web technology was successfully used to integrate world knowledge into a MT process. Thus, the translation gathered a better quality and it thus can be stated that the experiment was successful.

8 Related work

The project Monnet has, according to its mission statement[26], a similar idea to combine MT with Semantic Web technology. However, results are still pending or not publically accessible at this point.

We also acknowledge the work by Elita and Birladeanu (2005), who outlined the combination of the Semantic Web with Example Based Machine Translation (EBMT), which is very much related to our approach. However, there are major differences: Elita and Birladeanu (2005) only applied their technique on certain phrases of offical documents - sequences of words they call "fields" (Elita & Birladeanu 2005, p. 14). Our idea is however to aid translation of complete sentences. Another very important difference is the intensiveness of use of W3C technology. Unlike Elita and Birladeanu (2005), we heavily use RDF, SPARQL and - probably the most promising matter of fact - OWL reasoning and try to follow the Semantic Web standard tooling very strictly.

9 Outlook

At this point in our research, we have not yet combined existing MT technology, especially SMT, with SWMT. The combination of approaches has yet to be explored, but existing MT technologies and SWMT are certainly not mutually exclusive and we suspect that a combination of MT approaches will lead to yet even better results, especially in cases where the translation quality is based on world or expert knowledge.

10 Conclusion

In the recent past, MT researchers have already discussed the combination of RBMT and SMT (Hutchins 2009, pp. 13-20). We suggest to add yet another possibility in MT to existing MT approaches, namely a Semantic Web based MT (SWMT).

[26] `http://www.monnet-project.eu/Monnet/Monnet/English?init=true` (URL last access 2012-01-26).

In this paper we have taken a next logical step in MT technology by including not only the vast amounts of texts available in the Web to enhance MT quality applying statistical computations across online texts and translations, but going one step further by looking at the power of and knowledge contained in the Semantic Web.

By taking advantage of the knowledge in the Web of the future, our approach of combining Semantic Web technology with MT allows this world knowledge to be made available for machine translations, thus enhancing challenges in MT, such as lexical ambiguities. In our discussed sample sentences, we have shown that a solution for the disambiguation would traditionally involve a costly disambiguation process or would be left unsolved. Using our SWMT approach, the MT quality benefits from world knowledge extracted from the Semantic Web and by its technology.

This combination of MT with Semantic Web technology results in a new focus of MT which we suggest to be called Semantic Web based MT (SWMT).

11 Acknowledgements

We like to thank Rike Bacher from Linguatec and the reviewers of the ESIRMT-HyTra conference 2012 for their valuable hints.

References

Allemang, D. & Hendler, J. (2008), *Semantic Web for the Working Ontologist: Effective Modeling in RDFS and OWL*, Morgan Kaufmann.
URL: `http://www.amazon.com/Semantic-Web-Working-Ontologist-Effective/dp/0123735564`

Berners-Lee, T. (1999), *Weaving the Web : The Original Design and Ultimate Destiny of the World Wide Web by its Inventor*, HarperOne.
URL: `http://www.amazon.com/Weaving-Web-Original-Ultimate-Inventor/dp/0062515861`

Berners-Lee, T. & Hendler, J. (2001), 'Scientific American: The Semantic Web', *Scientific American, USA.* .
URL: `http://scholar.google.com/scholar?hl=en\&btnG=Search\&q=intitle:Scientific+American:+The+Semantic+Web\#3`

Boothroyd, D. (2011), 'Statistical machine translation to enable universal communication?'.
URL: `http://www.newelectronics.co.uk/electronics-technology/statistical-machine-translation-to-enable-universal-communication/33008/`

Elita, N. & Birladeanu, A. (2005), 'A first step in integrating an EBMT into the Semantic Web'.
URL: `www.mt-archive.info/MTS-2005-Elita.pdf`

Graves, A. & Gutierrez, C. (2005), 'Data representations for WordNet : A case for RDF'.
URL: `http://www.dcc.uchile.cl/~cgutierr/papers/wordnet-rdf.pdf`

Guha, R. (2004), 'RDF Vocabulary Description Language 1.0: RDF Schema'.
URL: `http://moodletest.ncnu.edu.tw/file.php/9506/references-2009/RDF\_schema\_1.pdf`

Hutchins, J. (2009), 'Multiple Uses of Machine Translation and Computerised Translation Tools', *Machine Translation* pp. 13–20.
URL: `http://www.hutchinsweb.me.uk/Besancon-2009.pdf`

Klyne, G. & Carroll, J. (2004), 'Resource description framework (RDF): Concepts and abstract syntax', *Changes* **10**(February), 1–20.
URL: `http://www.mendeley.com/research/w3c-gibt-recommendation-fr-resource-description-framework-rdf-frei/`

Knight, K. (1999), A statistical MT tutorial workbook, *in* 'Prepared for the 1999 JHU Summer Workshop'.
URL: `http://www.snlp.de/prescher/teaching/2007/StatisticalNLP/bib/1999jhu.knight.pdf`

Knight, K. & Koehn, P. (2004), 'What's New in Statistical Machine Translation', *Tutorial, HLT/NAACL* pp. 1–89.
URL: `http://www.auai.org/uai2003/Knight-UAI-03.pdf`

Koehn, P., Osborne, M., Haddow, B., Auli, M., Buck, C., Dugast, L., Guillou, L., Hasler, E., Matthews, D., Williams, P., Wilson, O. & Saint-Amand, H. (2012), 'Statistical Machine Translation at the University of Edinburgh'.

Kunze, C. & Lüngen, H. (2007), 'Repräsentation und Verknüpfung allgemeinsprachlicher und terminologischer Wortnetze in OWL', *Zeitschrift für Sprachwissenschaft* .

Mark van Assem, V. U. A., Aldo Gangemi, ISTC-CNR, R. & Guus Schreiber, V. U. A. (2006), 'RDF/OWL Representation of WordNet'.
URL: `http://www.w3.org/TR/wordnet-rdf/`

Miles, A. (2008), 'SKOS simple knowledge organization system reference', *W3C Recommendation* .
URL: `http://www.mendeley.com/research/skos-simple-knowledge-organization-system-reference/`

Measuring Comparability of Documents in Non-Parallel Corpora for Efficient Extraction of (Semi-)Parallel Translation Equivalents

Fangzhong Su
Centre for Translation Studies
University Of Leeds
LS2 9JT, Leeds, UK
smlfs@leeds.ac.uk

Bogdan Babych
Centre for Translation Studies
University Of Leeds
LS2 9JT, Leeds, UK
b.babych@leeds.ac.uk

Abstract

In this paper we present and evaluate three approaches to measure comparability of documents in non-parallel corpora. We develop a task-oriented definition of comparability, based on the performance of automatic extraction of translation equivalents from the documents aligned by the proposed metrics, which formalises intuitive definitions of comparability for machine translation research. We demonstrate application of our metrics for the task of automatic extraction of parallel and semi-parallel translation equivalents and discuss how these resources can be used in the frameworks of statistical and rule-based machine translation.

1 Introduction

Parallel corpora have been extensively exploited in different ways in machine translation (MT) — both in Statistical (SMT) and more recently, in Rule-Based (RBMT) architectures: in SMT aligned parallel resources are used for building translation phrase tables and calculating translation probabilities; and in RBMT, they are used for automatically building bilingual dictionaries of translation equivalents and automatically deriving bilingual mappings for frequent structural patterns. However, large parallel resources are not always available, especially for under-resourced languages or narrow domains. Therefore, in recent years, the use of cross-lingual comparable corpora has attracted considerable attention in the MT community (Sharoff et al., 2006; Fung and Cheung, 2004a; Munteanu and Marcu, 2005; Babych et al., 2008).

Most of the applications of comparable corpora focus on discovering translation equivalents to support machine translation, such as bilingual lexicon extraction (Rapp, 1995; Rapp, 1999; Morin et al., 2007; Yu and Tsujii, 2009; Li and Gaussier, 2010; Prachasson and Fung, 2011), parallel phrase extraction (Munteanu and Marcu, 2006), and parallel sentence extraction (Fung and Cheung, 2004b; Munteanu and Marcu, 2005; Munteanu et al., 2004; Smith et al., 2010).

Comparability between documents is often understood as belonging to the same subject domain, genre or text type, so this definition relies on these vague linguistic concepts. The problem with this definition then is that it cannot be exactly benchmarked, since it becomes hard to relate automated measures of comparability to such inexact and unmeasurable linguistic concepts. Research on comparable corpora needs not only good measures for comparability, but also a clearer, technologically-grounded and quantifiable definition of comparability in the first place.

In this paper we relate comparability to usefulness of comparable texts for MT. In particular, we propose a performance-based definition of comparability, as the possibility to extract parallel or quasi-parallel translation equivalents – words, phrases and sentences which are translations of each other. This definition directly relates comparability to texts' potential to improve the quality of MT by adding extracted phrases to phrase tables, training corpus or dictionaries. It also can be quantified as the rate of successful extraction of translation equivalents by automated tools, such as proposed in Munteanu and Marcu (2006).

Still, successful detection of translation equivalents from comparable corpora very much de-

Proceedings of the 13th Conference of the European Chapter of the Association for Computational Linguistics, pages 10–19,
Avignon, France, April 23 - 27 2012.

pends on the quality of these corpora, specifically on the degree of their textual equivalence and successful alignment on various text units. Therefore, the goal of this work is to provide comparability metrics which can reliably identify cross-lingual comparable documents from raw corpora crawled from the Web, and characterize the degree of their similarity, which enriches comparable corpora with the document alignment information, filters out documents that are not useful and eventually leads to extraction of good-quality translation equivalents from the corpora.

To achieve this goal, we need to define a scale to assess comparability qualitatively, metrics to measure comparability quantitatively, and the sources to get comparable corpora from. In this work, we directly characterize comparability by how useful comparable corpora are for the task of detecting translation equivalents in them, and ultimately to machine translation. We focus on document-level comparability, and use three categories for qualitative definition of comparability levels, defined in terms of granularity for possible alignment:

- Parallel: Traditional parallel texts that are translations of each other or approximate translations with minor variations, which can be aligned on the sentence level.

- Strongly-comparable: Texts that talk about the same event or subject, but in different languages. For example, international news about oil spill in the Gulf of Mexico, or linked articles in Wikipedia about the same topic. These documents can be aligned on the document level on the basis of their origin.

- Weakly-comparable: Texts in the same subject domain which describe different events. For example, customer reviews about hotel and restaurant in London. These documents do not have an independent alignment across languages, but sets of texts can be aligned on the basis of belonging to the same subject domain or sub-domain.

In this paper, we present three different approaches to measure the comparability of cross-lingual (especially under-resourced languages) comparable documents: a lexical mapping based approach, a keyword based approach, and a machine translation based approach. The experimental results show that all of them can effectively predict the comparability levels of the compared document pairs. We then further investigate the applicability of the proposed metrics by measuring their impact on the task of parallel phrase extraction from comparable corpora. It turns out that, higher comparability level predicted by the metrics consistently lead to more number of parallel phrase extracted from comparable documents. Thus, the metrics can help select more comparable document pairs to improve the performance of parallel phrase extraction.

The remainder of this paper is organized as follows. Section 2 discusses previous work. Section 3 introduces our comparability metrics. Section 4 presents the experimental results and evaluation. Section 5 describes the application of the metrics. Section 6 discusses the pros and cons of the proposed metrics, followed by conclusions and future work in Section 7.

2 Related Work

The term "comparability", which is the key concept in this work, applies to the level of corpora, documents and sub-document units. However, so far there is no widely accepted definition of comparability. For example, there is no agreement on the degree of similarity that documents in comparable corpora should have or on the criteria for measuring comparability. Also, most of the work that performs translation equivalent extraction in comparable corpora usually assumes that the corpora they use are reliably comparable and focuses on the design of efficient extraction algorithms. Therefore, there has been very little literature discussing the characteristics of comparable corpora (Maia, 2003). In this section, we introduce some representative work which tackles comparability metrics.

Some studies (Sharoff, 2007; Maia, 2003; McEnery and Xiao, 2007) analyse comparability by assessing corpus composition, such as structural criteria (e.g., format and size), and linguistic criteria (e.g., topic, domain, and genre). Kilgarriff and Rose (1998) measure similarity and homogeneity between monolingual corpora. They generate word frequency list from each corpus and then apply χ^2 statistic on the most frequent n (e.g., 500) words of the compared corpora.

The work which deals with comparability measures in cross-lingual comparable corpora is closer to our work. Saralegi et al. (2008) measure the degree of comparability of comparable corpora (English and Basque) according to the distribution of topics and publication dates of documents. They compute content similarity for all the document pairs between two corpora. These similarity scores are then input as parameters for the EMD (Earth Mover's Distance) distance measure, which is employed to calculate the global compatibility of the corpora. Munteanu and Marcu (2005; 2006) select more comparable document pairs in a cross-lingual information retrieval based manner by using a toolkit called Lemur[1]. The retrieved document pairs then serve as input for the tasks of parallel sentence and sub-sentence extraction. Smith et al. (2010) treat Wikipedia as a comparable corpus and use "interwiki" links to identify aligned comparable document pairs for the task of parallel sentence extraction. Li and Gaussier (2010) propose a comparability metric which can be applied at both document level and corpus level and use it as a measure to select more comparable texts from other external sources into the original corpora for bilingual lexicon extraction. The metric measures the proportion of words in the source language corpus translated in the target language corpus by looking up a bilingual dictionary. They evaluate the metric on the rich-resourced English-French language pair, thus good dictionary resources are available. However, this is not the case for under-resourced languages in which reliable language resources such as machine-readable bilingual dictionaries with broad word coverage or word lemmatizers might be not publicly available.

3 Comparability Metrics

To measure the comparability degree of document pairs in different languages, we need to translate the texts or map lexical items from the source language into the target languages so that we can compare them within the same language. Usually this can be done by using bilingual dictionaries (Rapp, 1999; Li and Gaussier, 2010; Prachasson and Fung, 2011) or existing machine translation tools. Based on this process, in this section we present three different approaches to measure the comparability of comparable documents.

3.1 Lexical mapping based metric

It is straightforward that we expect a bilingual dictionary can be used for lexical mapping between a language pair. However, unlike the language pairs in which both languages are rich-resourced (e.g., English-French, or English-Spanish) and dictionary resources are relatively easy to obtain, it is likely that bilingual dictionaries with good word coverage are not publicly available for under-resourced languages (e.g., English-Slovenian, or English-Lithuanian). In order to address this problem, we automatically construct dictionaries by using word alignment on large-scale parallel corpora (e.g., Europarl and JRC-Acquis[2]).

Specifically, GIZA++ toolkit (Och and Ney, 2000) with default setting is used for word alignment on the JRC-Acquis parallel corpora (Steinberger et al., 2006). The aligned word pairs together with the alignment probabilities are then converted into dictionary entries. For example, in Estonian-English language pair, the alignment example "kompanii company 0.625" in the word alignment table means the Estonian word "kompanii" can be translated as (or aligned with) the English candidate word "company" with a probability of 0.625. In the dictionary, the translation candidates are ranked by translation probability in descending order. Note that the dictionary collects inflectional form of words, but not only base form of words. This is because the dictionary is directly generated from the word alignment results and no further word lemmatization is applied.

Using the resulting dictionary, we then perform lexical mapping in a word-for-word mapping strategy. We scan each word in the source language texts to check if it occurs in the dictionary entries. If so, the first translation candidate are recorded as the corresponding mapping word. If there are more than one translation candidate, the second candidate will also be kept as the mapping result if its translation probability is higher than 0.3[3]. For non-English and English

[1] Available at http://www.lemurproject.org/

[2] The JRC-Acquis covers 22 European languages and provides large-scale parallel corpora for all the 231 language pairs.

[3] From the manual inspection on the word alignment results, we find that if the alignment probability is higher than 0.3, it is more reliable.

language pair, the non-English texts are mapped into English. If both languages are non-English (e.g., Greek-Romanian), we use English as a pivot langauge and map both the source and target language texts into English[4]. Due to the lack of reliable linguistic resources in non-English languages, mapping texts from non-English language into English can avoid language processing in non-English texts and allows us to make use of the rich resources in English for further text processing, such as stop-word filtering and word lemmatization[5]. Finally, cosine similarity measure is applied to compute the comparability strength of the compared document pairs.

3.2 Keyword based metric

The lexical mapping based metric takes all the words in the text into account for comparability measure, but if we only retain a small number of representative words (keywords) and discard all the other less informative words in each document, can we judge the comparability of a document pair by comparing these words? Our intuition is that, if two document share more keywords, they should be more comparable. To validate this, we then perform keyword extraction by using a simple TFIDF based approach, which has been shown effective for keyword or keyphrase extraction from the texts (Frank et al., 1999; Hulth, 2003; Liu et al., 2009).

More specifically, the keyword based metric can be described as below. First, similar to the lexical mapping based metric, bilingual dictionaries are used to map non-English texts into English. Thus, only the English resources are applied for stop-word filtering and word lemmatization, which are useful text preprocessing steps for keyword extraction. We then use TFIDF to measure the weight of words in the document and rank the words by their TFIDF weights in descending order. The top *n* (e.g., 30) words are extracted as keywords to represent the document. Finally, the comparability of each document pair is determined by applying cosine similarity to their keyword lists.

3.3 Machine translation based metrics

Bilingual dictionary is used for word-for-word translation in the lexical mapping based metric and words which do not occur in the dictionary will be omitted. Thus, the mapping result is like a list of isolated words and information such as word order, syntactic structure and named entities can not be preserved. Therefore, in order to improve the text translation quality, we turn to the state-of-the-art SMT systems.

In practice, we use Microsoft translation API[6] to translate texts in under-resourced languages (e.g, Lithuanian and Slovenian) into English and then explore several features for comparability metric design, which are listed as below.

- **Lexical feature**: Lemmatized bag-of-word representation of each document after stop-word filtering. Lexical similarity (denoted by W_L) of each document pair is then obtained by applying cosine measure to the lexical feature.

- **Structure feature**: We approximate it by the number of content words (adjectives, adverbs, nouns, verbs and proper nouns) and the number of sentences in each document, denoted by C_D and S_D respectively. The intuition is that, if two documents are highly comparable, their number of content words and their document length should be similar. The structure similarity (denoted by W_S) of two documents $D1$ and $D2$ is defined as bellow.

  $$W_S = 0.5 * (C_{D1}/C_{D2}) + 0.5 * (S_{D1}/S_{D2})$$

  suppose that $C_{D1} <= C_{D2}$, and $S_{D1} <= S_{D2}$.

- **Keyword feature**: Top-20 words (ranked by TFIDF weight) of each document. keyword similarity (denoted by W_K) of two documents is also measured by cosine.

- **Named entity feature**: Named entities of each document. If more named entities co-occur in two documents, they are very likely to talk about the same event or subject and

[4]Generally in JRC-Acquis, the size of parallel corpora for most of non-English langauge pairs is much smaller than that of language pairs which contain English. Therefore, the resulting bilingual dictionaries which contain English have better word coverage as they have many more dictionary entries.

[5]We use WordNet (Fellbaum, 1998) for word lemmatization.

[6]Available at http://code.google.com/p/microsoft-translator-java-api/

thus should be more comparable. We use Stanford named entity recognizer[7] to extract named entities from the texts (Finkel et al., 2005). Again, cosine is then applied to measure the similarity of named entities (denoted by W_N) between a document pair.

We then combine these four different types of score in an ensemble manner. Specifically, a weighted average strategy is applied: each individual score is associated with a constant weight, indicating the relative confidence (importance) of the corresponding type of score. The overall comparability score (denoted by SC) of a document pair is thus computed as below:

$$SC = \alpha * W_L + \beta * W_S + \gamma * W_K + \delta * W_N$$

where α, β, γ, and $\delta \in [0, 1]$, and $\alpha+\beta+\gamma+\delta = 1$. SC should be a value between 0 and 1, and larger SC value indicates higher comparability level.

4 Experiment and Evaluation

4.1 Data source

To investigate the reliability of the proposed comparability metrics, we perform experiments for 6 language pairs which contain under-resoured languages: German-English (DE-EN), Estonian-English (ET-EN), Lithuanian-English (LT-EN), Latvian-English (LV-EN), Slovenian-English (SL-EN) and Greek-Romanian (EL-RO). A comparable corpus is collected for each language pair. Based on the definition of comparability levels (see Section 1), human annotators fluent in both languages then manually annotated the comparability degree (parallel, strongly-comparable, and weakly-comparable) at the document level. Hence, these bilingual comparable corpora are used as gold standard for experiments. The data distribution for each language pair, i.e., number of document pairs in each comparability level, is given in Table 1.

4.2 Experimental results

We adopt a simple method for evaluation. For each language pair, we compute the average scores for all the document pairs in the same comparability level, and compare them to the gold

[7]Available at http://nlp.stanford.edu/software/CRF-NER.shtml

Language pair	#document pair	parallel	strongly-comparable	weakly-comparable
DE-EN	1286	531	715	40
ET-EN	1648	182	987	479
LT-EN	1177	347	509	321
LV-EN	1252	184	558	510
SL-EN	1795	532	302	961
EL-RO	485	38	365	82

Table 1: Data distribution of gold standard corpora

standard comparability labels. In addition, in order to better reveal the relation between the scores obtained from the proposed metrics and comparability levels, we also measure the Pearson correlation between them[8]. For the keyword based metric, top 30 keywords are extracted from each text for experiment. For the machine translation based metric, we empirically set $\alpha = 0.5$, $\beta = \gamma = 0.2$, and $\delta = 0.1$. This is based on the assumption that, lexical feature can best characterize the comparability given the good translation quality provided by the powerful MT system, while keyword and named entity features are also better indicators of comparability than the simple document length information.

The results for the lexical mapping based metric, the keyword based metric and the machine translation based metric are listed in Table 2, 3, and 4, respectively.

Language pair	parallel	strongly-comparable	weakly-comparable	correlation
DE-EN	0.545	0.476	0.182	0.941
ET-EN	0.553	0.381	0.228	0.999
LT-EN	0.545	0.461	0.225	0.964
LV-EN	0.625	0.494	0.179	0.973
SL-EN	0.535	0.456	0.314	0.987
EL-RO	0.342	0.131	0.090	0.932

Table 2: Average comparability scores for lexical mapping based metric

Overall, from the average scores for each comparability level presented in Table 2, 3, and 4, we can see that, the scores obtained from the three comparability metrics can reli-

[8]For correlation measure, we use numerical calibration to different comparability degrees: "Parallel", "strongly-comparable" and "weakly-comparable" are converted as 3, 2, and 1, respectively. The correlation is then computed between the numerical comparability levels and the corresponding average comparability scores automatically derived from the metrics.

Language pair	parallel	strongly-comparable	weakly-comparable	correlation
DE-EN	0.526	0.486	0.084	0.941
ET-EN	0.502	0.345	0.184	0.990
LT-EN	0.485	0.420	0.202	0.954
LV-EN	0.590	0.448	0.124	0.975
SL-EN	0.551	0.505	0.292	0.937
EL-RO	0.210	0.110	0.031	0.997

Table 3: Average comparability scores for keyword based metric

Language pair	parallel	strongly-comparable	weakly-comparable	correlation
DE-EN	0.912	0.622	0.326	0.999
ET-EN	0.765	0.547	0.310	0.999
LT-EN	0.755	0.613	0.308	0.984
LV-EN	0.770	0.627	0.236	0.966
SL-EN	0.779	0.582	0.373	0.988
EL-RO	0.863	0.446	0.214	0.988

Table 4: Average comparability scores for machine translation based metric

ably reflect the comparability levels across different language pairs, as the average scores for higher comparable levels are always significantly larger than those of lower comparable levels, namely SC(parallel)>SC(strongly-comparable)>SC(weakly-comparable). In addition, in all the three metrics, the Pearson correlation scores are very high (over 0.93) across different language pairs, which indicate that there is strong correlation between the comparability scores obtained from the metrics and the corresponding comparability level.

Moreover, from the comparison of Table 2, 3, and 4, we also have several other findings. Firstly, the performance of keyword based metric (see Table 3) is comparable to the lexical mapping based metric (see Table 2) as their comparability scores for the corresponding comparability levels are similar. This means it is reasonable to determine the comparability level by only comparing a small number of keywords of the texts. Secondly, the scores obtained from the machine translation based metric (see Table 4) are significantly higher than those in both the lexical mapping based metric and the keyword based metric. Clearly, this is due to the advantages of using the state-of-the-art MT system. In comparison to the approach of using dictionary for word-for-word mapping, it can provide much better text translation which allows detecting more proportion of lexical overlapping and mining more useful features in the translated texts. Thirdly, in the lexical mapping based metric and keyword based metric, we can also see that, although the average scores for EL-RO (both under-resourced languages) conform to the comparability levels, they are much lower than those of the other 5 language pairs. The reason is that, the size of the parallel corpora in JRC-Acquis for these 5 language pairs are significantly larger (over 1 million parallel sentences) than that of EL-EN, RO-EN[9], and EL-RO, thus the resulting dictionaries of these 5 language pairs also contain many more dictionary entries.

5 Application

The experiments in Section 4 confirm the reliability of the proposed metrics. The comparability metrics are thus useful for collecting high-quality comparable corpora, as they can help filter out weakly comparable or non-comparable document pairs from the raw crawled corpora. But are they also useful for other NLP tasks, such as translation equivalent detection from comparable corpora? In this section, we further measure the impact of the metrics on parallel phrase extraction (**PPE**) from comparable corpora. Our intuition is that, if document pairs are assigned higher comparability scores by the metrics, they should be more comparable and thus more parallel phrases can be extracted from them.

The algorithm of parallel phrase extraction, which develops the approached presented in Munteanu and Marcu (2006), uses lexical overlap and structural matching measures (Ion, 2012). Taking a list of bilingual comparable document pairs as input, the extraction algorithm involves the following steps.

---

1. Split the source and target language documents into phrases.

2. Compute the degree of parallelism for each candidate pair of phrases by using the bilingual dictionary generated from GIZA++ (base dictionary), and retain all the phrase pairs with a score larger than a predefined parallelism threshold.

[9]Remember that in our experiment, English is used as the pivot language for non-English langauge pairs.

3. Apply GIZA++ to the retained phrase pairs to detect new dictionary entries and add them to the base dictionary.

4. Repeat Step 2 and 3 for several times (empirically set at 5) by using the augmented dictionary, and output the detected phrase pairs.

Phrases which are extracted by this algorithm are frequently not exact translation equivalents. Below we give some English-German examples of extracted equivalents with their corresponding alignment scores:

1. But a successful mission — seiner überaus erfolgreichen Mission abgebremst — 0.815501989333333

2. Former President Jimmy Carter — Der ehemalige US-Präsident Jimmy Carter — 0.69708324976825

3. on the Korean Peninsula — auf der koreanischen Halbinsel — 0.8677432145

4. across the Muslim world — mit der muslimischen Welt ermöglichen — 0.893330864

5. to join the United Nations — der Weg in die Vereinten Nationen offensteht — 0.397418711927629

Even though some of the extracted phrases are not exact translation equivalents, they may still be useful resources both for SMT and RBMT if these phrases are passed through an extra pre-processing stage, of if the engines are modified specifically to work with semi-parallel translation equivalents extracted from comparable texts. We address this issue in the discussion section (see Section 6).

For evaluation, we measure how the metrics affect the performance of parallel phrase extraction algorithm on 5 language pairs (DE-EN, ET-EN, LT-EN, LV-EN, and SL-EN). A large raw comparable corpus for each language pair was crawled from the Web, and the metrics were then applied to assign comparability scores to all the document pairs in each corpus. For each language pair, we set three different intervals based on the comparability score (SC) and randomly select 500 document pairs in each interval for evaluation. For the MT based metric, the three intervals are (1) 0.1<=SC<0.3, (2) 0.3<=SC<0.5, and (3) SC>=0.5. For the lexical mapping based metric and keyword based metric, since their scores are lower than those of the MT based metric for each comparability level, we set three lower intervals at (1) 0.1<=SC<0.2, (2) 0.2<=SC<0.4, and (3) SC>=0.4. The experiment focuses on counting the number of extracted parallel phrases with parallelism score>=0.4[10], and computes the average number of extracted phrases per 100000 words (the sum of words in the source and target language documents) for each interval. In addition, the Pearson correlation measure is also applied to measure the correlation between the interval[11] of comparability scores and the number of extracted parallel phrases. The results which summarize the impact of the three metrics to the performance of parallel phrase extraction are listed in Table 5, 6, and 7, respectively.

Language pair	0.1<= SC<0.2	0.2<= SC<0.4	SC>=0.4	correlation
DE-EN	728	1434	2510	0.993
ET-EN	313	631	1166	0.989
LT-EN	258	419	894	0.962
LV-EN	470	859	1900	0.967
SL-EN	393	946	2220	0.975

Table 5: Impact of the lexical mapping based metric to parallel phrase extraction

Language pair	0.1<= SC<0.2	0.2<= SC<0.4	SC>=0.4	correlation
DE-EN	1007	1340	2151	0.972
ET-EN	438	650	1050	0.984
LT-EN	306	442	765	0.973
LV-EN	600	966	1722	0.980
SL-EN	715	1026	1854	0.967

Table 6: Impact of the keyword based metric to parallel phrase extraction

From Table 5, 6, and 7, we can see that for all the 5 language pairs, based on the average number of extracted aligned phrases, clearly we have interval (3)>(2)>(1). In other words, in any of the three metrics, a higher comparability level always leads to significantly more number

[10] A manual evaluation of a small set of extracted data shows that parallel phrases with parallelism score >=0.4 are more reliable.

[11] For the purpose of correlation measure, the three intervals are numerically calibrated as "1", "2", and "3", respectively.

Language pair	0.1<= SC<0.3	0.3<= SC<0.5	SC>=0.5	correlation
DE-EN	861	1547	2552	0.996
ET-EN	448	883	1251	0.999
LT-EN	293	483	1070	0.959
LV-EN	589	1072	2037	0.982
SL-EN	560	1151	2421	0.979

Table 7: Impact of the machine translation based metric to parallel phrase extraction

of aligned phrases extracted from the comparable documents. Moreover, although the lexical mapping based metric and the keyword based metric produce lower comparability scores than the MT based metric (see Section 4), they have similar impact to the task of parallel phrase extraction. This means, the comparability score itself does not matter much, as long as the metrics are reliable and proper thresholds are set for different metrics.

In all the three metrics, the Pearson correlation scores are very close to 1 for all the language pairs, which indicate that the intervals of comparability scores obtained from the metrics are in line with the performance of equivalent extraction algorithm. Therefore, in order to extract more parallel phrases (or other translation equivalents) from comparable corpora, we can try to improve the corpus comparability by applying the comparability metrics beforehand to add highly comparable document pairs in the corpora.

6 Discussion

We have presented three different approaches to measure comparability at the document level. In this section, we will analyze the advantages and limitations of the proposed metrics, and the feasibility of using semi-parallel equivalents in MT.

6.1 Pros and cons of the metrics

Using bilingual dictionary for lexical mapping is simple and fast. However, as it adopts the word-for-word mapping strategy and out-of-vocabulary (OOV) words are omitted, the linguistic structure of the original texts is badly hurt after mapping. Thus, apart from lexical information, it is difficult to explore more useful features for the comparability metrics. The TFIDF based keyword extraction approach allows us to select more representative words and prune a large amount of less informative words from the texts. The keywords are usually relevant to subject and domain terms, which is quite useful in judging the comparability of two documents. Both the lexical mapping based approach and the keyword based approach use dictionary for lexical translation, thus rely on the availability and completeness of the dictionary resources or large scale parallel corpora.

For the machine translation based metric, it provides much better text translation than the dictionary-based approach so that the comparability of two document can be better revealed from the richer lexical information and other useful features, such as named entities. However, the text translation process is expensive, as it depends on the availability of the powerful MT systems[12] and takes much longer than the simple dictionary based translation.

In addition, we use a translation strategy of translating texts from under-resourced (or less-resourced) languages into rich-resourced language. In case that both languages are under-resourced languages, English is used as the pivot langauge for translation. This can compensate the shortage of the linguistic resources in the under-resourced languages and take advantages of various resources in the rich-resourced languages.

6.2 Using semi-parallel equivalents in MT systems

We note that modern SMT and RBMT systems take maximal advantage of strictly parallel phrases, but they still do not use full potential of the semi-parallel translation equivalents, of the type that is illustrated in the application section (see Section 5). Such resources, even though they are not exact equivalents contain useful information which is not used by the systems.

In particular, the modern decoders do not work with under-specified phrases in phrase tables, and do not work with factored semantic features. For example, the phrase:

But a successful mission — seiner überaus erfolgreichen Mission abgebremst

The English side contains the word *but*, which pre-supposes contrast, and on the Greman side words *überaus erfolgreichen* ("generally successful") and *abgebremst* ("slowed down") – which taken together exemplify a contrast, since they

[12] Alternatively, we can also train MT systems for text translation by using the available SMT toolkits (e.g., Moses) on large scale parallel corpora.

have different semantic prosodies. In this example the semantic feature of contrast can be extracted and reused in other contexts. However, this would require the development of a new generation of decoders or rule-based systems which can successfully identify and reuse such subtle semantic features.

7 Conclusion and Future work

The success of extracting good-quality translation equivalents from comparable corpora to improve machine translation performance highly depends on "how comparable" the used corpora are. In this paper, we propose three different comparability measures at the document level. The experiments show that all the three approaches can effectively determine the comparability levels of comparable document pairs. We also further investigate the impact of the metrics on the task of parallel phrase extraction from comparable corpora. It turns out that higher comparability scores always lead to significantly more parallel phrases extracted from comparable documents. Since better quality of comparable corpora should have better applicability, our metrics can be applied to select highly comparable document pairs for the tasks of translation equivalent extraction.

In the future work, we will conduct more comprehensive evaluation of the metrics by capturing its impact to the performance of machine translation systems with extended phrase tables derived from comparable corpora.

Acknowledgments

We thank Radu Ion at RACAI for providing us the toolkit of parallel phrase extraction, and the three anonymous reviewers for valuable comments. This work is supported by the EU funded ACCURAT project (FP7-ICT-2009-4-248347) at the Centre for Translation Studies, University of Leeds.

References

Bogdan Babych, Serge Sharoff and Anthony Hartley. 2008. *Generalising Lexical Translation Strategies for MT Using Comparable Corpora*. Proceedings of LREC 2008, Marrakech, Morocco.

Yun-Chuang Chiao and Pierre Zweigenbaum. 2002. *Looking for candidate translational equivalents in specialized, comparable corpora*. Proceedings of COLING 2002, Taipei, Taiwan.

Christiane Fellbaum. 1998. *WordNet: An Electronic Lexical Database*. MIT Press, Cambridge, MA, USA.

Jenny Finkel, Trond Grenager, and Christopher Manning. 2005. *Incorporating Non-local Information into Information Extraction Systems by Gibbs Sampling*. Proceedings of ACL 2005, University of Michigan, Ann Arbor, USA.

Eibe Frank, Gordon Paynter and Ian Witten. 1999. *Domain-specific keyphrase extraction*. Proceedings of IJCAI 1999, Stockholm, Sweden.

Pascale Fung and Percy Cheung. 2004a. *Mining very non-parallel corpora: Parallel sentence and lexicon extraction via bootstrapping and EM*. Proceedings of EMNLP 2004, Barcelona, Spain.

Pascale Fung and Percy Cheung. 2004b. *Multi-level bootstrapping for extracting parallel sentences from a quasicomparable corpus*. Proceedings of COLING 2004, Geneva, Switzerland.

Anette Hulth. 2003. *Improved Automatic Keyword Extraction Given More Linguistic Knowledge*. Proceedings of EMNLP 2003, Sapporo, Japan.

Radu Ion. 2012. *PEXACC: A Parallel Data Mining Algorithm from Comparable Corpora*. Proceedings of LREC 2012, Istanbul, Turkey.

Adam Kilgarriff and Tony Rose. 1998. *Measures for corpus similarity and homogeneity*. Proceedings of EMNLP 1998, Granada, Spain.

Bo Li and Eric Gaussier. 2010. *Improving corpus comparability for bilingual lexicon extraction from comparable corpora*. Proceedings of COLING 2010, Beijing, China.

Feifan Liu, Deana Pennell, Fei Liu and Yang Liu. 2009. *Unsupervised Approaches for Automatic Keyword Extraction Using Meeting Transcripts*. Proceedings of NAACL 2009, Boulder, Colorado, USA.

Belinda Maia. 2003. *What are comparable corpora?* Proceedings of the Corpus Linguistics workshop on Multilingual Corpora: Linguistic requirements and technical perspectives, 2003, Lancaster, U.K.

Anthony McEnery and Zhonghua Xiao. 2007. *Parallel and comparable corpora?* In Incorporating Corpora: Translation and the Linguist. Translating Europe. Multilingual Matters, Clevedon, UK.

Emmanuel Morin, Beatrice Daille, Korchi Takeuchi and Kyo Kageura. 2007. *Bilingual terminology mining — using brain, not brawn comparable corpora*. Proceedings of ACL 2007, Prague, Czech Republic.

Dragos Munteanu and Daniel Marcu. 2006. *Extracting parallel sub-sentential fragments from non-parallel corpora*. Proceedings of ACL 2006, Syndey, Australia.

Dragos Munteanu and Daniel Marcu. 2005. *Improving machine translation performance by exploiting non-parallel corpora*. Computational Linguistics, 31(4): 477-504.

Dragos Munteanu, Alexander Fraser and Daniel Marcu. 2004. *Improved machine translation performance via parallel sentence extraction from comparable corpora*. Proceedings of HLT-NAACL 2004, Boston, USA.

Franz Och and Hermann Ney. 2000. *Improved Statistical Alignment Models*. Proceedings of ACL 2000, Hongkong, China.

Emmanuel Prochasson and Pascale Fung. 2011. *Rare Word Translation Extraction from Aligned Comparable Documents*. Proceedings of ACL-HLT 2011, Portland, USA.

Reinhard Rapp. 1995. *Identifying Word Translation in Non-Parallel Texts*. Proceedings of ACL 1995, Cambridge, Massachusetts, USA.

Reinhard Rapp. 1999. *Automatic identification of word translations from unrelated English and German corpora*. Proceedings of ACL 1999, College Park, Maryland, USA.

Xabier Saralegi, Inaki Vicente and Antton Gurrutxaga. 2008. *Automatic Extraction of Bilingual Terms from Comparable Corpora in a Popular Science Domain*. Proceedings of the Workshop on Comparable Corpora, LREC 2008, Marrakech, Morocco.

Serge Sharoff. 2007. *Classifying Web corpora into domain and genre using automatic feature identification*. Proceedings of 3rd Web as Corpus Workshop, Louvain-la-Neuve, Belgium.

Serge Sharoff, Bogdan Babych and Anthony Hartley. 2006. *Using Comparable Corpora to Solve Problems Difficult for Human Translators*. Proceedings of ACL 2006, Syndey, Australia.

Jason Smith, Chris Quirk and Kristina Toutanova. 2010. *Extracting Parallel Sentences from Comparable Corpora using Document Level Alignment*. Proceedings of NAACL 2010, Los Angeles, USA.

Ralf Steinberger, Bruno Pouliquen, Anna Widiger, Camelia Ignat and Dan Tufis. 2006. *The JRC-Acquis: A multilingual aligned parallel corpus with 20+ languages*. Proceedings of LREC 2006, Genoa, Italy.

Kun Yu and Junichi Tsujii. 2009. *Extracting bilingual dictionary from comparable corpora with dependency heterogeneity*. Proceedings of HLT-NAACL 2009, Boulder, Colorado, USA.

Full Machine Translation for Factoid Question Answering

Cristina España-Bonet and **Pere R. Comas**
TALP Research Center
Universitat Politècnica de Catalunya (UPC)
{cristinae,pcomas}@lsi.upc.edu

Abstract

In this paper we present an SMT-based approach to Question Answering (QA). QA is the task of extracting exact answers in response to natural language questions. In our approach, the answer is a translation of the question obtained with an SMT system. We use the n-best translations of a given question to find similar sentences in the document collection that contain the real answer. Although it is not the first time that SMT inspires a QA system, it is the first approach that uses a full Machine Translation system for generating answers. Our approach is validated with the datasets of the TREC QA evaluation.

1 Introduction

Question Answering (QA) is the task of extracting short, relevant textual answers from a given document collection in response to natural language questions. QA extends IR techniques because it outputs concrete answers to a question instead of references to full documents which are relevant to a query. QA has attracted the attention of researchers for some years, and several public evaluations have been recently carried in the TREC, CLEF, and NTCIR conferences (Dang et al., 2007; Peñas et al., 2011; Sakai et al., 2008). All the example questions of this paper are extracted from the TREC evaluations.

QA systems are usually classified according to what kind of questions they can answer; *factoid*, *definitional*, *how to* or *why* questions are treated in a distinct way. This work focuses on *factoid* questions, that is, those questions whose answers are semantic entities (e.g., organisation names, person names, numbers, dates, objects, etc.). For example, the question *Q1545: What is a female rabbit called?* is factoid and its answer, *"doe",* is a semantic entity (although not a named entity).

Factoid questions written in natural language contain implicit information about the relations between the concepts expressed and the expected outcomes of the search, and QA explicitly exploits this information. Using an IR engine to look up a boolean query would not consider the relations therefore losing important information. Consider the question *Q0677: What was the name of the television show, starring Karl Malden, that had San Francisco in the title?* and the candidate answer A. In this question, two types of constraints are expressed over the candidate answers. One is that the expected type of A is a kind of "television show." The rest of the question indicates that "Karl Malden" is related to A as being "starred" by, and that "San Francisco" is a substring of A. Many factoid questions explicitly express an hyponymy relation about the answer type, and also several other relations describing its context (i.e. spatial, temporal, etc.).

The QA problem can be approached from several points of view, ranging from simple surface pattern matching (Ravichandran and Hovy, 2002), to automated reasoning (Moldovan et al., 2007) or supercomputing (Ferrucci et al., 2010). In this work, we propose to use Statistical Machine Translation (SMT) for the task of factoid QA. Under this perspective, the answer is a translation of the question. It is not the first time that SMT is used for QA tasks, several works have been using translation models to determine the answers (Berger et al., 2000; Cui et al., 2005; Surdeanu et al., 2011). But to our knowledge this is the first

Proceedings of the 13th Conference of the European Chapter of the Association for Computational Linguistics, pages 20–29,
Avignon, France, April 23 - 27 2012. ©2012 Association for Computational Linguistics

approach that uses a full Machine Translation system for generating answers.

The paper is organised as follows: Section 2 reviews the previous usages of SMT in QA, Section 3 reports our theoretical approach to the task, Section 4 describes our QA system, Section 5 presents the experimental setting, Section 6 analyses the results and Section 7 draws conclusions.

2 Translation Models in QA

The use of machine translation in IR is not new. Berger and Lafferty (1999) firstly propose a probabilistic approach to IR based on methods of SMT. Under their perspective, the human user has an information need that is satisfied by an "ideal" theoretical document d from which the user draws important query words q. This process can be mirrored by a translation model: given the query q, they find the documents in the collection with words a most likely to translate to q. The key ingredient is the set of translation probabilities $p(q|a)$ from IBM model 1 (Brown et al., 1993).

In a posterior work, Berger et al. also introduce the formulation of the QA problem in terms of SMT (Berger et al., 2000). They estimate the likelihood that a given answer containing a word a_i corresponds to a question containing word q_j. This estimation relies on an IBM model 1. The method is tested with a collection of closed-domain Usenet and call-center questions, where each question must be paired with one of the recorded answers. Soricut and Brill (2004) implement a similar strategy but with a richer formulation and targeted to open-domain QA. Given a question Q, a web-search engine is used to retrieve 3-sentence-long answer texts from FAQ pages. These texts are later ranked with the likelihood of containing the answer to Q, and this likelihood is estimated via a noisy-channel architecture. The work of Murdock and Croft (2005) applies the same strategy to TREC data. They evaluate the TREC 2003 passage retrieval task. In this task, the system must output a single sentence containing the answer to a factoid question. Murdock and Croft tackle the length disparity in question-answer pairs and show that this MT-based approach outperforms traditional query likelihood techniques.

Riezler et al. (2007) define the problem of answer retrieval from FAQ and social Q/A websites as a query expansion problem. SMT is used to translate the original query terms to the language of the answers, thus obtaining an expanded list of terms usable in standard IR techniques. They also use SMT to perform question paraphrasing. In the same context, Lee et al. (2008) study methods for improving the translation quality removing noise from the parallel corpus.

SMT can be also applied to sentence representations different than words. Cui et al. (2005) approach the task of passage retrieval for QA with translations of dependency parsing relations. They extract the sequences of relations that link each pair of words in the question and, using the IBM translation model 1, score their similarity to the relations extracted from the candidate passage. Thus, an approximate relation matching score is obtained. Surdeanu et al. (2011) extend the scope of this approach by combining together the translation probabilities of words, dependency relations, and semantic roles in the context of answer searching in FAQ collections.

The works we have described so far use archives of question-answer pairs as information sources. They are really doing document retrieval and sentence retrieval rather than question answering, because every document/sentence is known to be the answer of a question written in the form of an answer, and no further information extraction is necessary, they just select the best answer from a given pool of answers. The difference with a standard IR task is that these systems are not searching for *relevant* documents but for *answer* documents. In contrast, Echihabi and Marcu (2003) introduce an SMT-based method for extracting the concrete answer in factoid QA. First, they use a standard IR engine to retrieve candidate sentences and process them with a constituent parser. Then, an elaborated process simplifies these parse trees converting them into sequences of relevant words and/or syntactic tags. This process reduces the length disparity between questions and answers. For the answer extraction, a special tag marking the position of the answer is sequentially added to all suitable positions in the sentence, thus yielding several candidate answers for each sentence. Finally, each answer is rated according to its likelihood of being a translation of the question, according to an IBM model 4 trained on a corpus of TREC and web-based question-answer pairs.

With the exception of the query expansion approaches (Riezler et al., 2007), all works discussed here use some form of noisy-channel model (translation model and target language model) but do not perform the decoding part of the SMT process to generate translations, nor use the rich set of features of a full SMT. In fact, the formulation of the noisy-channel in these works has very few differences with pure language modelling approaches to QA like the one of Heie et al. (2011), where two different models for retrieval and filtering are learnt from a corpus of question-answer pairs.

3 Question-to-Answer Translation

The core of our QA system is an SMT system for the Question-to-Answer language pair. In SMT, the best translation for a given source sentence is the most probable one, and the probability of each translation is given by the Bayes theorem. In our case, the source sentence corresponds to the question Q and the target or translation is the sentence containing the answer A. With this correspondence, the fundamental equation of SMT can be written as:

$$\begin{aligned} \mathcal{A}(Q) &= \hat{A} = \text{argmax}_A \, P(A|Q) \\ &= \text{argmax}_A \, P(Q|A)\, P(A), \quad (1) \end{aligned}$$

where $P(Q|A)$ is the translation model and $P(A)$ is the language model, and each of them can be understood as the sum of the probabilities for each of the segments or phrases that conform the sentence. The translation model quantifies the appropriateness of each segment of Q being answered by A; the language model is a measure of the fluency of the answer sentence and does not take into account which is the question. Since we are interested in identifying the concrete string that answers the question and not a full sentence, this probability is not as important as it is in the translation problem.

The log-linear model (Och and Ney, 2002), a generalisation of the original noisy-channel approach (Eq. 1), estimates the final probability as the logarithmic sum of several terms that depend on both the question Q and the answer sentence A. Using just two of the features, the model reproduces the noisy-channel approach but written in this way one can include as many features as desired at the cost of introducing the same number of free parameters. The model in its traditional form includes 8 terms:

$$\begin{aligned} \mathcal{A}(Q) &= \hat{A} = \text{argmax}_\text{A} \; \log P(A|Q) = \\ &+ \lambda_{lm} \log P(A) + \lambda_d \log P_d(A,Q) \\ &+ \lambda_{lg} \log lex(Q|A) + \lambda_{ld} \log lex(A|Q) \\ &+ \lambda_g \log P_t(Q|A) + \lambda_d \log P_t(A|Q) \\ &+ \lambda_{ph} \log ph(A) + \lambda_w \log w(A)\,, \quad (2) \end{aligned}$$

where $P(A)$ is the language model probability, $lex(Q|A)$ and $lex(A|Q)$ are the generative and discriminative lexical translation probabilities respectively, $P_t(Q|A)$ the generative translation model, $P_t(A|Q)$ the discriminative one, $P_d(A,Q)$ the distortion model, and $ph(A)$ and $w(A)$ correspond to the phrase and word penalty models. We start by using this form for the answer probability and analyse the importance and validity of the terms in the experiments Section. The λ weights, which account for the relative importance of each feature in the log-linear probabilistic model, are commonly estimated by optimising the translation performance on a development set. For this optimisation one may use Minimum Error Rate Training (MERT) (Och, 2003) where BLEU (Papineni et al., 2002) is the reference evaluation.

Once the weights are determined and the probabilities estimated from a corpus of question-answer pairs (a parallel corpus in this task), a decoder uses Eq. 2 to score the possible outputs and to find the best answer sentence given a question or, in general, an n-best list of answers.

This formulation, although possible from an abstract point of view, is not feasible in practice. The corpus from which probabilities are estimated is finite, and therefore new questions may not be represented. There is no chance that SMT can generate *ex nihilo* the knowledge necessary to answer questions such as *Q1201: What planet has the strongest magnetic field of all the planets?*. So, rather than generating answers via translation, we use translations as indicators of the sentence *context* where an answer can be found. Context here has not only the meaning of near words but also a context at a higher level of abstraction.

To achieve this, we use two different representations of the question-answer pairs and two different SMT models in our QA system. We call Level1 representation the original strings of text of the question-answer pairs. The Level2 representation, that aims at being more abstract, more general and more useful in SMT, is constructed applying this sequence of transformations: 1) Quoted expressions in the question are identified, paired with their counterpart in the answer (in case any exists) and substituted by a special tag QUOTED. 2) Each named entity is substituted by its entity class (e.g., "Karl Malone" by PERSON). 3) Each noun and verb is substituted by their WordNet supersense[1] (e.g. "nickname" by COMMUNICATION). 4) Any remaining word, such as adjectives, adverbs and stop words, is left as is. Additionally, in the answer sentence string, the correct answer entity is substituted by a special tag ANSWER. An example of this annotation is given in Figure 1.

An SMT system trained with Level1 examples will translate Q to answer sentences with vocabulary and structure similar to the learning examples. The Level2 system will translate to a mix of named entities, WordNet supersenses, bare words, and ANSWER markers that represent the abstract structure of the answer sentence. We call *patterns* to the Level2 translations. The rationale of this process is that the SMT model can learn the context where answers appear depending of the structure of the question. The obtained translations from both levels can be searched in the document collection to find sentences that are very similar.

Note that in Level2, the vocabulary size of the question-answer pairs is dramatically reduced with respect to the original Level1 sentences, as seen in Table 2. Thus, the sparseness is reduced, and the translation model gains in coverage; patterns are also easier to find than Level1 sentences, and give flexibility and generality to the translation. And the most important feature, patterns capture the context of the answer, pinpointing it with accuracy.

These Level1 and Level2 translations are the core of our QA system that is presented in the following Section.

Level1 Q: What is Karl Malone's nickname ?
Level1 A: Malone , whose overall consistency has earned him the nickname `ANSWER` , missed both of them with nine seconds remaining .

Level2 Q: What STATIVE B-PERSON 's COMMUNICATION ?
Level2 A: B-PERSON , whose overall ATTRIBUTE POSSESSION POSSESSION him the COMMUNICATION `ANSWER` , PERCEPTION both of them with B-NUM TIME CHANGE .

Figure 1: Example of the two annotation levels used.

4 The Question Answering System

Our QA system is a pipeline of three modules. In the first one, the question is analysed and annotated with several linguistic processors. This information is used by the rest of the modules. In the second one, relevant documents are obtained from the document collection with straightforward IR techniques and a list of candidate answers is generated. Finally, these candidate answers are filtered and ranked to obtain a final list of proposed answers. This pipeline is a common architecture for a simple QA system.

4.1 Question Analysis

Questions are processed with a tokeniser, a POS tagger, a chunker, and a NERC. Besides, each word is tagged with its most frequent sense in WordNet. Then, a maximum-entropy classifier determines the most probable expected answer types for the question (EAT). This classifier is built following the approach of Li and Roth (2005), it can classify questions into 53 different answer types and belongs to our in-house QA system. Finally, a weighted list of relevant keywords is extracted from the question. Their saliences are heuristically determined: the most salient tokens are the quoted expressions, followed by named entities, then sequences of nouns and adjectives, then nouns, and finally verbs and any remaining non-stop word. This list is used in the candidate answer generation module.

4.2 Candidate Answer Generation

The candidate answer generation comprises two steps. First a set of passages is retrieved from the document collection, and then the candidate answers are extracted from the text.

For the retrieval, we have used the passage retrieval module of our in-house QA system. The passage retrieval algorithm initially creates a boolean query with all nouns and more salient words, and sets a threshold t to 50. It uses the Lucene IR engine[2] to fetch the documents match-

[1] WordNet noun synsets are organised in 26 semantic categories based on logical groupings, e.g., ARTIFACT, ANIMAL, BODY, COMMUNICATION... The verbs are organised in 15 categories. (Fellbaum, 1998)

[2] `http://lucene.apache.org`

ing the current query and a subsequent passage construction module extracts passages as document segments where two consecutive keyword occurrences are separated by at most t words. If too few or too many passages are obtained this way, a relaxation procedure is applied. The process iteratively adjusts the salience level of the keywords used in the query by dropping low salient words when too few are obtained or adding them when too many, and it also adjusts their proximity threshold until the quality of the recovered information is satisfactory (see **?**) for further details).

When the passages have been gathered, they are split into sentences and processed with POS tagging, chunking and a NERC. The candidate answer list is composed of all named entities and all phrases containing a noun. Each candidate is associated to the sentence it has been extracted from.

4.3 Answer Ranking

This module selects the best answers from the candidates previously generated. It employs three families of scores to rank them.

Context scores B and R: The n-best list of Level2 question translations is generated. In this step retrieved sentences are also transformed to the Level2 representation. Then, each candidate answer is replaced by the special ANSWER tag in the associated sentence, thus, each sentence has a unique ANSWER tag, as in the training examples. Finally, each candidate is evaluated assessing the similarity of the source sentence with the n-best translations.

For this assessment we use two different metrics. One of them is a lexical metric commonly used in machine translation, BLEU (Papineni et al., 2002). A smoothed version is used to evaluate the pairs at sentence level yielding the score B. The other metric is ROUGE (Lin and Och, 2004), here named R. We use the skip-bigram overlapping measure with a maximum skip distance of 4 unigrams (ROUGE-S4). Contrary to BLEU, ROUGE-S does not require consecutive matches but is still sensitive to word order.

Both BLEU and ROUGE are well-known metrics that are useful for finding partial matchings in long strings of words. Therefore it is an easy way of implementing an approximated pattern matching algorithm with off-the-shelf components.

Although these scores can determine if a sentence is a candidate for asserting a certain property of a certain object, they do not have the power to discriminate if these objects are the actually required by the question. Level2 representation is very coarse and, for example, treats all named entities of the same categories as the same word. Thus, it is prone to introduce noise in the form of totally irrelevant answers. For example, consider the questions *Q1760: Where was C.S. Lewis born?* and *Q1519: Where was Hans Christian Anderson born?*. Both questions have the same Level2 representation: *Where STATIVE PERSON STATIVE?*, and the same n-best list of translations. Any sentence stating the birthplace (or even deathplace) of any person is equally likely to be the correct answer of both questions because the lexicalisation of Lewis and Anderson is lost.

On the other hand, B and R also show another limitation. Since they are based on n-gram matching, they cannot be discriminative enough when there is only one different token between options, and that happens when a same sentence has different candidates for the answer. In this case the system would be able to distinguish among answer sentences but then all the variations with the answer in a different position would have too much similar scores. In order to mitigate these drawbacks, we consider two other scores.

Language scores L_b, L_r, L_f: To alleviate the discriminative problem of the context matching metrics, we calculate the same B and R scores but with Level1 translations and the original lexicalised question. These are the L_b and L_r scores.

Additionally, we introduce a new score L_f that does not take into account the n-gram structure of the sentences: after the n-best list of Level1 question translations is generated, the frequency of each word present in the translations is computed. Then, the words in the candidate answer sentence are scored according to their normalised frequency in the translations list and added up together. This score lies in the $[0, 1]$ range.

Expected answer type score E: This score checks if the type of the answer we are evaluating matches the expected types we have determined in the question analysis. For this task, the expected answer types are mapped to named entities and/or supersenses (e.g., type ENTY:product is mapped to ARTIFACT). If the candidate answer is a named entity of the expected type, or contains a noun of the expected supersense, then this candidate receives a score E equal to the confidence of the question classification (the scores of the ME classifier have been previously normalised to probabilities).

These three families of scores can be combined in several ways in order to produce a ranked list of answers. In Section 6 the combination methods are discussed.

5 Experiments

5.1 Training and Test Corpora

We have used the datasets from the Question Answering Track of the TREC evaluation campaigns[3] ranging from TREC-9 to TREC-16 in our experiments. These datasets provide both a robust testbed for evaluation, and a source of question-answer pairs to use as a parallel corpus for training our SMT system. Each TREC evaluation provides a collection of documents composed of newspaper texts (three different collections have been used over the years), a set of new questions, and an answer key providing both the answer string and the source document. Description of these collections can be found in the TREC overviews (Voorhees, 2002; Dang et al., 2007).

We use the TREC-11 questions for test purposes, the remaining sets are used for training unless some parts of TREC-9, TREC-10 and TREC-12 that are kept for fitting the weights of our SMT system. To gather the SMT corpus, we select all the factoid questions whose answer can be found in the documents and extract the full sentence that contains the answer. With this methodology, a parallel corpus with 12,335 question-answer pairs is obtained. We have divided it into two subsets: the pairs with only a single answer found in the documents are used for the development set, and the remaining pairs (i.e. having multiple occurrences of the correct answer) are used for training. The test set are the 500 TREC-11 questions, 452 out of them have a correct answer in the documents. The numbers are summarised in Table 1.

In order to obtain the Level2 representation of these corpora, the documents and the test sets must be annotated. For the annotation pipeline

[3]http://trec.nist.gov/data/qamain.html

	Q	A	TRECs
Train	2264	12116	9,10,12,13,14,15,16
Dev	219	219	9,10,12
Test	500	2551	11

Table 1: Number of Questions and Answers in our data sets. The number of TREC evaluation from which are obtained is indicated.

	Tokens		Vocabulary	
	Q	A	Q	A
TrainL1	97028	393978	3232	32013
TrainL2	91567	373008	540	9130

Table 2: Statistics for the 12,116 Q-A pairs in the training corpus according to the annotation level.

we use the TnT POS tagger (Brants, 2000), WordNet (Fellbaum, 1998), the YamCha chunker (Kudo and Matsumoto, 2003), the Stanford NERC (Finkel et al., 2005), and an in-house temporal expressions recogniser.

Table 2 shows some statistics for the parallel corpus and the two different levels of annotation. From the SMT point of view the corpus is small in order to estimate the translation probabilities in a reliable way but, as stated before, Level2 representation diminishes the vocabulary considerably and alleviates the problem.

5.2 SMT system

The statistical system is a state-of-the-art phrase-based SMT system trained on the previously introduced corpus. Its development has been done using standard freely available software. The language model is estimated using interpolated Kneser-Ney discounting with SRILM (Stolcke, 2002). Word alignment is done with GIZA++ (Och and Ney, 2003) and both phrase extraction and decoding are done with the Moses package (Koehn et al., 2007). The model weights are optimised with Moses' script of MERT against the BLEU evaluation metric.

For the full model, we consider the language model, direct and inverse phrase probabilities, direct and inverse lexical probabilities, phrase and word penalties, and a non-lexicalised reordering.

5.3 QA system

The question answering system has three different modules as explained in Section 4. For the

	T1	T50	MRR
QA	0.006 (4)	0.206 (14)	0.024 (4)
SR	0.066 (8)	0.538 (9)	0.142 (8)
Upper bound	0.677	0.677	0.677

Table 3: Mean and standard deviation for 1000 realisations of the random baseline for QA and SR. The upper bound is also shown.

first module, questions are annotated using the same tools introduced in the corpora Section. The second module generates 2,866,098 candidate answers (373,323 different sentences), that is to say, a mean of 5,700 answers per question (750 sentences per question). These candidates are made available to the third module resulting in the experiments that will be discussed in Section 6.

The global QA system performance is evaluated with three measures. T1 is a measure of the system's precision and gives the percentage of correct answers in the first position; T50 gives the number of correct answers in the first 50 positions, in some cases that corresponds to all candidate answers; finally the Mean Reciprocal Rank (MRR) is a measure of the ranking capability of the system and is estimated as the mean of the inverse ranking of the first correct answer for every question: MRR= $Q^{-1}\sum_i \text{rank}_i^{-1}$.

6 Results Analysis

Given the set of answers retrieved by the candidate answer generation module, a naïve baseline system is estimated by selecting randomly 50 answers for each of the questions. Table 3 shows the mean of the three measures after applying this random process 1000 times. The upper bound of this task is the oracle that selects always the correct answer/sentence if it is present in the retrieved passages. An answer is considered correct if it perfectly matches the official TREC's answer key and a sentence is correct if it contains a correct answer. The random baseline has a precision of 0.6%.

We also evaluate a second task, sentence retrieval for QA (SR). In this task, the system has to provide a sentence that contains the answer, but not to extract it. Within our SMT approach, both tasks are done simultaneously, because the answer is extracted according to its context sentence. A random baseline for this second task, where only full sentences without marked answers are taken into account, can also be read in Table 3.

	QA			SR		
Metric	T1	T50	MRR	T1	T50	MRR
B	0.018	0.292	0.049	0.084	0.540	0.164
R	0.018	0.283	0.045	0.119	0.608	0.209
B+R	0.022	0.294	0.053	0.097	0.573	0.180
BR	0.027	0.294	0.057	0.137	0.591	0.211

Table 4: System performance using an SMT that generates a 100-best list, uses a 5-gram LM and all the features of the TM.

1st best: The B-ORGANIZATION B-LOCATION , B-DATE (B-ORGANIZATION) - B-PERSON , whose COMMUNICATION STATIVE " ANSWER . "

50th best: The ANSWER ANSWER , B-DATE (B-ORGANIZATION) - B-PERSON , the PERSON of ANSWER , the most popular ARTIFACT , serenely COGNITION COMMUNICATION .

100th best: The B-LOCATION , B-DATE (B-ORGANIZATION) - B-PERSON , the PERSON of ANSWER , COMMUNICATION B-LOCATION 's COMMUNICATION .

Figure 2: Example of patterns found in an n-best list.

We begin this analysis studying the performance of the SMT-based parts alone. Table 4 shows the results when using an SMT decoder that generates a 100-best list, uses a 5-gram language model and all the features of the translation model. An example of the generated patterns in Level2 representation can be found in Figure 2 for the question of Figure 1, *Q1565: What is Karl Malone's nickname?*.

Candidate answer sentences are ranked according to the similarity with the patterns generated by translation as measured by BLEU (B), ROUGE-S4 (R) or combinations of them. To calculate these metrics the n-best list with patterns is considered to be a list of reference translations (Fig. 2) to every candidate (Fig. 1). In general, a combination of both metrics is more powerful than any of them alone and the product outperforms the sum given that in most cases BLEU is larger than ROUGE and smooths its effect. The inclusion of the SMT patterns improves the baseline but it does not imply a quantum leap. T1 is at least three times better than the baseline's one but still the system answers less than a 3% of the questions. In the first 50 positions the answer is

SMT Features	T1	T50	MRR
Lex, LM5, 100-best	0.027	0.294	0.057
noLex, LM5, 100-best	0.015	0.281	0.045
Lex, LM3, 100-best	0.015	0.257	0.041
Lex, LM7, 100-best	0.033	0.288	0.050
Lex, LM5, 10-best	0.024	0.310	0.056
Lex, LM5, 1000-best	0.027	0.301	0.061
Lex, LM5, 10000-best	0.011	0.290	0.045

Table 5: System performance with different combinations of the SMT features used in decoding. BR is the metric used to score the answers.

found a 30% of the times. In the sentence retrieval task, results grow up to 14% and 59% respectively. Its difference between tasks shows one of the limitations of these metrics commented before, they are not discriminative enough when the only difference among options is the position of the ANSWER tag inside the sentence. This is the empirical indication of the need for a score like E. On the other hand, each question has a mean of 5,732 candidate answers, and although T50 is not a significant measure, its good results indicate that the context scores metrics are doing their job. The highest T50, 0.608, is reached by R and it is very close to the upper bound 0.667.

Taking BR as a reference measure, we investigate the impact of three features of the SMT in Table 5. Regarding the length of the language model used in the statistical translation, there is a trend to improve the accuracy with longer language models (T1 is 0.015 for a LM3, 0.027 for LM5 and 0.033 for LM7 with the product of metrics) but recall is not very much affected and the best values are obtained for LM5.

Second, the number of features in the translation model indicates that the best scores are reached when one reproduces the same number of features as a standard translation system. That is, all of the measures when the lexical translation probabilities are ignored are significantly lower than when the eight features are used. In a counterintuitive way, the token to token translation probability helps to improve the final system although word alignments here can be meaningless or nonexistent given the difference in length and structure between question and answer.

Finally, the length of the n-best list is not a decisive factor to take into account. Since the elements in a n-best list usually differ very little, and this is even more important for a system with a reduced vocabulary, increasing the size of the list does not enrich in a substantial way the variety of the generated answers and results show no significant variances. Given these observations, we fix an SMT system with a 5-gram language model, the full set of translation model features and the generation of a 100-best list for obtaining B and R scores.

	QA			SR		
Metric	T1	T50	MRR	T1	T50	MRR
L_f	0.016	0.286	0.046	0.137	0.605	0.236
L_b	0.022	0.304	0.054	0.100	0.581	0.192
L_r	0.018	0.326	0.060	0.131	0.627	0.225
L_{brf}	0.038	0.330	0.079	0.147	0.622	0.238
E	0.044	0.373	0.096	0.058	0.579	0.142
EL_{brf}	0.018	0.293	0.048	0.118	0.623	0.214
BL_{brf}	0.051	0.337	0.091	0.184	0.616	0.271
RL_{brf}	0.033	0.346	0.069	0.191	0.618	0.279
BRL_{brf}	0.042	0.350	0.082	0.182	0.616	0.273
$(B+R)L_{brf}$	0.044	0.346	0.085	0.187	0.618	0.273
BE	0.035	0.384	0.084	0.086	0.579	0.179
RE	0.035	0.377	0.086	0.131	**0.630**	0.228
BRE	0.049	0.377	0.098	0.135	0.608	0.220
(B+R)E	0.040	**0.386**	0.091	0.102	0.596	0.196
BEL_{brf}	0.093	0.379	0.137	0.200	0.621	0.283
REL_{brf}	0.071	0.377	0.123	**0.208**	0.619	**0.294**
$BREL_{brf}$	0.091	0.379	0.132	0.200	0.622	0.287
$(B+R)EL_{brf}$	**0.100**	0.377	**0.141**	0.204	0.621	0.286

Table 6: System performance according to three different ranking strategies: context score (B and R), the language scores (L_x) and EAT type checking (E).

Each score approaches different problems of the task and therefore, complement each other rather than overlapping. Table 6 introduces the results of a selected group of score combinations, where $L_{brf}=L_bL_rL_f$.

The scores L_{brf} and E alone are not very useful because L_{brf} gives the same score to all candidates in the same sentence and E gives the same score to all candidates of the same type. Experimental results confirm that, as expected, L_{brf} is more appropriate for the SR task and E for the QA task, although the figures are very low. When joining E and the Ls together, no improvement is obtained, and the results for the QA task are worse than L_{brf} alone, thus demonstrating that Level1 translations are not good enough for the QA task.

A better system combines all the metrics together.

The best results are achieved when adding B and R scores to the combination. All of these combinations (i.e. B, R, BR and B+R) are better when are multiplied by both E and L_{brf} than by only one of them alone. Otherwise, combinations of only E and L_{brf} yield very poor results. Thus, the Level2 representation boosts T1 scores from 0.018 (EL_{brf}) to 0.100 ((B+R)EL_{brf}) in QA and almost doubles it in SR. As a general trend, we see that combinations involving R but not B are better in the SR task than in the QA task. In fact the best results for SR are obtained with the REL_{brf} combination. The best MRR scores are achieved also with the best T1 scores.

7 Discussion and Conclusions

The results here presented are our approach to consider question answering a translation problem. Questions in an abstract representation (Level2) are translated into an abstract representation of the answer, and these generated answers are matched against all the candidates obtained with the retrieval module. The candidates are then ranked according to their similarity with the n-best list of translations as measured by three families of metrics that include R, B, E and L.

The best combination of metrics is able to answer a 10.0% of the questions in first place (T1). This result is in the lowest part of the table reported by the official TREC-11 overview (Voorhees, 2002). The approach of Echihabi and Marcu (2003) that uses translation probabilities to rank the answers achieves higher results on the same data set (an MRR of 0.325 versus our 0.141). Although both works use SMT techniques, the approach is quite different. In fact, our system is more similar in spirit to that of Ravichandran and Hovy (2002), which learns regular expressions to find answer contexts and shows significant improvements for out-of-domain test sets, that is web data. Besides the fact that Echihabi and Marcu use translation models instead of a full translation system, they explicitly treat the problem of the difference of length between the question and the answer. In our work, this is not further considered than by the word and phrase penalty features of the translation model. Future work will address this difficulty.

The results of sentence ranking of our system are similar to those obtained by Murdock and Croft (2005), however, since test sets are different they are not directly comparable. This is notable because we tackle QA, and sentence retrieval is obtained as collateral information.

Possible lines of future research include the study abstraction levels different from Level2. The linguistic processors provide us with intermediate information such as POS that is not currently used as it is WordNet and named entities. Several other levels combining this information can be also tested in order to find the most appropriate degree of abstraction for each kind of word.

The development part of the SMT system is a delicate issue. MERT is currently optimising towards BLEU, but the final score for ranking the answers is a combination of a smoothed BLEU, ROUGE, L and E. It has been shown that optimising towards the same metric used to evaluate the system is beneficial for translation, but also that BLEU is one of the most robust metrics to be used (Cer et al., 2010), so the issue has to be investigated for the QA problem. Also, refining BLEU and ROUGE for this specific problem can be useful. A first approximation could be an adaptation of the n-gram counting of BLEU and ROUGE so that it is weighted by its distance to the answer; this way sentences that differ only because of the candidate answer string would be better differentiated.

Related to this, the generation of the candidate answer strings is exhaustive; the suppression of the less frequent candidates could help to eliminate noise in the form of irrelevant answer sentences. Besides, the system correlates these answer strings with the expected answer type of the question (coincidence measured with E). This step should be replaced by an SMT-based mechanism to build a full system only based on SMT. Furthermore, we plan to include the Level1 translations into the candidate answer generation module in order to do query expansion in the style of Riezler et al. (2007).

Acknowledgements

This work has been partially funded by the European Community's Seventh Framework Programme (MOLTO project, FP7-ICT-2009-4-247914) and the Spanish Ministry of Science and Innovation projects (OpenMT-2, TIN2009-14675-C03-01 and KNOW-2, TIN2009-14715-C04-04).

References

A. Berger and J. Lafferty. 1999. Information retrieval as statistical translation. In *Proceedings of ACM SIGIR Conference*.

A. Berger, R. Caruana, D. Cohn, D. Freitag, and V. Mittal. 2000. Bridging the lexical chasm: statistical approaches to answer-finding. In *Proceedings of the ACM SIGIR Conference*.

T. Brants. 2000. TnT – a statistical part-of-speech tagger. In *Proceedings ANLP Conference*.

P. F. Brown, V. J. Della Pietra, S. A. Della Pietra, and R. L. Mercer. 1993. The mathematics of statistical machine translation: parameter estimation. *Computational Linguistics*, 19(2).

D. Cer, C. D. Manning, and D. Jurafsky. 2010. The best lexical metric for phrase-based statistical MT system optimization. In *Proceeding of the HLT Conference*.

H. Cui, R. Sun, K. Li, M.Y. Kan, and T.S. Chua. 2005. Question answering passage retrieval using dependency relations. In *Proceedings of the ACM SIGIR Conference*.

H.T. Dang, D. Kelly, and J. Lin. 2007. Overview of the TREC 2007 question answering track. *In Proceedings of the Text REtrieval Conference, TREC*.

A. Echihabi and D. Marcu. 2003. A noisy-channel approach to question answering. In *Proceedings of the ACL Conference*. ACL.

C. Fellbaum. 1998. *WordNet: An Electronic Lexical Database*. Cambridge, MA: MIT Press.

D. Ferrucci, E. Brown, J. Chu-Carroll, J. Fan, D. Gondek, A. Kalyanpur, A. Lally, J. Murdock, E. Nyberg, J. Prager, N. Schlaefer, and C. Welty. 2010. Building Watson: An overview of the DeepQA project. *AI Magazine*, 31(3):59–79.

J. R. Finkel, T. Grenager, and C. D. Manning. 2005. Incorporating non-local information into information extraction systems by gibbs sampling. In *ACL*.

M.H. Heie, E.W.D. Whittaker, and S. Furui. 2011. Question answering using statistical language modelling. *Computer Speech & Language*.

P. Koehn, H. Hoang, A. Mayne, C. Callison-Burch, M. Federico, N. Bertoldi, B. Cowan, W. Shen, C. Moran, R. Zens, C. Dyer, O. Bojar, A. Constantin, and E. Herbst. 2007. Moses: Open source toolkit for statistical machine translation. In *Annual Meeting of the ACL, Demonstration Session*.

T. Kudo and Y. Matsumoto. 2003. Fast methods for kernelbased text analysis. In *Proceedings of ACL Conference*.

J.T. Lee, S.B. Kim, Y.I. Song, and H.C. Rim. 2008. Bridging lexical gaps between queries and questions on large online Q&A collections with compact translation models. In *Proceedings of the EMNLP Conference*. ACL.

X. Li and D. Roth. 2005. Learning question classifiers: The role of semantic information. *Journal of Natural Language Engineering*.

C-Y. Lin and F. Och. 2004. Automatic Evaluation of Machine Translation Quality Using Longest Common Subsequence and Skip-Bigram Statics. In *Proceedings of the ACL Conference*.

D. Moldovan, C. Clark, S. Harabagiu, and D. Hodges. 2007. Cogex: A semantically and contextually enriched logic prover for question answering. *Journal of Applied Logic*, 5(1).

V. Murdock and W.B. Croft. 2005. Simple translation models for sentence retrieval in factoid question answering. In *Procedings of the ACM SIGIR Conference*.

F. Och and H. Ney. 2002. Discriminative Training and Maximum Entropy Models for Statistical Machine Translation. In *Proceedings of the ACL Conference*.

F. Och and H. Ney. 2003. A systematic comparison of various statistical alignment models. *Computational Linguistics*, 29(1).

F. Och. 2003. Minimum error rate training in statistical machine translation. In *Proceedings of the ACL Conference*.

K. Papineni, S. Roukos, T. Ward, and W-J. Zhu. 2002. BLEU: a Method for Automatic Evaluation of Machine Translation. In *Proceedings of the ACL Conference*.

A. Peñas, E. Hovy, P. Forner, Á. Rodrigo, R. Sutcliffe, C. Forascu, and C. Sporleder. 2011. Overview of QA4MRE at CLEF 2011: Question answering for machine reading evaluation. *Working Notes of CLEF*.

D. Ravichandran and E. Hovy. 2002. Learning surface text patterns for a question answering system. In *Proceedings of the ACL Conference*.

S. Riezler, A. Vasserman, I. Tsochantaridis, V. Mittal, and Y. Liu. 2007. Statistical machine translation for query expansion in answer retrieval. In *Proceedings of the ACL Conference*.

T. Sakai, N. Kando, C.J. Lin, T. Mitamura, H. Shima, D. Ji, K.H. Chen, and E. Nyberg. 2008. Overview of the NTCIR-7 ACLIA IR4QA task. In *Proceedings of NTCIR Conference*.

R. Soricut and E. Brill. 2004. Automatic question answering: Beyond the factoid. In *Proceedings of HLT-NAACL Conference*.

A. Stolcke. 2002. SRILM – An extensible language modeling toolkit. In *Proc. Intl. Conf. on Spoken Language Processing*.

M. Surdeanu, M. Ciaramita, and H. Zaragoza. 2011. Learning to rank answers to non-factoid questions from web collections. *Computational Linguistics*, 37(2).

E.M. Voorhees. 2002. Overview of the TREC 2002 Question Answering track. In *In Proceedings of the Text REtrieval Conference, TREC*.

An Empirical Evaluation of Stop Word Removal in Statistical Machine Translation

Chong Tze Yuang
School of Computer Engineering, Nanyang Technological University, 639798
Singapore
tychong@ntu.edu.sg

Rafael E. Banchs
Institute for Infocomm Research, A*STAR, 138632,
Singapore
rembanchs@i2r.a-star.edu.sg

Chng Eng Siong
School of Computer Engineering Nanyang Technological University, 639798
Singapore.
aseschng@ntu.edu.sg

Abstract

In this paper we evaluate the possibility of improving the performance of a statistical machine translation system by relaxing the complexity of the translation task by removing the most frequent and predictable terms from the target language vocabulary. Afterwards, the removed terms are inserted back in the relaxed output by using an *n*-gram based word predictor. Empirically, we have found that when these words are omitted from the text, the perplexity of the text decreases, which may imply the reduction of confusion in the text. We conducted some machine translation experiments to see if this perplexity reduction produced a better translation output. While the word prediction results exhibits 77% accuracy in predicting 40% of the most frequent words in the text, the perplexity reduction did not help to produce better translations.

1 Introduction

It is a characteristic of natural language that a large proportion of running words in a corpus corresponds to a very small fraction of the vocabulary. An analysis of the Brown Corpus has shown that the hundred most frequent words account for 42% of the corpus, while only 0.1% in the vocabulary. On the other hand, words occurring only once account merely 5.7% in the corpus but 58% in the vocabulary (Bell et al. 1990). This phenomenon can be explained in terms of Zipf's Law, which states that the product of word ranks and their frequencies approximates a constant, i.e. word-frequency plot is close to a hyperbolic function, and hence the few top ranked words would account for a great portion of the corpus. Also, it appears that the top ranked words are mainly function words. For instance, the eight most frequent words in the Brown Corpus are *the*, *of*, *and*, *to*, *a*, *in*, *that* and *is* (Bell et al. 1990).

It is a common practice in Information Retrieval (IR) to filter the most frequent words out from processed documents (which are referred to as stop words), as these function words are semantically non-informative and constitute weak indexing terms. By removing this great amount of stop words, not only space and time complexities can be reduced, but document content can be better discriminated by the remaining content words (Fox, 1989; Rijsbergen, 1979; Zou et al., 2006; Dolamic & Savoy 2009).

Inspired by the concept of stop word removal in Information Retrieval, in this work we study the feasibility of stop word removal in Statistical Machine Translation (SMT). Different from Information Retrieval, that ranks or classifies documents; SMT hypothesizes sentences in target language. Therefore, without explicitly removing frequent words from the documents, we proposed to ignore such words in the target language vocabulary, i.e. by replacing those words with a null token. We term this process as "relaxation" and the omitted words as "relaxed words".

Relaxed SMT here refers to a translation task in which target vocabulary words are intentionally omitted from the training dataset for reducing translation complexity. Since the most frequent words are targeted to be relaxed, as a result, there will be vast amount of null tokens in the output text, which later shall be recovered in a post processing stage. The idea of relaxation in SMT is motivated by one of our experimental findings, in which the perplexity measured over a test set decreases when most frequent words are relaxed. For instance, a 15% of perplexity reduction is observed when the twenty most frequent words are relaxed in the English EPPS dataset. The reduction of perplexity allows us to conjecture

Proceedings of the 13th Conference of the European Chapter of the Association for Computational Linguistics, pages 30–37,
Avignon, France, April 23 - 27 2012.

about the decrease of confusion in the text, from which a SMT system might be benefited.

After applying relaxed SMT, the resulting null tokens in the translated sentences have to be replaced by the corresponding words from the set of relaxed words. As relaxed words are chosen from the top ranked words, which possess high occurrences in the corpus, their *n*-gram probabilities could be reliably trained to serve for word prediction. Also, these words are mainly function words and, from the human perspective, function words are usually much easier to predict from their neighbor context than content words. Consider for instance the sentence *the house of the president is very nice*. Function words like *the*, *of*, and *is*, are certainly easier to be predicted than content words such as *house*, *president*, and *nice*.

The rest of the paper is organized into four sections. In section 2, we discuss the relaxation strategy implemented for a SMT system, which generates translation outputs that contain null tokens. In section 3, we present the word prediction mechanism used to recover the null tokens occurring in the relaxed translation outputs. In section 4, we present and discuss the experimental results. Finally, in section 5 we present the most relevant conclusion of this work.

2 Relaxation for Machine Translation

In this paper, relaxation refers to the replacement of the most frequent words in text by a null token. In the practice, a set of frequent words is defined and the cardinality of such set is referred to as the relaxation order. For example, lets the relaxation order be two and the two words on the top rank are *the* and *is*. By relaxing the sample sentence previously presented in the introduction, the following relaxed sentence will be obtained: *NULL house of NULL President NULL very beautiful.*

From some of our preliminary experimental results with the EPPS dataset, we did observe that a relaxation order of twenty leaded to a perplexity reduction of about a 15%. To see whether this contributes to improving the translation performance, we trained a translation system by relaxing the top ranked words in the vocabulary of the target language. In this way, there will be a large number of words in the source language that will be translated to a null token. For example: *la* (*the* in Spanish) and *es* (*is* in Spanish) will be both translated to a null token in English.

This relaxation of terms is only applied to the target language vocabulary, and it is conducted after the word alignment process but before the extraction of translation units and the computation of model probabilities. The main objective of this relaxation procedure is twofold: on the one hand, it attempts to reduce the complexity of the translation task by reducing the size of the target vocabulary while affecting a large proportion of the running words in the text; on the other hand, it should also help to reduce model sparseness and improve model probability estimates.

Of course, different from the Information Retrieval case, in which stop words are not used at all along the search process, in the considered machine translation scenario, the removed words need to be recovered after decoding in order to produce an acceptable translation. The relaxed word replacement procedure, which is based on an *n*-gram based predictor, is implemented as a post-processing step and applied to the relaxed machine translation output in order to produce the final translation result.

Our bet here is that the gain in the translation step, which is derived from the relaxation strategy, should be enough to compensate the error rate of the word prediction step, producing, in overall, a significant improvement in translation quality with respect to the non-relaxed baseline procedure.

The next section describes the implemented word prediction model in detail. It constitutes a fundamental element of our proposed relaxed SMT approach.

3 Frequent Word Prediction

Word prediction has been widely studied and used in several different tasks such as, for example, augmented and alternative communication (Wandmacher and Antoine, 2007) and spelling correction (Thiele et al., 2000). In addition to the commonly used word *n*-gram, various language modeling techniques have been applied, such as the semantic model (Luís and Rosa, 2002; Wandmacher and Antoine, 2007) and the class-based model (Thiele et al., 2000; Zohar and Roth, 2000; Ruch et al., 2001).

The role of such a word predictor in our considered problem is to recover the null tokens in the translation output by replacing them with the words that best fit the sentence. This task is essentially a classification problem, in which the most suitable relaxed word for recovering a given null token must be selected. In other words, $w_i = \max_{v_i \in R} P_{\text{sentence}}(\ldots w_{i-1} v_i w_{i+1} \ldots)$, where $P_{\text{sentence}}(\cdot)$ is the probabilistic model, e.g. *n*-

gram, that estimates the likelihood of a sentence when a null token is recovered with word v_i, drawn from the set of relaxed words R. The cardinality $|R|$ is referred to as the relaxation order, e.g. $|R| = 5$ implies that the five most frequent words have been relaxed and are candidates to be recovered.

Notice that the word prediction problem in this task is quite different from other works in the literature. This is basically because the relaxed words to be predicted in this case are mainly function words. Firstly, it may not be effective to predict a function word semantically. For example, we are more certain in predicting *equity* than *for* given the occurrence of *share* in the sentence. Secondly, although class-based modeling is commonly used for prediction, its original intention is to tackle the sparseness problem, whereas our task focuses only on the most frequent words.

In this preliminary work, our predicting mechanism is based on an *n*-gram model. It predicts the word that yields the maximum a posteriori probability, conditioned on its predecessors. For the case of the trigram model, it can be expressed as follows:

$$w_i = \max_{v_i \in R} P(v_i | w_{i-2} w_{i-1}) \quad (1)$$

Often, there are cases in which more than one null token occur consecutively. In such cases predicting a null token is conditioned on the previous recovered null tokens. To prevent a prediction error from being propagated, one possibility is to consider the marginal probability (summed over the relaxed word set) over the words that were previously null tokens. For example, if v_{i-1} is a relaxed word, which has been recovered from earlier predictions, then the prediction of v_i should no longer be conditioned by v_{i-1}. This can be computed as follows:

$$w_i = \max_{v_i \in R} \bigcup_{v_{i-1} \in R} P(v_i | w_{i-2} v_{i-1}) = \max_{v_i \in R} \sum_{v_{i-1} \in R} P(v_i | w_{i-2} v_{i-1}) \quad (2)$$

The traditional *n*-gram model, as discussed previously, can be termed as the forward *n*-gram model as it predicts the word ahead. Additionally, we also tested the backward *n*-gram to predict the word behind (i.e. on the left hand side of the target word), which can be formulated as:

$$w_i = \max_{v_i \in R} P(v_i | w_{i+1} w_{i+2}) \quad (3)$$

and the bidirectional *n*-gram to predict the word in middle, which can be formulated as follows:

$$w_i = \max_{v_i \in R} P(v_i | w_{i-1}, w_{i+1}) \quad (4)$$

Notice that the backward *n*-gram model can be estimated from the word counts as:

$$P(w_i | w_{i+1} w_{i+2}) = \frac{C(w_i w_{i+1} w_{i+2})}{C(w_{i+1} w_{i+2})} \quad (5)$$

or, it can be also approximated from the forward *n*-gram model, as follows:

$$P(w_i | w_{i+1} w_{i+2}) = \frac{P(w_{i+2} | w_i w_{i+1}) P(w_{i+1} | w_i) P(w_i)}{P(w_{i+2} | w_{i+1}) P(w_{i+1})} \quad (6)$$

Similarly, the bidirectional *n*-gram model can be estimated from the word counts:

$$P(w_i | w_{i-1} w_{i+1}) = \frac{P(w_{i+1} | w_{i-1} w_i) P(w_i | w_{i-1}) P(w_{i-1})}{\sum_{v_i \in V} P(w_{i+1} | w_{i-1} v_i) P(v_i | w_{i-1}) P(w_{i-1})} \quad (7)$$

or approximated from the forward model:

$$P(w_i | w_{i-1} w_{i+1}) = \frac{P(w_{i+1} | w_{i-1} w_i) P(w_i | w_{i-1}) P(w_{i-1})}{\sum_{v_i \in V} P(w_{i+1} | w_{i-1} v_i) P(v_i | w_{i-1}) P(w_{i-1})} \quad (8)$$

The word prediction results of using the forward, backward, and bidirectional *n*-gram models will be presented and discussed in the experimental section.

The three *n*-gram models discussed so far predict words based on the local word ordering. There are two main drawbacks to this: first, only the neighboring words can be used for prediction as building higher order *n*-gram models is costly; and, second, prediction may easily fail when consecutive null tokens occur, especially when all words conditioning the prediction probability are recovered null tokens. Hence, instead of predicting words by maximizing the local probability, predicting words by maximizing a global score (i.e. a sentence probability in this case), may be a better alternative.

At the sentence level, the word predictor considers all possible relaxed word permutations and searchs for the one that yields the maximum a posteriori sentence probability. For the trigram model, a relaxed word that maximizes the sentence probability can be predicted as follows:

$$w_i = \max_{v_i \in R} \prod_{i=1}^{N} P(v_i | w_{i-2} w_{i-1}) \quad (9)$$

where, N is the number of words in the sentence.

Although the forward, backward, and interpolated models have been shown to be applicable for local word prediction, they make no difference at sentence level predictions as they produce identical sentence probabilities. It is not hard to prove the following identity:

$$\prod_{i=1}^{N} P(w_i|w_{i-2}w_{i-1}) = \prod_{i=1}^{N} P(w_i|w_{i+1}w_{i+2}) \quad (10)$$

4 Experimental Results and Discussion

In this section, we first highlight the Zipfian distribution in the corpus and the reduction of perplexity after removing the top ranked words. The *n*-gram probabilities estimated were then used for word prediction, and we report the resulting prediction accuracy at different relaxation orders. The performance of the SMT system with a relaxed vocabulary is presented and discussed in the last subsection of this section.

4.1 Corpus Analysis

The data used in our experiments is taken from the EPPS (Europarl Corpus). We used the version available through the shared task of the 2007's ACL Workshops on Statistical Machine Translation (Burch et al., 2007). The training set comprises 1.2M sentences with 35M words while the development set and test sets contains 2K sentences each.

From the train set, we computed the twenty most frequent words and ranked them accordingly. We found them to be mainly function words. Their counts follow closely a Zipfian distribution (Figure 1) and account for a vast proportion of the text (Figure 2). Indeed, the 40% of the running words is made up by these twenty words.

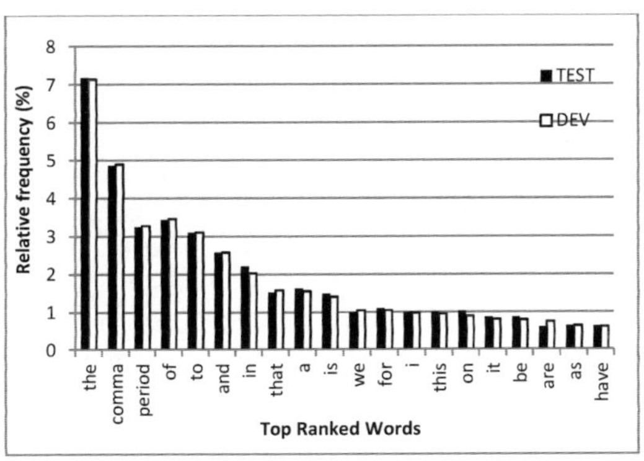

Figure 1. The twenty top ranked words and their relative frequencies

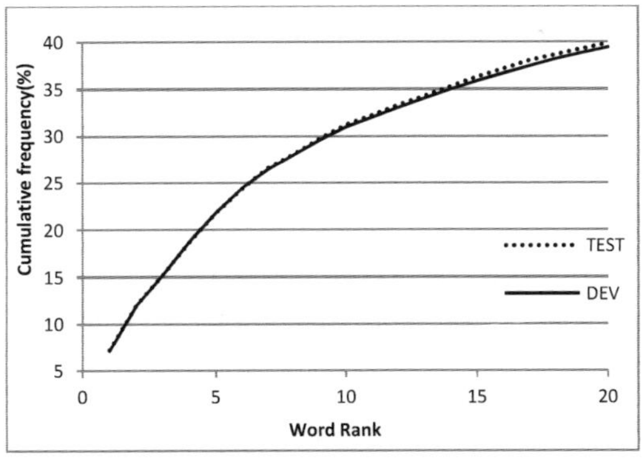

Figure 2. Cumulative relative frequencies of the top ranked words (up to order 20)

We found that when the most frequent words were relaxed from the vocabulary, which means being replaced by a null token, the perplexity (measured with a trigram model) decreased up to 15% for the case of a relaxation order of twenty (Figure 3). This implies that the relaxation causes the text becoming less confusing, which might benefit natural language processing tasks such as machine translation.

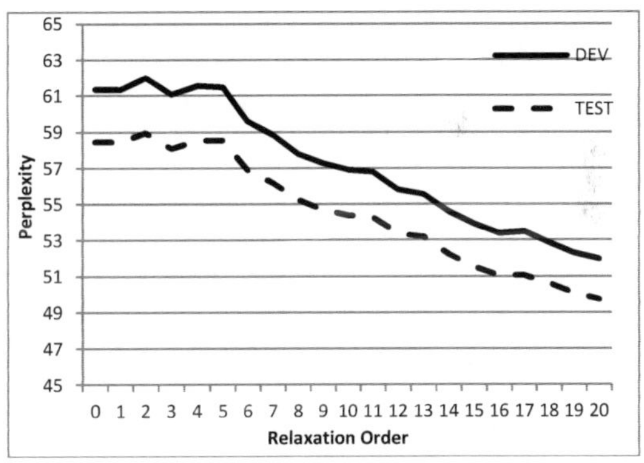

Figure 3. Perplexity decreases with the relaxation of the most frequent words

4.2 Word Prediction Accuracy

In order to evaluate the quality of the different prediction strategies, we carried out some experiments for replacing null tokens with relaxed words. For this, frequent words were dropped manually from text (i.e. replaced with null tokens) and were recovered later by using the word predictor. As discussed earlier, a word can be predicted locally, to yield maximum *n*-gram probability, or globally, to yield maximum sentence probability. In a real application, a text may comprise up to 40% of null tokens that must be recovered from the twenty top ranked words.

For n-gram level prediction (local), we evaluated word accuracy at different orders of relaxation. More specifically, we tested the forward trigram model, the backward trigram model, the bidirectional model, and the linear interpolation between forward and backward trigram models (with weight 0.5). The accuracy was computed as the percentage of null tokens recovered successfully with respect to the original words. These results are shown in Figure 4. Notice that the accuracy of the relaxation of order one is 100%, so it has not been depicted in the plots.

Notice from the figure how the forward and backward models performed very alike throughout the different relaxation orders. This can be explained in terms of their similar perplexities (both models exhibit a perplexity of 58). Better accuracy was obtained by the interpolated model, which demonstrates the advantage of incorporating the left and right contexts in the prediction.

Different from the interpolated model, which simply adds probabilities from the two models, the bidirectional model estimates the probability from the left and right contexts simultaneously during the training phase; thus it produces a better result. However, due to its heavy computational cost (Equation 8), it is infeasible to apply it at orders higher than five.

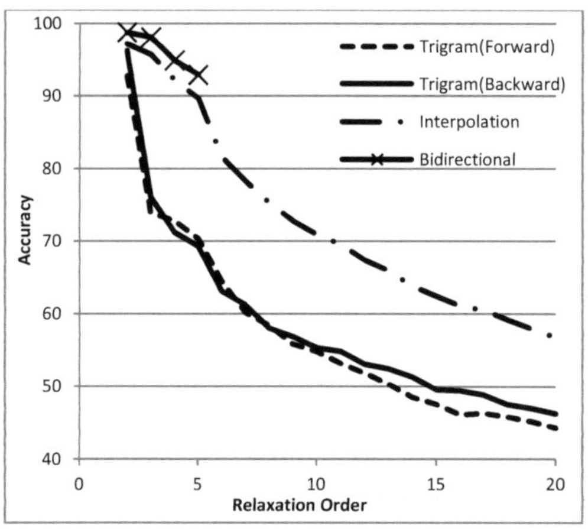

Figure 4. Accuracy of word prediction at n-gram level. Models incorporating left and right context yield about a 20% improvement over one-sided models.

Better accuracy has been obtained for sentence-level prediction by using a bigram model and a trigram model. These results are shown in Figure 5. From the cumulative frequency showed in Figure 2, we could see that 40% of the words in text could now be predicted with an accuracy of about 77%.

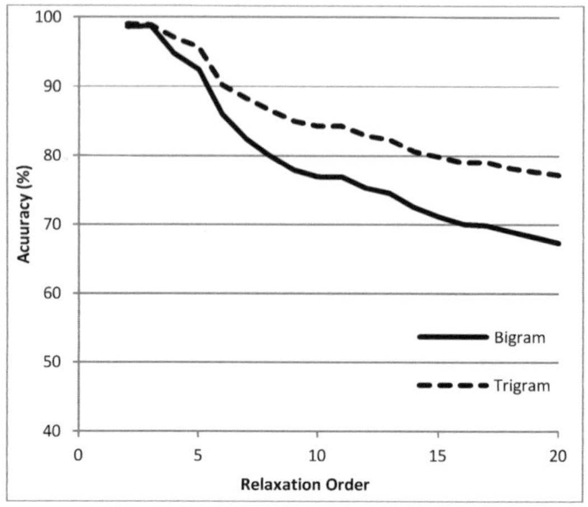

Figure 5. Accuracy of word prediction at the sentence level.

For predicting words by maximizing the sentence probability, two methods have been tried: first, a brute force method that attempts all possible relaxed word permutations for the occurring null tokens within a sentence and finds the one producing the largest probability estimate; and, second, applying Viterbi decoding over a word lattice, which is built from the sentence by replacing the arcs of null tokens with a parallel network of all relaxed words.

All the arcs in the word lattice have to be weighted with n-gram probabilities in order to search for the best route. In the case of the trigram model, we expand the lattice with the aid of the SRILM toolkit (Stolcke 2002). Both methods yield almost identical prediction accuracy. However, we discarded the brute force approach for the later experiments because of its heavy computational burden.

Figure 4 and 5 have been plotted with the same scale on the vertical axis for easing their visual comparison. The global prediction strategy, which optimizes the overall sentence perplexity, is much more useful for prediction as compared to the local predictions. Furthermore, as seen from Figure 5, the global prediction has better resistance against higher order relaxations.

We also observed that the local bidirectional model performed closely to the global bigram model, up to relaxation order five, for which the computation of the bidirectional model is still feasible. In Figure 6 we present a scaled version of the plots to focus on the lower orders for comparison purposes. Although the global bigram prediction makes use of all words in the sentence in order to yield the prediction, locally, a given word is only covered by two consecutive bigrams. Thus, the prediction of a word does not depend on the second word before or the second word after. In other words, we could see the bidirectional model as a global model that is applied to a "short segment" (in this case, a three word segment). The only difference here is that the local bidirectional model estimates the probabilities from the corpus and keeps all seen "short segment" probabilities in the language model (in our case, it is derived from forward bigram), while the global bigram model optimizes the probabilities by searching for the best two consecutive bigrams. The global prediction might only show its advantage when predicting two or more consecutive null tokens.

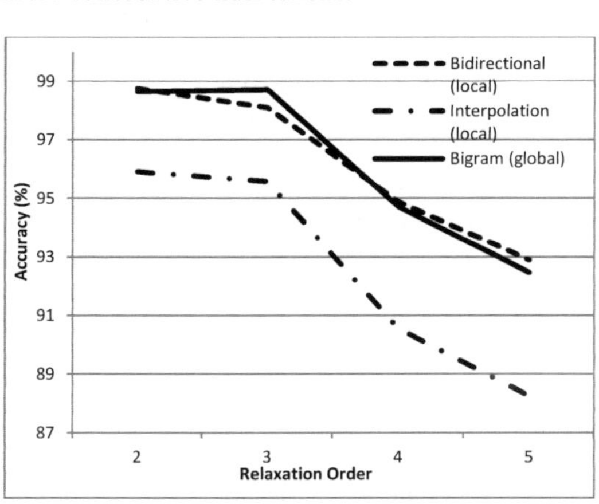

Figure 6. Comparison among local bidirectional, local interpolation, and global bigram models.

Hence, we believe that, if the bidirectional bigram model is computed from counts and stored, it could perform as good as global bigram model at much faster speed (as it involves only querying the language model). Similarly, a local bidirectional trigram model (actually a 5-gram) may be comparable to a global trigram model.

Deriving bidirectional *n*-gram probabilities from a forward model is computationally expensive. In the worst case scenario, where both companion words are relaxed words, the computation complexity is in the order of $O(|V||R|^3)$, where $|V|$ is the vocabulary size and $|R|$ is the number of relaxed words in V. Building a bidirectional bigram/trigram model from scratch is worth to be considered. As all known language model toolkits do not offer this function (even the backward *n*-gram model is built by first reversing the sentences manually), the discounting/smoothing of the trigram has to be derived. The methods of Good-Turing, Kneser Ney, Absolute discounting, etc. (Chen and Goodman, 1998) can be imitated.

4.3 Translation Performance

As frequent words have been ignored in the target language vocabulary of the machine translation system, the translation outputs will contain a great number of null tokens. The amount of null tokens should approximate the cumulative frequencies shown in Figure 2.

In this experiment, a word predictor was used to recover all null tokens in the translation outputs, and the recovered translations were evaluated with the BLEU metric. All BLEU scores have been computed up to trigram precision.

The word predictor used was the global trigram model, which was the best performing system in word prediction experiments previously described. In this case, the predictor was used to recover the null tokens in the translation outputs. In order to apply the prediction mechanism as a post-processing step, a word lattice was built from each translation output, for which the null word arcs were expanded with the words of the relaxed set. Finally, the lattice was decoded to produce the best word list as the complete translation output.

To evaluate whether a SMT system benefits from the relaxation strategy, we set up a baseline system in which the relaxed words in the translation output were replaced manually with null tokens. After that, we used the same word predictor as in the relaxed SMT case (global trigram predictor) for recovering the null tokens and regenerating the complete sentences. We then compared the translation output of the relaxed SMT system to the baseline system.

The results for the baseline (BL) and the relaxed (RX) systems are shown in Figure 7. We evaluated the translation performance for relaxation orders of five and twenty.

From the results shown in Figure 7, it becomes evident that the translation task is not gaining any advantage from relaxation strategy and did not outperform the baseline translator, neither at low nor at high orders of relaxation.

Notice how the BLEU score of the baseline systems are better than those of the relaxed systems.

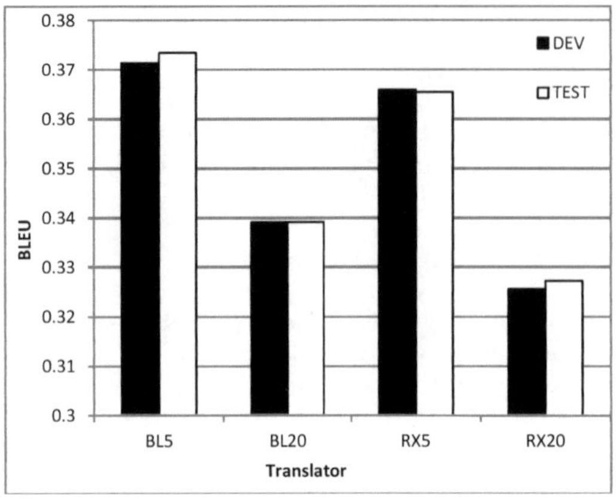

Figure 7. BLEU scores for baseline (BL) and relaxed (RX) translation systems at relaxation orders of five and twenty.

We further analyzed these results by computing BLEU scores for the translation outputs before and after the word prediction step. These results are shown in Figure 8. Notice from Figure 8 that the relaxed translators did not produce any better BLEU score than the corresponding baseline systems, even before word recovery. Although the text after relaxation is less confusing (perplexity decreases about 15% after the twenty most frequent words are relaxed), the resulting perplexity drop was not translated into a BLEU score improvement.

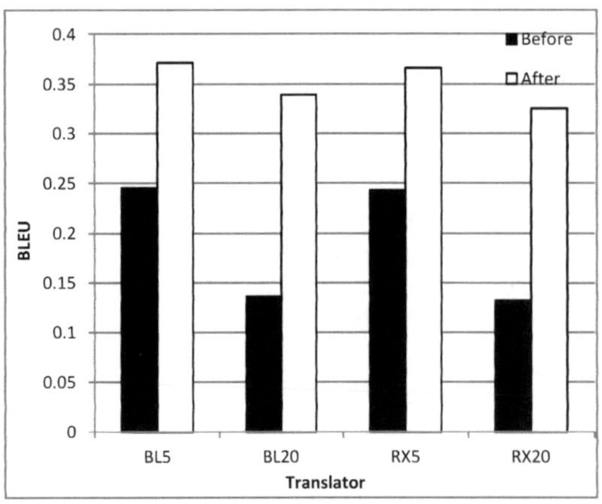

Figure 8. The BLEU scores before and after word prediction

In terms of the word predictions shown in Figure 8, we can see that this post-processing step performed consistently for the relaxed SMT systems, as for the baseline systems (for which the null tokens were inserted manually into sentences). Since the word prediction is based on an *n*-gram model, we may deduce that the relaxed SMT system preserves the syntactic structure of the sentence as the null tokens in the translation output could be recovered as accurate as in the case of the baseline system.

5 Conclusion and Future Work

We have looked into the problem of predicting the most frequently occurring words in a text. The best of the studied word predictors, which is based on an *n*-gram language model and a global search at the sentence level, has achieved 77% of accuracy when predicting 40% words in the text.

We also proposed the idea of relaxed SMT, which consists of replacing top ranked words in the target language vocabulary with a null token. This strategy was originally inspired by the concept of stop word removal in Information Retrieval, and later motivated by the finding that text will become less confusing after relaxation. However, when relaxation is applied to the machine translation system, our results indicate that the relaxed translation task is performing poorer than the conventional non-relaxed system. In other words, the SMT system does not seem to be benefiting from the word relaxation strategy, at least in the case of the specific implementation studied here.

As future work, we will attempt to re-tailor the set of relaxed words by, for instance, imposing some constraints to also include some less frequent function words, which may not be informative to the translation system or, alternatively, excluding some frequent semantically important words from the relaxed set. This remark is based on the observation of the fifty most frequent words in the EPPS dataset, such as *president*, *union*, *commission*, *European*, and *parliament*, which could be harmful when ignored by the translation system but also easy to predict. Hence there is a need to study the effects of different sets of relaxed words on translation performance, as it have already been done for the search problem by researchers in the area of Information Retrieval (Fox, 1990; Ibrahim, 2006).

Acknowledgements

The authors would like to thank their corresponding institutions: the Nanyang Technological University and the Institute for Infocomm Research, for their support regarding the development and publishing of this work.

References

Andreas Stolcke, 2002, SRILM - An Extensible Language Modeling Toolkit, in *Proceedings of ICSLP*, 901-904.

Chris Callison-Burch, Cameron Fordyce, Philipp Koehn, Christof Monz and Josh Schroeder, 2007, (Meta-)evaluation of machine translation, in *Proceedings of the SMT Workshop*, 136-158

Christopher Fox, 1990, A stop list for general text, *SIGIR Forum*, 24:19-35.

Cornelis Joost van Rijsbergen, 1979, *Information Retrieval*, Butterworth-Heinemann.

Feng Zou, Fu Lee Wang, Xiaotie Deng and Song Han, 2006, Automatic identification of Chinese stop words, *Research on Comp. Science*, 18:151-162.

Frank Thiele, Bernhard Rueber and Dietrich Klakow, 2000, Long range language models for free spelling recognition, in *Proceeding of the 2000 IEEE ICASSP*, 3:1715-1718.

Ibrahim Abu El-Khair, 2006, Effects of stop words elimination for Arabic information retrieval: a comparative study, International Journal of Computing & Information Sciences, 4(3):119-133.

João Luís and Garcia Rosa, 2002, Next word prediction in a connectionist distributed representation system, in *Proceedings of the 2002 IEEE Int. Conference on Systems, Man and Cybernetics*, 6-11.

Keith Trnka, John McCaw, Debra Yarrington, Kathleen F. McCoy, User interaction with word prediction: the effects of prediction quality, *ACM Transaction on Accessible Computing*, 1(17):1-34.

Ljiljana Dolamic and Jacques Savoy., 2009, When stopword lists make the difference, *Journal of the American Society for Information Science and Technology*, 61(1):1-4.

Patrick Ruch, Robert Baud and Antoine Geissbuhler, 2001, Toward filling the gap between interactive and fully-automatic spelling correction using the linguistic context, in *Proceedings of the 2001 IEEE International Conference on Systems, Man and Cybernetics*, 199-204.

Stanley F. Chen and Joshua Goodman, 1998, An empirical study of smoothing techniques for language modeling, in *Proceedings of the 34th Annual Meeting of the Association for Computational Linguistics*, 310-318.

Timothy C. Bell, John G. Cleary and Ian H. Witten., 1990, *Text Compression*, Prentice Hall.

Tonio Wandmacher and Jean-Yves Antoine, 2007, Methods to integrate a language model with semantic information for a word prediction component, in *Proceedings of the 2007 Joint Conference on Empirical Methods in Natural Language Processing and Computational Natural Language Learning*, 506-513.

Yair Even-Zohar and Dan Roth, 2000, A classification approach to word prediction, in *Proceedings of the 1st North American chapter of the Association for Computational Linguistics*, 124-131.

Natural Language Descriptions of Visual Scenes: Corpus Generation and Analysis

Muhammad Usman Ghani Khan **Rao Muhammad Adeel Nawab** **Yoshihiko Gotoh**
University of Sheffield, United Kingdom
{ughani, r.nawab, y.gotoh}@dcs.shef.ac.uk

Abstract

As video contents continue to expand, it is increasingly important to properly annotate videos for effective search, mining and retrieval purposes. While the idea of annotating images with keywords is relatively well explored, work is still needed for annotating videos with natural language to improve the quality of video search. The focus of this work is to present a video dataset with natural language descriptions which is a step ahead of keywords based tagging. We describe our initial experiences with a corpus consisting of descriptions for video segments crafted from TREC video data. Analysis of the descriptions created by 13 annotators presents insights into humans' interests and thoughts on videos. Such resource can also be used to evaluate automatic natural language generation systems for video.

1 Introduction

This paper presents our experiences in manually constructing a corpus, consisting of natural language descriptions of video segments crafted from a small subset of TREC video[1] data. In a broad sense the task can be considered one form of machine translation as it translates video streams into textual descriptions. To date the number of studies in this field is relatively small partially because of lack of appropriate dataset for such task. Another obstacle may be inherently larger variation for descriptions that can be produced for videos than a conventional translation from one language to another. Indeed humans are very subjective while annotating video streams, *e.g.*, two humans may produce quite different descriptions for the same video. Based on these descriptions we are interested to identify the most important and frequent high level features (HLFs); they may be 'keywords', such as a particular object and its position/moves, used for a semantic indexing task in video retrieval. Mostly HLFs are related to humans, objects, their moves and properties (*e.g.*, gender, emotion and action) (Smeaton et al., 2009).

In this paper we present these HLFs in the form of ontologies and provides two hierarchical structures of important concepts — one most relevant for humans and their actions, and another for non human objects. The similarity of video descriptions is quantified using a bag of word model. The notion of sequence of events in a video was quantified using the order preserving sequence alignment algorithm (longest common subsequence). This corpus may also be used for evaluation of automatic natural language description systems.

1.1 Background

The TREC video evaluation consists of on-going series of annual workshops focusing on a list of information retrieval (IR) tasks. The TREC video promotes research activities by providing a large test collection, uniform scoring procedures, and a forum for research teams interested in presenting their results. The high level feature extraction task aims to identify presence or absence of high level semantic features in a given video sequence (Smeaton et al., 2009). Approaches to video summarisation have been explored using rushes video[2] (Over et al., 2007).

[1] www-nlpir.nist.gov/projects/trecvid/

[2] Rushes are the unedited video footage, sometimes referred to as a pre-production video.

Proceedings of the 13th Conference of the European Chapter of the Association for Computational Linguistics, pages 38–47,
Avignon, France, April 23 - 27 2012.

TREC video also provides a variety of meta data annotations for video datasets. For the HLF task, speech recognition transcripts, a list of master shot references, and shot IDs having HLFs in them are provided. Annotations are created for shots (*i.e.*, one camera take) for the summarisation task. Multiple humans performing multiple actions in different backgrounds can be shown in one shot. Annotations typically consist of a few phrases with several words per phrase. Human related features (*e.g.*, their presence, gender, age, action) are often described. Additionally, camera motion and camera angle, ethnicity information and human's dressing are often stated. On the other hand, details relating to events and objects are usually missing. Human emotion is another missing information in many of such annotations.

2 Corpus Creation

We are exploring approaches to natural language descriptions of video data. The step one of the study is to create a dataset that can be used for development and evaluation. Textual annotations are manually generated in three different flavours, *i.e.*, selection of HLFs (keywords), title assignment (a single phrase) and full description (multiple phrases). Keywords are useful for identification of objects and actions in videos. A title, in a sense, is a summary in the most compact form; it captures the most important content, or the theme, of the video in a short phrase. On the other hand, a full description is lengthy, comprising of several sentences with details of objects, activities and their interactions. Combination of keywords, a title, and a full descriptions will create a valuable resource for text based video retrieval and summarisation tasks. Finally, analysis of this dataset provides an insight into how humans generate natural language description for video.

Most of previous datasets are related to specific tasks; PETS (Young and Ferryman, 2005), CAVIAR (Fisher et al., 2005) and Terrascope (Jaynes et al., 2005) are for surveillance videos. KTH (Schuldt et al., 2004) and the Hollywood action dataset (Marszalek et al., 2009) are for human action recognition. MIT car dataset is for identification of cars (Papageorgiou and Poggio, 1999). Caltech 101 and Caltech 256 are image datasets with 101 and 256 object categories respectively (Griffin et al., 2007) but there is no information about human actions or emotions. There are some datasets specially generated for scene settings such as MIT outdoor scene dataset (Oliva and Torralba, 2009). Quattoni and Torralba (2009) created indoor dataset with 67 different scenes categories. For most of these datasets annotations are available in the form of keywords (*e.g.*, actions such as sit, stand, walk). They were developed for keyword search, object recognition or event identification tasks. Rashtchian et al. (2010) provided an interesting dataset of 1000 images which contain natural language descriptions of those images.

In this study we select video clips from TREC video benchmark for creating annotations. They include categories such as news, meeting, crowd, grouping, indoor/outdoor scene settings, traffic, costume, documentary, identity, music, sports and animals videos. The most important and probably the most frequent content in these videos appears to be a human (or humans), showing their activities, emotions and interactions with other objects. We do not intend to derive a dataset with a full scope of video categories, which is beyond our work. Instead, to keep the task manageable, we aim to create a compact dataset that can be used for developing approaches to translating video contents to natural language description.

Annotations were manually created for a small subset of data prepared form the rushes video summarisation task and the HLF extraction task for the 2007 and 2008 TREC video evaluations. It consisted of 140 segments of videos — 20 segments for each of the following seven categories:

Action videos: Human posture is visible and human can be seen performing some action such as 'sitting', 'standing', 'walking' and 'running'.

Close-up: Human face is visible. Facial expressions and emotions usually define mood of the video (*e.g.*, happy, sad).

News: Presence of an anchor or reporters. Characterised by scene settings such as weather boards at the background.

Meeting: Multiple humans are sitting and communicating. Presence of objects such as chairs and a table.

Grouping: Multiple humans interaction scenes that do not belong to a meeting scenario. A table or chairs may not be present.

Traffic: Presence of vehicles such as cars, buses and trucks. Traffic signals.

Indoor/Outdoor: Scene settings are more obvious than human activities. Examples may be park scenes and office scenes (where computers and files are visible).

Each segment contained a single camera shot, spanning between 10 and 30 seconds in length. Two categories, 'Close-up' and 'Action', are mainly related to humans' activities, expressions and emotions. 'Grouping' and 'Meeting' depict relation and interaction between multiple humans. 'News' videos explain human activities in a constrained environment such as a broadcast studio. Last two categories, 'Indoor/Outdoor' and 'Traffic', are often observed in surveillance videos. They often shows for humans' interaction with other objects in indoor and outdoor settings. TREC video annotated most video segments with a brief description, comprising of multiple phrases and sentences. Further, 13 human subjects prepared additional annotation for these video segments, consisting of keywords, a title and a full description with multiple sentences. They are referred to as **hand annotations** in the rest of this paper.

2.1 Annotation Tool

There exist several freely available video annotation tools. One of the popular video annotation tool is *Simple Video Annotation tool*[3]. It allows to place a simple tag or annotation on a specified part of the screen at a particular time. The approach is similar to the one used by *YouTube*[4]. Another well-known video annotation tool is *Video Annotation Tool*[5]. A video can be scrolled for a certain time period and place annotations for that part of the video. In addition, an annotator can view a video clip, mark a time segment, attach a note to the time segment on a video timeline, or play back the segment. '*Elan*' annotation tool allows to create annotations for both audio and visual data using temporal information (Wittenburg et al., 2006). During that annotation process, a user selects a section of video using the timeline capability and writes annotation for the specific time.

[3]videoannotation.codeplex.com/

[4]www.youtube.com/t/annotations_about

[5]dewey.at.northwestern.edu/ppad2/documents/help/video.html

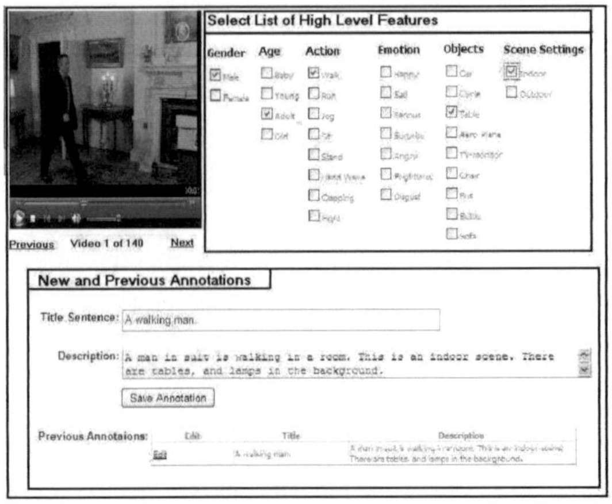

Figure 1: *Video Description Tool* (VDT). An annotator watches one video at one time, selects all HLFs present in the video, describes a theme of the video as a title and creates a full description for important contents in the video.

We have developed our own annotation tool because of a few reasons. None of existing annotation tools provided the functionality of generating a description and/or a title for a video segment. Some tools allows selection of keywords in a free format, which is not suitable for our purpose of creating a list of HLFs. Figure 1 shows a screen shot of the video annotation tool developed, which is referred to as *Video Description Tool* (VDT). VDT is simple to operate and assist annotators in creating quality annotations. There are three main items to be annotated. An annotator is shown one video segment at one time. Firstly a restricted list of HLFs is provided for each segment and an annotator is required to select all HLFs occurring in the segment. Second, a title should be typed in. A title may be a theme of the video, typically a phrase or a sentence with several words. Lastly, a full description of video contents is created, consisting of several phrases and sentences. During the annotation, it is possible to stop, forward, reverse or play again the same video if required. Links are provided for navigation to the next and the previous videos. An annotator can delete or update earlier annotations if required.

2.2 Annotation Process

A total of 13 annotators were recruited to create texts for the video corpus. They were undergraduate or postgraduate students and fluent in English. It was expected that they could produce descriptions of good quality without detailed instructions or further training. A simple instruction set was given, leaving a wide room for individual interpretation about what might be included in the description. For quality reasons each annotator was given one week to complete the full set of videos.

Each annotator was presented with a complete set of 140 video segments on the annotation tool VDT. For each video annotators were instructed to provide

- a title of one sentence long, indicating the main theme of the video;
- description of four to six sentences, related to what are shown in the video;
- selection of high level features (*e.g.*, male, female, walk, smile, table).

The annotations are made with open vocabulary — that is, they can use any English words as long as they contain only standard (ASCII) characters. They should avoid using any symbols or computer codes. Annotators were further guided not to use proper nouns (*e.g.*, do not state the person name) and information obtained from audio. They were also instructed to select all HLFs appeared in the video.

3 Corpus Analysis

13 annotators created descriptions for 140 videos (seven categories with 20 videos per category), resulting in 1820 documents in the corpus. The total number of words is 30954, hence the average length of one document is 17 words. We counted 1823 unique words and 1643 keywords (nouns and verbs).

Figure 2 shows a video segment for a meeting scene, sampled at 1 fps (frame per second), and three examples for hand annotations. They typically contain two to five phrases or sentences. Most sentences are short, ranging between two to six words. Descriptions for human, gender, emotion and action are commonly observed. Occasionally minor details for objects and events are also stated. Descriptions for the background are often associated with objects rather than humans. It is interesting to observe the subjectivity with the task; the variety of words were selected by individual annotators to express the same video contents. Figure 3 shows another example of a video segment for a human activity and hand annotations.

Hand annotation 1
(title) interview in the studio;
(description) three people are sitting on a red table; a tv presenter is interviewing his guests; he is talking to the guests; he is reading from papers in front of him; they are wearing a formal suit;

Hand annotation 2
(title) tv presenter and guests
(description) there are three persons; the one is host; others are guests; they are all men;

Hand annotation 3
(title) three men are talking
(description) three people are sitting around the table and talking each other;

Figure 2: A montage showing a meeting scene in a news video and three sets of hand annotations. In this video segment, three persons are shown sitting on chairs around a table — extracted from TREC video '*20041116_150100_CCTV4_DAILY_NEWS_CHN33050028*'.

3.1 Human Related Features

After removing function words, the frequency for each word was counted in hand annotations. Two classes are manually defined; one class is related directly to humans, their body structure, identity, action and interaction with other humans. (Another class represents artificial and natural objects and scene settings, *i.e.*, all the words not directly related to humans, although they are important for semantic understanding of the visual scene — described further in the next section.) Note that some related words (*e.g.*, '*woman*' and '*lady*') were replaced with a single concept ('*female*'); concepts were then built up into a hierarchical structure for each class.

Figure 4 presents human related information observed in hand annotations. Annotators paid full attention to human gender information as the number of occurrences for '*female*' and '*male*' is

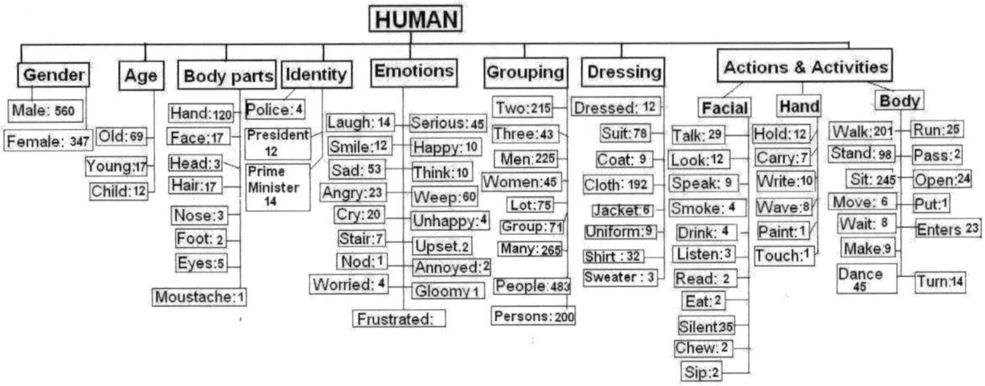

Figure 4: Human related information found in 13 hand annotations. Information is divided into structures (gender, age, identity, emotion, dressing, grouping and body parts) and activities (facial, hand and body). Each box contains a high level concept (*e.g.*, '*woman*' and '*lady*' are both merged into '*female*') and the number of its occurrences.

Hand annotation 1
(title) outdoor talking scene;
(description) young woman is sitting on chair in park and talking to man who is standing next to her;

Hand annotation 2
(title) A couple is talking;
(description) two person are talking; a lady is sitting and a man is standing; a man is wearing a black formal suit; a red bus is moving in the street; people are walking in the street; a yellow taxi is moving in the street;

Hand annotation 3
(title) talk of two persons;
(description) a man is wearing dark clothes; he is standing there; a woman is sitting in front of him; they are saying to each other;

Figure 3: A montage of video showing a human activity in an outdoor scene and three sets of hand annotations. In this video segment, a man is standing while a woman is sitting in outdoor — from TREC video '*20041101_160000_CCTV4_DAILY_NEWS_CHN_41504210*'.

the highest among HLFs. This highlights our conclusion that most interesting and important HLF is humans when they appear in a video. On the other hand age information (*e.g.*, '*old*', '*young*', '*child*') was not identified very often. Names for human body parts have mixed occurrences ranging from high ('*hand*') to low ('*moustache*'). Six basic emotions — anger, disgust, fear, happiness, sadness, and surprise as discussed by Paul Ekman[6] — covered most of facial expressions.

Dressing became an interesting feature when a human was in a unique dress such as a formal suit, a coloured jacket, an army or police uniform. Videos with multiple humans were common, and thus human grouping information was frequently recognised. Human body parts were involved in identification of human activities; they included actions such as standing, sitting, walking, moving, holding and carrying. Actions related to human body and posture were frequently identified. It was rare that unique human identities, such as police, president and prime minister, were described. This may indicate that a viewer might want to know a specific type of an object to describe a particular situation instead of generalised concepts.

3.2 Objects and Scene Settings

Figure 5 shows the hierarchy created for HLFs that did not appear in Figure 4. Most of the words are related to artificial objects. Humans interact with these objects to complete an activity —

[6] en.wikipedia.org/wiki/Paul_Ekman

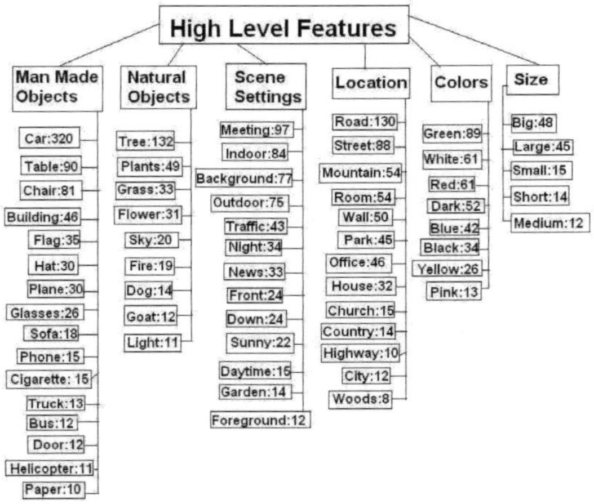

Figure 5: Artificial and natural objects and scene settings were summarised into six groups.

e.g., '*man is sitting on a chair*', '*she is talking on the phone*', '*he is wearing a hat*'. Natural objects were usually in the background, providing the additional context of a visual scene — *e.g.*, '*human is standing in the jungle*, '*sky is clear today*'. Place and location information (*e.g.*, room, office, hospital, cafeteria) were important as they show the position of humans or other objects in the scene — *e.g.*, '*there is a car on the road*, '*people are walking in the park*'.

Colour information often plays an important part in identifying separate HLFs — *e.g.*, '*a man in black shirt is walking with a woman with green jacket*', '*she is wearing a white uniform*'. The large number of occurrences for colours indicates human's interest in observing not only objects but also their colour scheme in a visual scene. Some hand descriptions reflected annotator's interest in scene settings shown in the foreground or in the background. Indoor/outdoor scene settings were also interested in by some annotators. These observations demonstrate that a viewer is interested in high level details of a video and relationships between different prominent objects in a visual scene.

3.3 Spatial Relations

Figure 6 presents a list of the most frequent words and phrases related to spatial relations found in hand annotations. Spatial relations between HLFs are important when explaining the semantics of visual scenes. Their effective use leads to the smooth description. Spatial relations can be categorised into

in (404); with (120); on (329); near (68); around (63); at (55); on the left (35); in front of (24); down (24); together (24); along (16); beside (16); on the right (16); into (14); far (11); between (10); in the middle (10); outside (8); off (8); over (8); pass-by (8); across (7); inside (7); middle (7); under (7); away (6); after (7)

Figure 6: List of frequent spatial relations with their counts found in hand annotations.

static: relations between stationary objects;

dynamic: direction and path of moving objects;

inter-static and dynamic: relations between moving and not moving objects.

Static relations can establish the scene settings (*e.g.*, '*chairs around a table*' may imply an indoor scene). Dynamic relations are used for finding activities present in the video (*e.g.*, '*a man is running with a dog*'). Inter-static and dynamic relations are a mixture of stationary and non stationary objects; they explain semantics of the complete scene (*e.g.*, '*persons are sitting on the chairs around the table*' indicates a meeting scene).

3.4 Temporal Relations

Video is a class of time series data formed with highly complex multi dimensional contents. Let video X be a uniformly sampled frame sequence of length n, denoted by $X = \{x_1, \ldots, x_n\}$, and each frame x_i gives a chronological position of the sequence (Figure 7). To generate full description of video contents, annotators use temporal information to join descriptions of individual frames. For example,

> *A man is walking. After sometime he enters the room. Later on he is sitting on the chair.*

Based on the analysis of the corpus, we describe temporal information in two flavors:

1. temporal information extracted from activities of a single human;

2. interactions between multiple humans.

Most common relations in video sequences are '*before*', '*after*', '*start*' and '*finish*' for single humans, and '*overlap*', '*during*' and '*meeting*' for multiple humans.

Figure 8 presents a list of the most frequent words in the corpus related to temporal relations. It can be observed that annotators put much focus

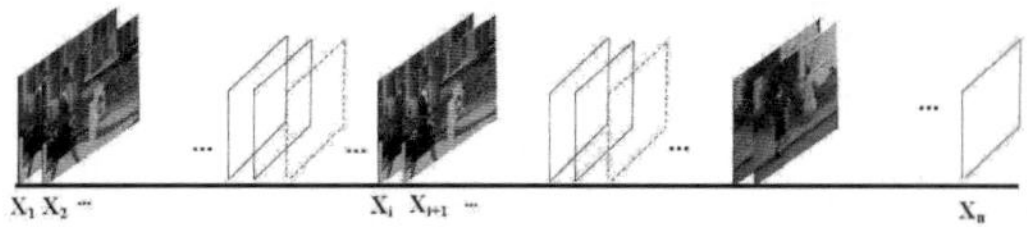

Figure 7: Illustration of a video as a uniformly sampled sequence of length n. A video frame is denoted by x_i, whose spatial context can be represented in the d dimensional feature space.

single human:
then (25); end (24); before (22); after (16); next (12); later on (12); start (11); previous (11); throughout (10); finish (8); afterwards (6); prior to (4); since (4)
multiple humans:
meet (114); while (37); during (27); at the same time (19); overlap (12); meanwhile (12); throughout (7); equals (4)

Figure 8: List of frequent temporal relations with their counts found in hand annotations.

on keywords related to activities of multiple humans as compared to single human cases. '*Meet*' keyword has the highest frequency, as annotators usually consider most of the scenes involving multiple humans as the meeting scene. '*While*' keyword is mostly used for showing separate activities of multiple humans such as '*a man is walking while a woman is sitting*'.

3.5 Similarity between Descriptions

A well-established approach to calculating human inter-annotator agreement is kappa statistics (Eugenio and Glass, 2004). However in the current task it is not possible to compute inter-annotator agreement using this approach because no category was defined for video descriptions. Further the description length for one video can vary among annotators. Alternatively the similarity between natural language descriptions can be calculated; an effective and commonly used measure to find the similarity between a pair of documents is the overlap similarity coefficient (Manning and Schütze, 1999):

$$Sim_{overlap}(X, Y) = \frac{|S(X, n) \cap S(Y, n)|}{\min(|S(X, n)|, |S(Y, n)|)}$$

where $S(X, n)$ and $S(Y, n)$ are the set of distinct n-grams in documents X and Y respectively. It is a similarity measure related to the Jaccard index (Tan et al., 2006). Note that when a set X is a subset of Y or the converse, the overlap coefficient is equal to one. Values for the overlap coefficient range between 0 and 1, where '0' presents the situation where documents are completely different and '1' describes the case where two documents are exactly the same.

Table 1 shows the average overlap similarity scores for seven scene categories within 13 hand annotations. The average was calculated from scores for individual description, that was compared with the rest of descriptions in the same category. The outcome demonstrate the fact that humans have different observations and interests while watching videos. Calculation were repeated with two conditions; one with stop words removed and Porter stemmer (Porter, 1993) applied, but synonyms NOT replaced, and the other with stop words NOT removed, but Porter stemmer applied and synonyms replaced. It was found the latter combination of preprocessing techniques resulted in better scores. Not surprisingly synonym replacement led to increased performance, indicating that humans do express the same concept using different terms.

The average overlap similarity score was higher for 'Traffic' videos than for the rest of categories. Because vehicles were the major entity in 'Traffic' videos, rather than humans and their actions, contributing for annotators to create more uniform descriptions. Scores for some other categories were lower. It probably means that there are more aspects to pay attention when watching videos in, *e.g.*, 'Grouping' category, hence resulting in the wider range of natural language expressions produced.

3.6 Sequence of Events Matching

Video is a class of time series data which can be partitioned into time aligned frames (images). These frames are tied together sequentially and temporally. Therefore, it will be useful to know how a person captures the temporal information present in a video. As the order is preserved in a sequence of events, a suitable measure to quantify sequential and temporal information of a description is the longest common subsequence (LCS). This approach computes the similarity between a pair of token (*i.e.*, word) sequences by simply counting the number of edit operations (insertions and deletions) required to transform one sequence into the other. The output is a sequence of common elements such that no other longer string is

	Action	Close-up	Indoor	Grouping	Meeting	News	Traffic
unigram (A)	0.3827	0.3913	0.4217	0.3809	0.3968	0.4378	0.4687
(B)	0.4135	0.4269	0.4544	0.4067	0.4271	0.4635	0.5174
bigram (A)	0.1483	0.1572	0.1870	0.1605	0.1649	0.1872	0.1765
(B)	0.2490	0.2616	0.2877	0.2619	0.2651	0.2890	0.2825
trigram (A)	0.0136	0.0153	0.0301	0.0227	0.0219	0.0279	0.0261
(B)	0.1138	0.1163	0.1302	0.1229	0.1214	0.1279	0.1298

Table 1: Average overlapping similarity scores within 13 hand annotations. For each of unigram, bigram and trigram, scores are calculated for seven categories in two conditions: (A) stop words removed and Porter stemmer applied, but synonyms NOT replaced; (B) stop words NOT removed, but Porter stemmer applied and synonyms replaced.

	raw	synonym	keyword
Action	0.3782	0.3934	0.3955
Close-up	0.4181	0.4332	0.4257
Indoor	0.4248	0.4386	0.4338
Grouping	0.3941	0.4104	0.3832
Meeting	0.3939	0.4107	0.4124
News	0.4382	0.4587	0.4531
Traffic	0.4036	0.4222	0.4093

Table 2: Similarity scores based on the longest common subsequence (LCS) in three conditions: scores without any preprocessing (raw), scores after synonym replacement (synonym), and scores by keyword comparison (keyword). For keyword comparison, verbs and nouns were presented as keywords after stemming and removing stop words.

available. In the experiments, the LCS score between word sequences is normalised by the length of the shorter sequence.

Table 2 presents results for identifying sequences of events in hand descriptions using the LCS similarity score. Individual descriptions were compared with the rest of descriptions in the same category and the average score was calculated. Relatively low scores in the table indicate the great variation in annotators' attention on the sequence of events, or temporal information, in a video. Events described by one annotator may not have been listed by another annotator. The News videos category resulted in the highest similarity score, confirming the fact that videos in this category are highly structured.

3.7 Video Classification

To demonstrate the application of this corpus with natural language descriptions, a supervised document classification task is outlined. *Tf-idf* score can express textual document features (Dumais et al., 1998). Traditional *tf-idf* represents the relation between term t and document d. It provides a measure of the importance of a term within a particular document, calculated as

$$tfidf(t,d) = tf(t,d) \cdot idf(d) \qquad (1)$$

where the term frequency $tf(t,d)$ is given by

$$tf(t,d) = \frac{N_{t,d}}{\sum_k N_{k,d}} \qquad (2)$$

In the above equation $N_{t,d}$ is the number of occurrences of term t in document d, and the denominator is the sum of the number of occurrences for all terms in document d, that is, the size of the document $|d|$. Further the inverse document frequency $idf(d)$ is

$$idf(d) = \log \frac{N}{W(t)} \qquad (3)$$

where N is the total number of documents in the corpus and $W(t)$ is the total number of document containing term t.

A term-document matrix X is presented by $T \times D$ matrix $tfidf(t,d)$. In the experiment Naive Bayes probabilistic supervised learning algorithm was applied for classification using *Weka* machine learning library (Hall et al., 2009). Tenfold cross validation was applied. The performance was measured using precision, recall and F1-measure (Table 3). F1-measure was low for 'Grouping' and 'Action' videos, indicating the difficulty in classifying these types of natural language descriptions. Best classification results were achieved for 'Traffic' and 'Indoor/Outdoor' scenes. Absence of humans and their actions might have contributed obtaining the high classification scores. Human actions and activities were present in most videos in various categories, hence the 'Action' category resulted in the lowest results. 'Grouping' category also showed

	precision	recall	F1-measure
Action	0.701	0.417	0.523
Close-up	0.861	0.703	0.774
Grouping	0.453	0.696	0.549
Indoor	0.846	0.915	0.879
Meeting	0.723	0.732	0.727
News	0.679	0.823	0.744
Traffic	0.866	0.869	0.868
average	0.753	0.739	0.736

Table 3: Results for supervised classification using the *tf-idf* features.

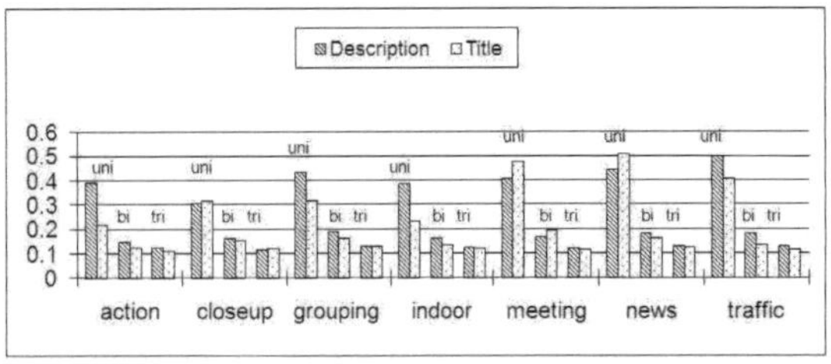

Figure 9: The average overlap similarity scores for titles and for descriptions. 'uni', 'bi', and 'tri' indicate the unigram, bigram, and trigram based similarity scores, respectively. They were calculated without any preprocessing such as stop word removal or synonym replacement.

weaker result; it was probably because processing for interaction between multiple people, with their overlapped actions, had not been fully developed. Overall classification results are encouraging which demonstrates that this dataset is a good resource for evaluating natural language description systems of short videos.

3.8 Analysis of Title and Description

A title may be considered a very short form of summary. We carried out further experiments to calculate the similarity between a title and a description manually created for a video. The length of a title varied between two to five words. Figure 9 shows the average overlapping similarity scores between titles and descriptions. It can be observed that, in general, scores for titles were lower than those for descriptions, apart from 'News' and 'Meeting' videos. It was probably caused by the short length of titles; by inspection we found phrases such as '*news video*' and '*meeting scene*' for these categories.

Another experiment was performed for classification of videos based on title information only. Figure 10 shows comparison of classification per-

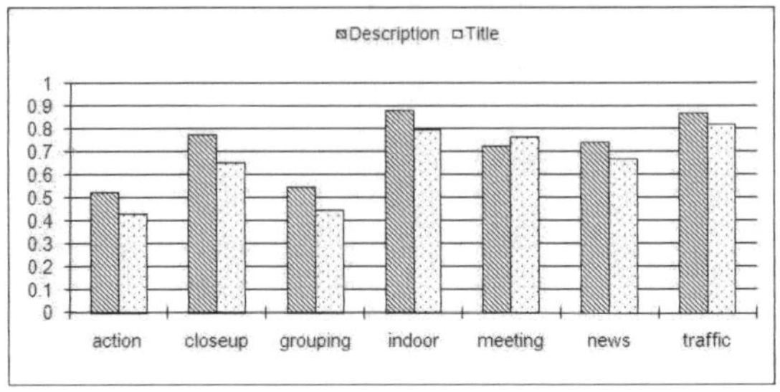

Figure 10: Video classification by titles, and by descriptions.

formance with titles and with descriptions. We were able to make correct classification in many videos with titles alone, although the performance was slightly less for titles only than for descriptions.

4 Conclusion and Future Work

This paper presented our experiments using a corpus created for natural language description of videos. For a small subset of TREC video data in seven categories, annotators produced titles, descriptions and selected high level features. This paper aimed to characterise the corpus based on analysis of hand annotations and a series of experiments for description similarity and video classification. In the future we plan to develop automatic machine annotations for video sequences and compare them against human authored annotations. Further, we aim to annotate this corpus in multiple languages such as Arabic and Urdu to generate a multilingual resource for video processing community.

Acknowledgements

M U G Khan thanks University of Engineering & Technology, Lahore, Pakistan and R M A Nawab thanks COMSATS Institute of Information Technology, Lahore, Pakistan for funding their work under the Faculty Development Program.

References

S. Dumais, J. Platt, D. Heckerman, and M. Sahami. 1998. Inductive learning algorithms and representations for text categorization. In *Proceedings of the seventh international conference on Information and knowledge management*, pages 148–155. ACM.

B.D. Eugenio and M. Glass. 2004. The kappa statistic: A second look. *Computational linguistics*, 30(1):95–101.

R. Fisher, J. Santos-Victor, and J. Crowley. 2005. Caviar: Context aware vision using image-based active recognition.

G. Griffin, A. Holub, and P. Perona. 2007. Caltech-256 object category dataset.

M. Hall, E. Frank, G. Holmes, B. Pfahringer, P. Reutemann, and I.H. Witten. 2009. The weka data mining software: an update. *ACM SIGKDD Explorations Newsletter*, 11(1):10–18.

C. Jaynes, A. Kale, N. Sanders, and E. Grossmann. 2005. The terrascope dataset: A scripted multi-camera indoor video surveillance dataset with ground-truth. In *Proceedings of the IEEE Workshop on VS PETS*, volume 4. Citeseer.

Christopher Manning and Hinrich Schütze. 1999. *Foundations of Statistical Natural Language Processing*. MIT Press.

M. Marszalek, I. Laptev, and C. Schmid. 2009. Actions in context.

A. Oliva and A. Torralba. 2009. Mit outdoor scene dataset.

P. Over, A.F. Smeaton, and P. Kelly. 2007. The trecvid 2007 bbc rushes summarization evaluation pilot. In *Proceedings of the international workshop on TRECVID video summarization*, pages 1–15. ACM.

C. Papageorgiou and T. Poggio. 1999. A trainable object detection system: Car detection in static images. Technical Report 1673, October. (CBCL Memo 180).

M.F. Porter. 1993. An algorithm for suffix stripping. *Program: electronic library and information systems*, 14(3):130–137.

A. Quattoni and A. Torralba. 2009. Recognizing indoor scenes.

C. Rashtchian, P. Young, M. Hodosh, and J. Hockenmaier. 2010. Collecting image annotations using amazon's mechanical turk. In *Proceedings of the NAACL HLT 2010 Workshop on Creating Speech and Language Data with Amazon's Mechanical Turk*, pages 139–147. Association for Computational Linguistics.

C. Schuldt, I. Laptev, and B. Caputo. 2004. Recognizing human actions: A local svm approach. In *Pattern Recognition, 2004. ICPR 2004. Proceedings of the 17th International Conference on*, volume 3, pages 32–36. IEEE.

A.F. Smeaton, P. Over, and W. Kraaij. 2009. High-level feature detection from video in trecvid: a 5-year retrospective of achievements. *Multimedia Content Analysis*, pages 1–24.

P.N. Tan, M. Steinbach, V. Kumar, et al. 2006. *Introduction to data mining*. Pearson Addison Wesley Boston.

P. Wittenburg, H. Brugman, A. Russel, A. Klassmann, and H. Sloetjes. 2006. Elan: a professional framework for multimodality research. In *Proceedings of LREC*, volume 2006. Citeseer.

D.P. Young and J.M. Ferryman. 2005. Pets metrics: On-line performance evaluation service. In *Joint IEEE International Workshop on Visual Surveillance and Performance Evaluation of Tracking and Surveillance (VS-PETS)*, pages 317–324.

Combining EBMT, SMT, TM and IR Technologies for Quality and Scale

Sandipan Dandapat[1], **Sara Morrissey**[1], **Andy Way**[2], **Joseph van Genabith**[1]
[1] CNGL, School of Computing
Dublin City University, Glasnevin, Dublin 9, Ireland
{sdandapat,smorri,josef}@computing.dcu.ie
[2] Applied Language Solutions, Delph, UK
andy.way@appliedlanguage.com

Abstract

In this paper we present a hybrid statistical machine translation (SMT)-example-based MT (EBMT) system that shows significant improvement over both SMT and EBMT baseline systems. First we present a runtime EBMT system using a subsentential translation memory (TM). The EBMT system is further combined with an SMT system for effective hybridization of the pair of systems. The hybrid system shows significant improvement in translation quality (0.82 and 2.75 absolute BLEU points) for two different language pairs (English–Turkish (En–Tr) and English–French (En–Fr)) over the baseline SMT system. However, the EBMT approach suffers from significant time complexity issues for a runtime approach. We explore two methods to make the system scalable at runtime. First, we use an heuristic-based approach. Secondly, we use an IR-based indexing technique to speed up the time-consuming matching procedure of the EBMT system. The index-based matching procedure substantially improves run-time speed without affecting translation quality.

1 Introduction

State-of-the-art phrase-based SMT (Koehn, 2010a) is the most successful MT approach in many large scale evaluations, such as WMT,[1] IWSLT[2] etc. At the same time, work continues in the area of EBMT. Some recent EBMT systems include Cunei (Phillips, 2011), CMU-EBMT (Brown, 2011) and OpenMaTrEx (Dandapat et al., 2010). The success of an SMT system often depends on the amount of parallel training corpora available for the particular language pair. However, low translation accuracy has been observed for language pairs with limited training resources (Islam et al., 2010; Khalilov et al., 2010). SMT systems effectively discard the actual training data once the models (translation model and language model) have been estimated. This can lead to their inability to guarantee good quality translation for sentences closely matching those in the training corpora. By contrast, EBMT systems usually maintain a linked relationship between the full sentence pairs in source and target texts. Because of this EBMT systems can often capture long range dependencies and rich morphology at runtime. In contrast to SMT, however, most EBMT models lack a well-formed probability model, which restricts the use of statistical information in the translation process.

Keeping these in mind, our objective is to develop a good quality MT system choosing the best approach for each input in the form of a hybrid SMT-EBMT approach. It is often the case that an EBMT system produces a good translation where SMT systems fail and vice versa (Dandapat et al., 2011).

An EBMT system relies on past translations to derive the target output for a given input. Runtime EBMT approaches generally do not include any training stage, which has the advantage of not having to depend on time-consuming preprocessing. On the other hand, their runtime complexity can be considerable. This is due to the time-consuming matching stage at runtime that finds the example

[1] http://www.statmt.org/wmt11/
[2] http://www.iwslt2011.org/

Proceedings of the 13th Conference of the European Chapter of the Association for Computational Linguistics, pages 48–58,
Avignon, France, April 23 - 27 2012. ©2012 Association for Computational Linguistics

(or set of examples) which most closely matches the source-language sentence to be translated. This matching step often uses some variation of string edit-distance measures (Levenshtein, 1965) which has quadratic time complexity.[3] This is quite time-consuming even when a moderate amount of training examples are used for the matching procedure.

We adopt two alternative approaches to tackle the above problem. First we use heuristics which are often useful to avoid some of the computations. For a input sentence, in the matching process, we may not need to compute the string edit distance with all sentences in the example base. In order to prune some of the computation, we rely on the fact that the input sentence and its closest match sentence from the example-base are likely to have a similar sentence length. Search engine indexing is an effective way of storing data for fast and accurate retrieval of information. During retrieval, a set of documents are extracted based on their similarity to the input query. In our second approach, we use this concept to efficiently retrieve a potential set of suitable candidate sentences from the example-base to find the closest match. We index the entire example-base considering each source-side sentence as a document for the indexer. We show that improvements can be made with our approach in terms of time complexity without affecting the translation quality.

The remainder of this paper is organized as follows. The next section presents work related to our EBMT approach. Section 3 describes the MT systems used in our experiments. Section 4 focuses on the two techniques used to make the system scalable. Section 5 presents the experiments in detail. Section 6 presents and discusses the results and provides an error analysis. We conclude in Section 7.

2 Related Work

The EBMT framework was first introduced by Nagao (1984) as the "MT by analogy principle". The two main approaches to EBMT are distinguished by the inclusion or exclusion of a preprocessing/training stage. Approaches that incorporate a training stage are commonly called "compiled approaches" (Cicekli and Güvenir, 2001). Approaches that do not include a training stage are often referred to as "pure" or "runtime" EBMT approaches, e.g. (Lepage and Denoual, 2005). These approaches have the advantage that they do not depend on any time-consuming preprocessing stages. On the other hand, their runtime complexity can be considerable.

EBMT is often linked with the related concept of *translation memory* (TM). A TM essentially stores source- and target-language translation pairs for effective reuse of previous translations originally created by human translators. TMs are often used to store examples for EBMT systems. After retrieving a set of examples with associated translations, EBMT systems automatically extract translations of suitable fragments and combine them to produce a grammatical target output.

Phrase-based SMT systems (Koehn, 2010a), produce a source–target aligned subsentential phrase table which can be adapted as an additional TM to be used in a CAT environment (Simard, 2003; Biçici and Dymetman, 2008; Bourdaillet et al., 2009; Simard and Isabelle, 2009). Koehn and Senellart (2010b) use SMT to produce the translation of the non-matched fragments after obtaining the TM-based match. EBMT phrases have also been used to populate the knowledge database of an SMT system (Groves et al., 2006). However, to the best of our knowledge, the use of SMT phrase tables within an EBMT system as an additional sub-sentential TM has not been attempted so far. Some work has been carried out to integrate MT in a CAT environment to translate the whole segment using the MT system when no sufficiently well matching translation unit (TU) is found in the TM. The TransType system (Langlais et al., 2002) integrates an SMT system within a text editor to suggest possible continuations of the translations being typed by the translator. By contrast, our approach attempts to integrate the subsentential TM obtained using SMT techniques within an EBMT system.

3 MT Systems

The SMT system used in our hybrid SMT-EBMT approach is the vanilla Moses[4] decoder.

[3]Ukkonen (1983) gave an algorithm for computing edit-distance with the worst case complexity $O(md)$, where m is the length of the string and d is their edit distance. This is effective when $m \gg d$. We use word-based edit distance, so m is shorter in length.

[4]`http://www.statmt.org/moses/`

Moses (Koehn et al., 2007) is a set of SMT tools that include routines to automatically train a translation model for any language pair and an efficient decoder to find the most probable translation. Due to lack of space and the wide usage of Moses, here we focus more on the novel EBMT system we have developed for our hybrid SMT-EBMT approach. The EBMT system described in this section is based on previous work (Dandapat et al., 2010) and some of the material has been reproduced here to make the paper complete.

Like all other EBMT systems, our particular approach comprises three stages: matching, alignment and recombination. Our EBMT system also uses a subsentential TM in addition to the sentence aligned example-base. Using the original TM as a training set, additional subsentential TUs (words and phrases) are extracted from it based on word alignments and phrase pairs produced by Moses. These subsentential TUs are used for alignment and recombination stages of our EBMT system.

3.1 Building a Subsentential TM for EBMT

A TM for EBMT usually contains TUs linked at the sentence, phrasal and word level. TUs can be derived manually or automatically (e.g. using the marker-hypothesis (Groves et al., 2006)). Usually, TUs are linguistically motivated translation units. In this paper however, we explore a different route, as manual construction of high-quality TMs is time consuming and expensive. Furthermore, only considering linguistically motivated TUs may limit the matching potential of a TM. Because of this, we used SMT technology to automatically create the subsentential part of our TM at the phrase (i.e. no longer necessarily linguistically motivated) and word level. Based on Moses word alignment (using GIZA++ (Och and Ney, 2003)) and phrase table construction, we construct the additional TM for further use within an EBMT approach.

Firstly, we add entries to the TM based on the aligned phrase pairs from the Moses phrase table using the following two scores:

1. Direct phrase translation probabilities: $\phi(t|s)$
2. Direct lexical weight: $lex(t|s)$

Table 1 shows an example of phrase pairs with the associated probabilities learned by Moses. We keep all target equivalents in a sorted order based on the above probabilities. This helps us in the matching procedure, but during recombination we only consider the most probable target equivalent. The following shows the resulting TUs in the TM for the English source phrase *a hotel.*

Table 1: Moses phrase equivalence probabilities.

English (s)	Turkish (t)	$p(t\|s)$	$lex(t\|s)$
a hotel	bir otel	0.826087	0.12843
a hotel	bir otelde	0.086957	0.07313
a hotel	otel mi	0.043478	0.00662
a hotel	otel	0.043478	0.22360

a hotel ⇔ {*bir otel, bir otelde, otel, otem mi*}

Secondly, we add entries to the TM based on the source-to-target word-aligned file. We also keep the multiple target equivalents for a source word in a sorted order. This essentially adds source- and target-language equivalent word pairs into the TM. Note that the entries in the TM may contain incorrect source-target equivalents due to unreliable word/phrase alignments produced by Moses.

3.2 EBMT Engine

The overview of the three stages of the EBMT engine is given below:

Matching: In this stage, we find a sentence pair $\langle s_c, t_c \rangle$ from the example-base that closely matches with the input sentence s. We used a fuzzy-match score (FMS) based on a word-level edit distance metric (Wagner and Fischer, 1974) to find the closest matching source-side sentence from the example-base ($\{s_i\}_1^N$) based on Equation (i).

$$\text{score}(s, s_i) = 1 - \text{ED}(s, s_i) / \max(|s|, |s_i|) \quad (i)$$

where $|x|$ denotes the length (in words) of a sentence, and $\text{ED}(x, y)$ refers to the word-level edit distance between x and y. The EBMT system considers the associated translation t_c of the closest matching source sentence s_c, to build a skeleton for the translation of the input sentence s.

Alignment: After retrieving the closest fuzzy-matched sentence pair $\langle s_c, t_c \rangle$, we identify the non-matching fragments from the skeleton translation t_c in two steps.

Firstly, we find the matched and non-matched segments between s and s_c using edit distance trace. Given the two sentences (s and s_c), the algorithm finds the minimum possible number of operations (substitutions, additions and deletions) required to change the closest match s_c into the input sentence s. For example, consider the input sentence $s = w_1\, w_2\, w_3\, w_4\, w_5\, w_6\, w_7\, w_8$ and $s_c = w'_1\, w'_3\, w_4\, w_5\, w_7\, w_8\, w'_9$. Figure 1 shows the matched and non-matched sequence between s and s_c using edit-distance trace.

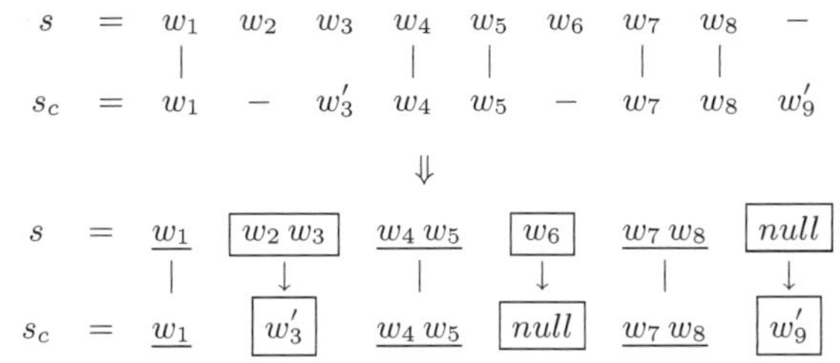

Figure 1: Extraction of matched (underlined) and non-matched (boxed) segments between s and s_c.

Secondly, we align each non-matched segment in s_c with its associated translation using the TM and the GIZA++ alignment. Based on the source-target aligned pair in the TM, we mark the mismatched segment in t_c. We find the longest possible segment from the non-matched segment in s_c that has a matching target equivalent in t_c based on the source-target equivalents in the TM. We continue the process recursively until no further segments of the non-matched segment in s_c can be matched with t_c using the TM. Remaining non-matching segments in s_c are then aligned with segments in t_c using the GIZA++ word alignment information.

Recombination: In the recombination stage, we add or substitute segments from the input sentence s with the skeleton translation equivalent t_c. We also delete some segments from t_c that have no correspondence in s. After obtaining the source segments (needs to be added or substituted in t_c) from the input s, we use our subsentential TM to translate these segments. Details of the recombination process are given in Algorithm 1.

3.3 An Illustrative Example

As a running example, for the input sentence in (1a) the corresponding closest fuzzy-matched sentence pair $\langle s_c, t_c \rangle$ is shown in (1b) and (1c). The portion marked with angled brackets in (1c) are aligned with the mismatched portion in (1b). The character and the following number in angled brackets indicate the edit operation ('s' indicates substitution) and the index of the mismatched segment from the alignment process respectively.

Algorithm 1 recombination(X, TM)

In: source segment X,
subsentential translation memory TM
Out: translation of source segment X

```
mark all words of X as untranslated (untranslatedPortions(X) ← {X})
repeat
    U = untranslatedPortions(X)
    x = longest subsegment in untranslatedPortions(X) such that (x, t_x) ∈ TM;
    substitute(X, x → t_x) {substitute x with its target equivalent t_x in X}
    remove x from untranslatedPortions(X)
until (untranslatedPortions(X) = U)
return X
```

1. (a) s: i 'd like a <s#0:*present*> for <s#1:*my mother*> .
   (b) s_c: i 'd like a <s#0:*shampoo*> for <s#1:*greasy hair*> .
   (c) t_c: <s#1:*yağlı saçlar*> için bir <s#0:*şampuan*> istiyorum .

During recombination, we need to replace two segments in (1c) {*yağlı saçlar* (greasy hair) and *şampuan* (shampoo)} with the two corresponding source segments in (1a) {*my mother* and *present*} as an intermediate stage (2) along the way towards producing a target equivalent.

(2)<1:*my mother*> için bir <0:*present*> istiyorum .

Furthermore, replacing the untranslated segments in (2) with the translations obtained using TM, we derive the output translation in (3) of the original input sentence in (1).

(3) <*annem*> için bir <*hediye*> istiyorum .

4 Scalability

The main motivation of scalability is to improve the speed of the EBMT system when using a large example-base. The matching procedure in an EBMT system finds the example (or a set of examples) which closely matches the source-language string to be translated. All matching processes necessarily involve a distance or similarity measure. The most widely used distance measure in EBMT matching is Levenshtein distance (Levenshtein, 1965; Wagner and Fischer, 1974) which has quadratic time complexity. In our EBMT system, we find the closest sentence at runtime from the whole example-base for a given input sentence using the edit distance matching score. Thus, the matching step of the EBMT system is a time-consuming process with a runtime complexity of $O(nm^2)$, where n denotes the size of the example-base and m denotes the average length (in words) of a sentence. Due to a significant runtime complexity, the EBMT system can only handle a moderate size example-base in the matching stage. However, it is important to handle a large example-base to improve the quality of an MT system. In order to make the system scalable with a larger example-base, we adopt two approaches for finding the closest matching sentences efficiently.

4.1 Grouping

Our first attempt is heuristic-based. We divide the example-base into bins based on sentence length. It is anticipated that the sentence from the example-base that most closely matches an input sentence will fall into the group which has comparable length to the length of the input sentence. First, we divide the example-base E into different bins based on their word-level length $E = \bigcup_{i=1}^{l} E_i$ and $E_i \bigcap E_j = \emptyset$ for all $i \neq j$ where $0 \leq i, j \leq l$. E_i denotes the set of sentences with length i and l is the maximum length of a sentence in E. In order to find the closest match for a test sentence (s of length k), we only consider examples $E_G = \bigcup_{m=0}^{x} E_{k \pm m}$, where x indicates the window size. In our experiment, we consider the value of x from 0 to 2. We find the closest-match s_c from E_G for a given test sentence s. E_G has fewer sentences compared to E which will effectively reduce the time of the matching procedure.

4.2 Indexing

Our second approach to addressing time complexity is to use indexing. We index the complete example-base using an open-source IR engine SMART[5] and retrieve a potential set of candidate sentences (likely to contain the closest match sentence) from the example-base. Unigrams extracted from the sentences of the example-base are indexed using the language model (LM) and complete sentences are considered as retrievable units. In LM-based retrieval we assume that a given query is generated from a unigram document language model. The application of the LM retrieval model in our case returns a sorted list of sentences from the example-base ordered by the estimated probabilities of generating the given input sentence.

In order to improve the run-time performance, we integrate the SMART retrieval engine within the matching procedure of our EBMT system. The retrieval engine estimates a potential set of candidate close-matching sentences from the example-base E for a test sentence s. We assume that the closest source-side match s_c of the input sentence s can take the value from the set $\mathrm{E_{IR}}(s)$, where $\mathrm{E_{IR}}(s)$ is the potential set of close-matching sentences computed by the LM-based retrieval engine. We have used the top 50 candidate sentences from $\mathrm{E_{IR}}(s)$. Since the IR engine tries to retrieve the document (sentences from E) for a given query (input) sentence, it is likely to retrieve the closest match sentence s_c in the set $\mathrm{E_{IR}}(s)$. Due to a much reduced set of possibilities, this approach improves the run-time performance of the EBMT system without hampering system accuracy. Finding this potential set of candidate sentences will be much faster than traditional edit-distance-based retrieval on the full example-base as the worst case run time of the retriever is $O(\sum_{\forall w_i} s_i)$, where w_i is a word in the input sentence and s_i is the number of sentences in the example-base that contain w_i. Finding a set of candidate sentences took only 0.3 seconds and 116 seconds, respectively, for 414 and 10,000 example input sentences given 20k and 250k sentence example-base in our En–Tr and En–Fr experiment on a 3GHz Core 2 Duo machine with 4GB RAM.

5 Experiments

We conduct different experiments to report the accuracy of our EBMT systems for En–Tr and En–Fr translation tasks. In order to compare the performance of our approaches we use two baseline systems. We use the Moses **SMT** system as one base-

[5]An open source IR system from Cornell University. `ftp://ftp.cs.cornell.edu/pub/smart/`

line. Furthermore, based on the matching step (Section 3.2) of the EBMT approach, we obtain the closest target-side equivalent (the skeleton sentence) and consider this as the baseline output for the input to be translated. This is referred to as **TM** in the experiment below. We will consider this as the baseline accuracy for our EBMT using TM approach.

In addition, we conduct two experiments with our EBMT system. After obtaining the skeleton translation through the matching and alignment steps, in the *recombination* step, we use TM to translate any unmatched segments based on Algorithm 1. We call this $\mathbf{EBMT_{TM}}$.

We found that there are cases where the $\mathrm{EBMT_{TM}}$ system produces the correct translation but SMT fails and vice-versa (Dandapat et al., 2011). In order to further improve translation quality, we use a combination of EBMT and SMT. Here we use some features to decide whether to rely on the output produced by the $\mathrm{EBMT_{TM}}$ system. These features include *fuzzy match score***FMS** (as in (i)) and the number of mismatched segments in each of s, s_c, t_c (**EqUS**[6] as in (1)). We assume that the translations of an input sentence s produced by $\mathrm{EBMT_{TM}}$ and SMT systems are respectively $\mathrm{T_{EBMT}}(s)$ and $\mathrm{T_{SMT}}(s)$. If the value of FMS is greater than some threshold and EqUS exists between s and s_c, we rely on the output $\mathrm{T_{EBMT}}(s)$; otherwise we take the output from $\mathrm{T_{SMT}}(s)$. We refer to this system as $\mathbf{EBMT_{TM} + SMT}$.

To test the scalability of the system, we conducted two more experiments based on the approach described in Section 4. First, we conducted an experiment based on the sentence length-based grouping heuristics (Section 4.1). We refer to this system as $\mathbf{EBMT_{TM} + SMT} + \mathit{group_i}$, where i indicates the window size while comparing the length of the input sentence with the bins. We conduct a second experiment based on the LM-based indexing technique (Section 4.2) we have used to retrieve a potential set of candidate sentences from the indexed example-base. We call this system $\mathbf{EBMT_{TM} + SMT} + \mathit{index}$. Note that the $\mathrm{EBMT_{TM} + SMT}$ system is used as the baseline accuracy while conducting the experiments for scalability of the EBMT system.

[6]If s, s_c and t_c agree in the number of mismatched segments, EqUS evaluates to 1, otherwise 0.

5.1 Data Used for Experiments

We used two data sets for all our experiments representing two language pairs of different size and type. In the first data-set, we have used the En–Tr corpus from IWSLT09.[7] The training data consists of 19,972 parallel sentences. We used the IWSLT09 development set as our testset which consists of 414 sentences. The IWSLT09 data set is comprised of short sentences (with an average of 9.5 words per sentence) from a particular domain (the C-STAR project's Basic Travel Expression Corpus).

Our second data set consists of an En–Fr corpus from the European Medicines Agency (EMEA)[8] (Tiedemann and Nygaard, 2009). The training data consists of 250,806 unique parallel sentences.[9] As a testset we use a set of 10,000 randomly drawn sentences disjoint from the training corpus. This data also represents a particular domain (medicine) but with longer sentence lengths (with an average of 18.8 words per sentence) compared to the IWSLT09 data.

6 Results and Observations

We used BLEU (Papineni et al., 2002) for automatic evaluation of our EBMT systems. Table 2 shows the accuracy obtained for both En–Tr and En–Fr by the $\mathrm{EBMT_{TM}}$ system described in Section 3. Here we have two baseline systems (SMT and TM) as described in the first two experiments in Section 5.

Table 2: Baseline BLEU scores of the two systems and the scores for $\mathrm{EBMT_{TM}}$ system.

System	Language pairs	
	En–Tr	En–Fr
SMT	23.59	55.04
TM	15.60	40.23
$\mathrm{EBMT_{TM}}$	20.08	48.31

Table 2 shows that $\mathrm{EBMT_{TM}}$ has a lower system accuracy than SMT for both the language pairs, but

[7]http://mastarpj.nict.go.jp/IWSLT2009/2009/12/downloads.html

[8]`http://opus.lingfil.uu.se/EMEA.php`

[9]A large number of duplicate sentences exists in the original corpus (approximately 1M sentences). We remove duplicates and consider sentences with unique translation equivalents.

better scores than TM alone. Tables 3 and 4 show that combining EBMT with SMT systems shows improvements of 0.82 and 2.75 BLEU absolute over the SMT baseline (Table 2) for both the En–Tr and the En–Fr data sets. In each case, the improvement of $\mathrm{EBMT_{TM}} + \mathrm{SMT}$ over the baseline SMT is statistically significant (reliability of 98%) using bootstrap resampling (Koehn, 2004).

Table 3: En–Tr MT system accuracies of the combined systems ($\mathrm{EBMT_{TM}} + \mathrm{SMT}$) with different combining factors. The second column indicates the number (and percentage) of sentences translated by the $\mathrm{EBMT_{TM}}$ system during combination.

System: $\mathrm{EBMT_{TM}} + \mathrm{SMT}$		
Condition	**times** $\mathrm{EBMT_{TM}}$ **used**	**BLEU (in %)**
FMS>0.85	35 (8.5%)	24.22
FMS>0.80	114 (27.5%)	23.99
FMS>0.70	197 (47.6%)	22.74
FMS>0.80 OR (FMS>0.70 & EqUS)	165 (40.0%)	23.87
FMS>0.85 & EqUS	24 (5.8%)	**24.41**
FMS>0.80 & EqUS	76 (18.4%)	24.19
FMS>0.70 & EqUS	127 (30.7%)	24.08

Table 4: En–Fr MT system accuracies for the combined systems ($\mathrm{EBMT_{TM}} + \mathrm{SMT}$) with different combining factors.

System: $\mathrm{EBMT_{TM}} + \mathrm{SMT}$		
Condition	**times** $\mathrm{EBMT_{TM}}$ **used**	**BLEU (in %)**
FMS>0.85	3323 (33.2%)	**57.79**
FMS>0.80	4300 (43.0%)	57.55
FMS>0.70	5283 (52.8%)	57.05
FMS>0.60	6148 (61.5%)	56.25
FMS>0.80 OR (FMS>0.70 & EqUS)	4707 (47.1%)	57.46
FMS>0.85 & EqUS	2358 (23.6%)	57.24
FMS>0.80 & EqUS	2953 (29.5%)	57.16
FMS>0.70 & EqUS	3360 (33.6%)	57.08

A particular objective of our work is to scale the runtime EBMT system to a larger amount of training examples. We experiment with the two approaches described in Section 4 to improve the run time of the system. Table 5 compares the run time of the three systems ($\mathrm{EBMT_{TM}}$, $\mathrm{EBMT_{TM}} + \mathit{group_i}$ and $\mathrm{EBMT_{TM}} + \mathit{index}$) for both En–Tr and En–Fr translation. Note that the SMT decoder takes 140 seconds and 310 minutes respectively for En–Tr and En–Fr translation test sets.

Table 5: Running time of the three different systems.

System	Language pairs	
	En–Tr (*seconds*)	En–Fr (*minutes*)
SMT	140.0	310.0
$\mathrm{EBMT_{TM}}$	295.9	2267.0
$\mathrm{EBMT_{TM}} + \mathit{group_0}$	34.0	63.4
$\mathrm{EBMT_{TM}} + \mathit{group_1}$	96.2	183.5
$\mathrm{EBMT_{TM}} + \mathit{group_2}$	148.5	301.4
$\mathrm{EBMT_{TM}} + \mathit{index}$	**2.7**	**2.6**

Both the grouping and indexing methodologies proved successful for system scalability with a maximum speedup of almost 2 orders of magnitude. We also need to estimate the accuracy while combining grouping and indexing techniques with the baseline system ($\mathrm{EBMT_{TM}} + \mathrm{SMT}$) to understand their relative performance. Table 6 provides the system accuracy using the grouping and indexing techniques for both the language pairs. We report the translation quality under three conditions. Similar trends have been observed for other conditions.

6.1 Observations and Discussions

We find that the $\mathrm{EBMT_{TM}}$ system has a lower accuracy on its own compared to baseline SMT for both the language pairs (Table 2). Nevertheless, there are sentences which are better translated by the $\mathrm{EBMT_{TM}}$ approach compared to SMT, although the overall document translation score is higher with SMT. Thus, we combined the two systems based on different features and found that the combined system performs better. The highest relative improvements in BLEU score are 3.47% and 1.05% respectively for En–Tr and En–Fr translation. We found that if an input has a high fuzzy match score (FMS) with the example-base, then the $\mathrm{EBMT_{TM}}$ system does better compared to SMT. With our current experimental setup, we found that an FMS over 0.8 showed an improvement for En–Tr and a FMS over 0.6 showed improvement for En–Fr over the SMT system. Figure 2 shows the effect in the translation

Table 6: BLEU scores of the three different systems for En–Tr and En–Fr under different conditions. i denotes the number of bins considered during grouping.

Condition	System				
	$\mathrm{EBMT_{TM}}$ + SMT	$\mathrm{EBMT_{TM}}$ + SMT +*group*$_i$			$\mathrm{EBMT_{TM}}$ + SMT +*index*
		i=0	i=±1	i=±2	
En–Tr					
FMS>0.85	24.22	24.18	24.18	24.23	24.24
FMS>0.80 OR (FMS>0.70 & EqUS)	23.87	23.34	23.90	24.40	24.37
FMS>0.85 & EqUS	24.41	24.17	24.38	24.34	24.39
En–Fr					
FMS>0.85	57.79	56.47	57.48	57.76	57.92
FMS>0.80 OR (FMS>0.70 & EqUS)	57.46	55.69	57.07	57.33	57.56
FMS>0.85 & EqUS	57.24	56.48	57.23	57.29	57.32

quality when different FMS thresholds were used to combine the two systems.

However, FMS might not be the only factor for triggering the $\mathrm{EBMT_{TM}}$ system. We considered EqUs as another factor which showed improvement for En–Tr but showed negative effect for En–Fr. Though an FMS over 0.7 for En–Tr shows no improvement in overall system accuracy, inclusion of the EqUs feature along with FMS shows improvement. Thus, the $\mathrm{EBMT_{TM}}$ system is sometimes more effective when the number of unmatched segment matches in s, s_c and t_c.

These observations show the effective use of our EBMT approach in terms of translation quality. However, we found that the $\mathrm{EBMT_{TM}}$ system has a very considerable runtime complexity. In order to translate 414 test sentences from English into Turkish, the basic EBMT system takes 295.9 seconds. The situation becomes worse when using the large example-base for En–Fr translation. Here, we found that the system takes around 38 hours to translate 10k source English sentences into French. This is a significant time complexity by any standard for a runtime approach. However, both grouping and indexing reduce the time complexity of the approach considerably. The time reduction with grouping depends on the number of bins considered to find the closest sentence during the matching stage. Systems with a lower number of bins take less time but cause more of a drop in translation quality. The effect is more prominent with the En–Fr system which uses a larger example-base. We found a drop of absolute 1.32 BLEU points while considering a single bucket whose length is equal to the length of the test sentence. This configuration takes 63 minutes to translate 10k English sentences into French. There is only a drop of 0.03 BLEU points when considering the 5 nearest bins (±2) for a given test sentence. Nevertheless, there is not much of a reduction but it increases the run time to 5 hours for the translation of 10k sentences. Thus, the group-based method is not effective enough to balance system accuracy and run time.

Incorporation of the indexing technique into the matching stage of EBMT shows the highest efficiency gains in run time. Translating 10k sentences from English into French takes only 158 seconds. It is also interesting to note that with indexing, the BLEU score remained the same or even increased. This is due to the fact that, compared to FMS-based matching, a different closest-matching sentence s_c is selected for some of the input sentences while using indexing, thus resulting in a different outcome to the system. Figure 3 compares the number of times the $\mathrm{EBMT_{TM}}$ + SMT + *index* system is used in the hybrid system and the number of same closest-matching sentences selected by $\mathrm{EBMT_{TM}}$ + SMT + *index* systems under different conditions for En–Tr. The use of index-based candidate selection for EBMT matching shows effective

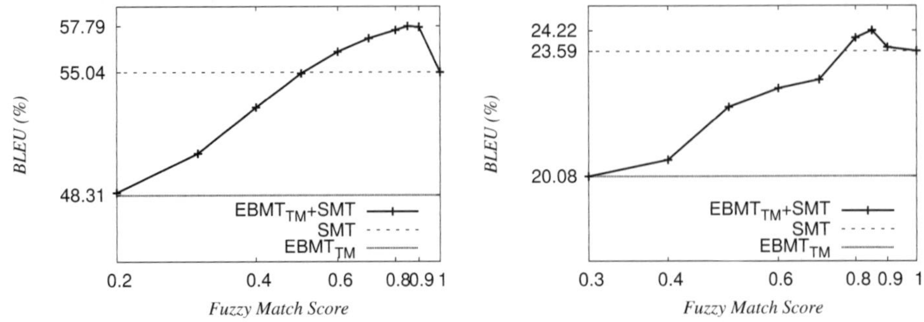

(a) En—Fr (b) En—Tr

Figure 2: Effect of FMS in the combined $\mathrm{EBMT_{TM}} + \mathrm{SMT}$ system.

Table 7: The effect of indexing in selection s_c and in final translation.

Input:	zeffix belongs to a group of medicines called antivirals.
Ref:	**zeffix appartient à une classe de médicaments appelés antiviraux.**
baseline $\mathrm{EBMT_{TM}}$ system	
s_c:	*simulect* belongs to a group of medicines called *immunosuppressants*.
s_t:	*simulect* fait parti d ' une classe de médicaments appelés *immunosuppresseurs*.
Output:	**zeffix fait parti d ' une classe de médicaments appelés antiviraux.**
$\mathrm{EBMT_{TM}} + \mathrm{SMT} +$ *index* system	
s_c:	*diacomit* belongs to a group of medicines called *antiepileptics*.
s_t:	*diacomit* appartient à un groupe de médicaments appelés *antiépileptiques*.
Output:	**zeffix appartient à un groupe de médicaments appelés antiviraux.**

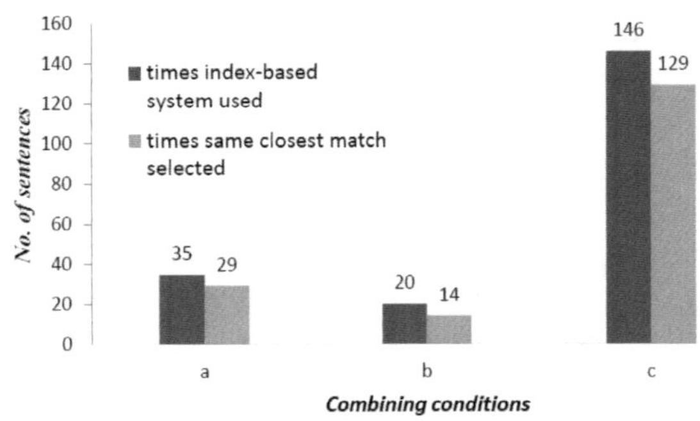

Figure 3: Number of times $\mathrm{EBMT_{TM}} + \mathrm{SMT} +$ *index* used in the hybrid system and the number of times the same closest-matching sentences are selected by the systems. a=FMS>0.85, b=FMS>0.85 & EqUS and c=FMS>0.80 OR (FMS>0.70 & EqUS)

improvement in translation time, and BLEU scores remained the same or increased. Due to the selection of different closest-matching sentence s_c, sometimes the system produces better quality translation which increases the system level BLEU score. Table 7 shows one such En—Fr example where an index-based technique produced a better translation than the baseline ($\mathrm{EBMT_{TM}} + \mathrm{SMT}$) system.

7 Conclusion

Our experiments show that EBMT approaches work better compared to the SMT-based system for certain sentences when a high fuzzy match score is obtained for the input sentence with the example-base. Thus a feature-based combination of EBMT- and SMT-based systems produces better translation quality than either of the individual systems. Integration of a SMT technology-based sub-sentential TM with the EBMT framework ($\mathrm{EBMT_{TM}}$) has improved translation quality in our experiments.

Our baseline $\mathrm{EBMT_{TM}}$ system is a runtime approach which has high time complexity when using a large example-base. We found that the integration of IR-based indexing substantially improves run time without affecting BLEU score. So far our systems have been tested using moderately sized example-bases from a closed domain corpus. In our future work, we plan to use a much larger example-base and wider-domain corpora.

Acknowledgments

This research is supported by Science Foundation Ireland (Grants 07/CE/I1142, Centre for Next Generation Localisation).

References

S. Armstrong, C. Caffrey, M. Flanagan, D. Kenny, M. O'Hagan and A. Way. 2006. Improving the Quality of Automated DVD Subtitles via Example-Based Machine Translation. Translating and the Computer **28**, [no page number], London: Aslib, UK.

E. Biçici and M. Dymetman. 2008. Dynamic Translation Memory: Using Statistical Machine Translation to Improve Translation Memory. In Gelbukh, Alexander F., editor, In *Proceedings of the 9th International Conference on Intelligent Text Processing and Computational Linguistics (CICLing),* volume 4919 of *Lecture Notes in Computer Science,* pp 3-57 Springer Verlag.

J. Bourdaillet, S. Huet, F. Gotti, G. Lapalme and P. Langlais. 2009. Enhancing the bilingual concordancer TransSearch with word-level alignment. In *Proceedings, volume 5549 of Lecture Notes in Artificial Intelligence: 22nd Canadian Conference on Artificial of Intelligence (Canadian AI 2009),* Springer-Verlag, pp. 27-38.

R. D. Brown. 2011. The CMU-EBMT machine translation system. *Machine Translation*, **25**(2):179–195.

I. Cicekli and H. A. Güvenir. 2001. Learning translation templates from bilingual translation examples. *Applied Intelligence*, **15**(1):57–76.

S. Dandapat, S. Morrissey, A. Way and M.L. Forcada. 2011. Using Example-Based MT to Support Statistical MT when Translating Homogeneous Data in Resource-Poor Settings. In *Proceedings of the 15th Annual Meeting of the European Association for Machine Translation (EAMT 2011),* pp. 201-208. Leuven, Belgium.

S. Dandapat, M.L. Forcada, D. Groves, S. Penkale, J. Tinsley and A. Way. 2010. OpenMaTrEx: a free/open-source marker-driven example-based machine translation system. In *Proceedings of the 7th International Conference on Natural Language Processing (IceTAL 2010),* pp. 121-126. Reykjavík, Iceland.

D. Groves and A. Way. 2006. Hybridity in MT: Experiments on the Europarl Corpus. In *Proceedings of the 11th Conference of the European Association for Machine Translation (EAMT 2006),* pp. 115-124. Oslo, Norway.

M. Islam, J. Tiedemann and A. Eisele. 2010. English–Bengali Phrase-based Machine Translation. In *Proceedings of the 14th Annual Conference of the European Association of Machine Translation, (EAMT 2010),* [no page number], Saint-Raphaël, France.

M. Khalilov, J.A.R. Fonollosa, I. Skadina, E. Bralitis and L. Pretkalnina. 2010. English–Latvian SMT: the Challenge of Translating into a Free Word Order Language. In *Proceedings of the 2nd International Workshop on Spoken Language Technologies for Under-resourced Languages (SLTU 2010),* [no page number], Saint-Raphaël, France.

P. Koehn. 2010. *Statistical Machine Translation*, Cambridge University Press, Cambridge, UK.

P. Koehn, H. Hoang, A. Birch, C. Callison-Burch, M. Federico, N. Bertoldi, B. Cowan, W. Shen, C. Moran, R. Zens, C. Dyer, O. Bojar, A. Constantin and E. Herbst. 2007. Moses: open source toolkit for statistical machine translation. In *Proceedings of the Demonstration and Poster Sessions at the 45th Annual Meeting of the Association of Computational Linguistics (ACL 2007),* pp. 177-180. Prague, Czech Republic.

P. Koehn. 2004. Statistical significance tests for machine translation evaluation. In *Proceedings of the Conference on Empirical Methods in Natural Language Processing (EMNLP 2004),* pp. 388-395. Barcelona, Spain.

P. Koehn and J. Senellart. 2004. Convergence of Translation Memory and Statistical Machine Translation. In *Proceedings of the AMTA workshop on MT Research and the Translation Industry,* pp. 21-23. Denever, CO.

P. Langlais, G. Lapalme and M. Loranger. 2002. Development-evaluation cycles to boost translator's productivity. *Machine Translation*, **15**(4):77–98.

Y. Lepage and E. Denoual. 2005. Purest ever example-based machine translation: Detailed presentation and assessment. *Machine Translation*, **19**(3-4):251–282.

V. I. Levenshtein. 1965. Binary Codes Capable of Correcting Deletions, Insertions, and Reversals. *Doklady Akademii Nauk SSSR,* **163**(4):845-848., English translation in Soviet Physics Doklady,**10**(8), 707-710.

C. D. Manning, P. Raghavan and H. Schütze. 2008. *Introduction to Information Retrieval.* Cambridge University Press, Cambridge, UK.

M. Nagao. 1984. A Framework of a Machine Translation between Japanese and English by Analogy Principle. In Elithorn, A. and Banerji, R., editors, *Artificial Human Intelligence,* pp. 173–180, North-Holland, Amsterdam.

F. Och and H. Ney. 2003. A Systematic Comparison of Various Statistical Alignment Models. *Computational Linguistics*, **29**(1):19–51.

K. Papineni, S. Roukos, T. Ward and W. J. Zhu. 2002. BLEU: a Method for Automatic Evaluation of Machine Translation. In *Proceedings of the 40th Annual Meeting of the Association for Computational Linguistics, (ACL 2002),* pp. 311–318, Philadelphia, PA.

A. B. Phillips. 2011. Cunei: open-source machine translation with relevance-based models of each translation instance. *Machine Translation*, **25**(2):161–177.

M. Simard and P. Isabelle. 2009. Phrase-based Machine Translation in a Computer-assisted Translation Memory. In *Proceedings of the 12th Machine Translation Summit, (MT Summit XII),* pp. 120–127, Ottawa, Canada.

M. Simard. 2003. Translation spotting for translation memories. In *Proceedings of the HLT-NAACL 2003, Workshop on Building and Using Parallel Texts: Data Driven Machine Translation and Beyond,* pp. 65–72, Edmonton, Canada.

H. Somers. 2003. An Overview of EBMT. In M. Carl and A. Way , editors, *Recent Advances in Example-based Machine Translation,* pp. 3-57, Kluwer Academic Publishers, Dordrecht, The Netherlands.

J. Tiedemann and L. Nygaard. 2009. News from OPUS - A Collection of Multilingual Parallel Corpora with Tools and Interfaces, in N. Nicolov, K. Bontcheva, G. Angelova, R. Mitkov. (eds.), *Recent Advances in Natural Language Processing*, **V**:237–248, John Benjamins, Amsterdam, The Netherlands.

E. Ukkonen. 1983. On Approximate String Matching. In *Proceedings of International Conference on Foundations of Computing Theory, (FCT 1983),* pp. 487–496, Borgholm, Sweden.

R. Wagner and M. Fischer. 1974. The String-to-String Correction Problem. *Journal of the Association for Computing Machinery*, **21**:168–173.

Two approaches for integrating translation and retrieval in real applications

Cristina Vertan
University of Hamburg
Research Group "Computerphilology"
Von-Mell Park 6, 20146 Hamburg, germany
cristina.vertan@uni-hamburg.de

Abstract

In this paper we present two approaches for integrating translation into cross-lingual search engines: the first approach relies on term translation via a language ontology, the other one is based on machine translation of specific information.

1 Introduction

The explosion of on-line available multilingual information during the last years, raised the necessity of building applications able to manage this type of content. People are more and more used to search for information not only in English, but also in their mother tongue and often in some other languages they understand. Moreover there are dedicated web-platforms where the information is a-priori multilingual, like eLearning Systems and Content Management Systems. eLearning systems are used more an more as real alternatives to face-to-face courses and include often materials in the mother languages and also English (either because a lot of literature is available in English or because the content should be made available to exchange students). Content management systems used by multinational corporates, share materials in several languages as well.

On such platforms the search facility is an essential one: usually the implemented methods are based on term indexes, which are created per language. This prohibits or at least makes very difficult the access to multilingual material: the user is forced to repeat the query in several languages, which is time consuming and error – prone.
Cross-lingual retrieval methods are only slowly introduced in real applications like those ones quoted above. In this paper we will describe two applications and two different ways of combining term-translation and information retrieval. In the first one, an eLearning system, we implement a language ontology on which we map the multilingual lexical entries. The search engine makes then use of the mapping between the lexical material and the ontology. The second application is a content management system, in which we use machine translation as backbone to the search engine

The rest of the paper is organised as follows: in Section 2 we describe the eLearning environment in which we embedded the search engine and present this one. In Section 3 we describe the content management system and the symbiosis between the machine translation and the search engines. In Section 4 we conclude with some observations on these two approaches and introduce possible approaches for further work.

2 Crosslingual search based on language independent ontology and lexical information

The system we describe in this section was developed within the EU-Project LT4eL – Language Technology for eLearning (http://www.lt4el.eu). The main goal of the project was to enhance an eLearning system with language technology tools. The system dealt with nine languages (Bulgarian, Czech, Dutch, English, German, Maltese, Polish, Portuguese, Romanian). eLearning documents were processed through language specific pipelines and keywords and definitions were automatic extracted. The kernel of the system is however the crosslingual semantic search engine which makes use of a language

Proceedings of the 13th Conference of the European Chapter of the Association for Computational Linguistics, pages 59–64,
Avignon, France, April 23 - 27 2012.

independent ontology and mapping of language specific lexicons.

As prototype we implemented a domain specific ontology of about 1000 concepts, from the field „Computer Science for non computer science specialists". The concepts were not collected from English texts, but from analyzed keywords from al involved languages. In this way we avoided a bias towards English specific concepts. For the keywords in each language each partner provided an English translation (one word, one expression or even several sentences). The analysis of these translations conducted to the construction of the ontology. The concepts were represented in OWL-DL. The domain specific ontology was mapped on the DOLCE-upper ontology as well as WordNeT to ensure consistency.

The two main components that define the ontology-to-text relation necessary to support the crosslingual retrieval are: (terminological) lexicon and concept annotation grammar (Lemnitzer et. Al, 2007).

The lexicon plays twofold role in the architecture. First, it interrelates the concepts in the ontology to the lexical knowledge used by the grammar in order to recognize the role of the concepts in the text. Second, the lexicon represents the main interface between the user and the ontology. This interface allows for the ontology to be navigated or represented in a natural way for the user. For example, the concepts and relations might be named with terms used by the users in their everyday activities and in their own natural language (e.g. Bulgarian). This could be considered as a first step to a contextualized usage of the ontology in a sense that the ontology could be viewed through different terms depending on the context. For example, the color names will vary from very specific terms within the domain of carpet production to more common names used when the same carpet is part of an interior design.

Thus, the lexical items contain the following information: a term, contextual information determining the context of the term usage, grammatical features determining the syntactic realization within the text. In the current implementation of the lexicons the contextual information is simplified to a list of a few types of users (producer, retailer, etc). With respect to the relations between the terms in the lexicon and the concepts in the ontology, there are two main problems: (1) there is no lexicalized term for some of the concepts in the ontology, and (2) there are lexical terms in the language of the domain which lack corresponding concepts in the ontology, which represent the meaning of the terms. The first problem is overcomed by writing down in the lexicon also non-lexicalized (fully compositional) phrases to be represented. Even more, we encourage the lexicon builders to add more terms and phrases to the lexicons for a given concept in order to represent as many ways of expressing the concept in the language as possible.

These different phrases or terms for a given concept are used as a basis for construction of the annotation grammar. Having them, we might capture different wordings of the same meaning in the text. The concepts are language independent and they might be represented within a natural language as form(s) of a lexicalized term, or as a free phrase. In general, a concept might have a few terms connected to it and a (potentially) unlimited number of free phrases expressing this concept in the language

Some of the free phrases receive their meaning compositionally regardless their usage in the text, other free phrases denote the corresponding concept only in a particular context. In our lexicons we decided to register as many free phrases as possible in order to have better recall on the semantic annotation task.

In case of a concept that is not-lexicalized in a given language we require at least one free phrase to be provided for this concept. We could summarize the connection between the ontology and the lexicons in the following way: the ontology represents the semantic knowledge in form of concepts and relations with appropriate axioms; and the lexicons represent the ways in which these concepts can be realized in texts in the corresponding languages.

Of course, the ways in which a concept could be represented in the text are potentially infinite in number, thus, we could hope to represent in our lexicons only the most frequent and important terms and phrases. Here is an example of an entry from the Dutch lexicon:

```
<entry id="id60">
<owl:Class
rdf:about="lt4el:BarWithButt
ons">
<rdfs:subClassOf>
<owl:Class
rdf:about="lt4el:Window"/>
</rdfs:subClassOf>
</owl:Class>
<def>A horizontal or
vertical bar as a part of a
window, that contains
buttons, icons.</def>
<termg lang="nl">
<term
shead="1">werkbalk</term>
<term>balk</term>
<term type="nonlex">balk met
knoppen</term>
<term>menubalk</term>
</termg>
</entry>
```

Each entry of the lexicons contains three types of information: (1) information about the concept from the ontology which represents the meaning for the terms in the entry; (2) explanation of the concept meaning in English; and (3) a set of terms in a given language that have the meaning expressed by the concept. The concept part of the entry provides minimum information for formal definition of the concept.

The English explanation of the concept meaning facilitates the human understanding. The set of terms stands for different wordings of the concept in the corresponding language. One of the terms is the representative for the term set. Note that this is a somewhat arbitrary decision, which might depend on frequency of term usage or specialist's intuition. This representative term will be used where just one of terms from the set is necessary to be used, for example as an item of a menu. In the example above we present the set of Dutch terms for the concept `lt4el:BarWithButtons`.

One of the term is non-lexicalized - attribute type with value nonlex. The first term is representative for the term set and it is marked-up with attribute shead with value 1. In this way we determine which term to be used for ontology browsing if there is no contextual information for the type of users. The second component of the ontology-to-text relation, the concept annotation grammar, is ideally considered as an extension of a general language deep grammar which is adopted to the concept annotation task. Minimally, the concept annotation grammar consists of a chunk grammar for concept annotation and (sense) disambiguation rules. The chunk grammar for each term in the lexicon contains at least one grammar rule for recognition of the term.

As a preprocessing step we consider annotation with grammatical features and lemmatization of the text. The disambiguation rules exploit the local context in terms of grammatical features, semantic annotation and syntactic structure, and alsp the global context such as topic of the text, discourse segmentation, etc. Currently we have implemented chunk grammars for several languages.

The disambiguation rules are under development. For the implementation of the annotation grammar we rely on the grammar facilities of the CLaRK System (Simov et al., 2001). The structure of each grammar rule in CLaRK is defined by the following DTD fragment:

```
<!ELEMENT line (LC?, RE, RC?,
RM, Comment?) >
<!ELEMENT LC (#PCDATA)>
<!ELEMENT RC (#PCDATA)>
<!ELEMENT RE (#PCDATA)>
<!ELEMENT RM (#PCDATA)>
<!ELEMENT Comment (#PCDATA)>
```

Each rule is represented as a line element. The rule consists of regular expression (RE) and category (RM = return markup). The regular expression is evaluated over the content of a given XML element and could recognize tokens and/or annotated data. The return markup is represented as an XML fragment which is substituted for the recognized part of the content of the element.

Additionally, the user could use regular expressions to restrict the context in which the regular expression is evaluated successfully. The LC element contains a regular expression for the left context and the RC for the right one. The element Comment is for human use. The application of the grammar is governed by Xpath expressions which provide additional mechanism for accurate annotation of a given XML document.

Thus, the CLaRK grammar is a good choice for implementation of the initial annotation grammar. The creation of the actual annotation grammars started with the terms in the lexicons for the corresponding languages. Each term was lemmatized and the lemmatized form of the term was converted into regular expression of grammar rules. Each concept related to the term is stored in the return markup of the corresponding rule. Thus, if a term is ambiguous, then the corresponding rule in the grammar contains reference to all concepts related to the term.

The relations between the different elements of the models are as follows. A lexical item could have more than one grammar rule associated to it depending on the word order and the grammatical realization of the lexical item. Two lexical items could share a grammar rule if they have the same wording, but they are connected to different concepts in the ontology. Each grammar rule could recognize zero or several text chunks.

The relation ontology-to-text implemented in this way is the basis fort the crosslingual search engine which works in the following way:
Words in any of the covered languages can be entered and are looked up in the lexicon; the concepts that are linked to the matching lexicon entries are used for ontology-based search in an automatic fashion.

Before lexicon lookup, the words are orthographically normalised, and combinations for multi-word terms are created (e.g. if the words "text" and "editor" are entered, the combinations "texteditor", "text editor" and "text-editor" are created and looked up, in addition to the individual words). For each of the found concepts, the set of all its (direct or indirect) subconcepts is determined, and is used to retrieve Learning Objects (Los) .

The use of these language-independent concepts as an intermediate step makes it possible to retrieve LOs in any of the covered languages, thus realising the crosslingual aspect of the retrieval. When the found LOs are displayed, at the same time the relevant parts of the ontology are presented in the language that the user prefers. In a second step, the user can select (by marking a checkbox) the concept(s) he wants to look for and repeat the search. If an entered word was ambiguous, the intended meaning can be explicated now by selecting the appropriate concept. Furthermore, by clicking on a concept, related concepts are displayed; navigation through the ontology is possible in this way. A list of retrieval languages (only LOs written in one of those languages will be found) is specified as an input parameter. The retrieved LOs are sorted by language. The next ordering criterion is a ranking, based on the number of different search concepts and the number of occurrences of those concepts in the LO. For each found LO, its title, language, and matching concepts are shown.

3 Crosslingual search based on machine Translation

The second case study is the embedding of a crosslingual search engine into a web-based content management system. The system is currently implemented within the EU-PSP project ATLAS (http://www.atlasproject .eu) and aims to be domain independent. Thus, a model as presented in section 2 is impossible to be realised, as the automatic construction of a domain ontology is too unreliable and the human construction too cost effective. Also a general lexicon coverage is practically impossible.

Therefore in this project we adopted a different solution (Karagiozov et al 2011), namely we ensure the translation of keywords and short generated abstracts, and all these translations are part of the RDF-generate index. The ATLAS system ensures the lingustic processing of uploaded documents and extraction of most important keywords. A separate module generates short abstracts. These two elements can be further submitted for translation.

For the MT-Engine of the ATLAS –System on a hybrid architecture combining example (EBMT) and statistical (SMT) machine translation on surface forms (no syntactic
trees will be used) is chosen. For the SMT-component PoS and domain factored models as in (Niehues and Waibel 2010) are used, in order to ensure domain adaptability. An original approach of our system is the interaction of the MT-engine with other modules of the system:

The document categorization module assigns to each document one or more domains. For each domain the system administrator has the possibility to store information regarding the availability of a correspondent specific training corpus. If no specific trained model for the respective domain exists, the user is provided with a warning, telling that the translation may be inadequate with respect to the lexical coverage.

The output of the summarization module is processed in such way that ellipses and anaphora are omitted, and lexical material is adapted to the training corpus.

The information extraction module is providing information about metadata of the document including publication age. For documents previous to 1900 we will not provide translation, explaining the user that in absence of a training corpus the translation may be misleading. The domain and dating restrictions can be changed at any time by the system administrator when an adequate training model is provides.

The translation results are then embedded in a document model which is used further for crosslingual search.
Each document is thus converted to the following format

```
<foaf:Document
rdf:about=http://atlas.eu/item
#20>
<dc:title>Internet Ethics
</dc:title>
<dc:creator
rdf:resource=http://atlas.eu/p
ers#950 />
<atlas:summary
xmnls:lang="en">
Default english summary
<atlas:summary>
<atlas:summary
xmnls:lang="de">
 Deutsche Zusammenfassung
</atlas:summary>
</foaf:Document>
<foaf:Personrdf:about=http://atla
s.eu/pers#950>
<foaf:name>Name </foaf:name>
<foaf:mbox>    name@some.address.eu
</foaf:mbox>
</foaf:Person>
```

This ist he basis for creation of the RDF-Index. The crosslingual serch engine is in this case a classic Lucene search engine, which operates however not with word-indexes but with these RDF-indexes, which automatically include multilingual information. This engine is currently under construction.

4 Conclusions

In this paper we presented two approaches of embedding multilingual information into search engines.

One is based on the construction of a language independent ontology and corresponding lexical material, the other one on machine translation.

The first approach relies on a manual constructed ontology, therefore it is highly domain dependent and requires the involvement of domain specialists.

The second approach relies on machine translation quality, and also lacks a deep semantic analysis of the query.

However the mechanism can be implemented completely automatically, and is domain independent (assuming that the machine translation engine contains domain adaptation models)

Therefore it is difficult to asses which approach performs better. Further work concerns the selection of a certain domain and comparison of retrieval quality fort the two approaches.

5 Acknowledgements

The work described here was realized within two projects: LT4eL (http://www.lt4el.eu) and ATLAS (http://www.atlasproject.eu).

The author is indebted especially to following persons who contributed essentially for the fulfillment of the described modules: Kiril Simov and Petya Osenova (Bulgarian Academy of Sciences), Eelco Mosel (former at the university of Hamburg), Ronald Winnemöller (University of Hamburg).

References

Karagiozov, D. Koeva,S. Ogrodniczuk, M. and Vertan, C. *ATLAS — A Robust Multilingual Platform for the Web.* In Proceedings of the German Society for Computational Linguistics and Language Technology Conference (GSCL 2011), Hamburg, Germany, 2011

Lemnitzer, L. and Vertan, C. and Simov, K. and Monachesi, P. and Kiling A. and Cristea D. and Evans, D., *„Improving the search for learning objects with keywords and ontologies".* In Proceedings of Technologically enhanced learning conference 2007, p. 202-216

Niehues J. and Waibel,A. Domain Adaptation in Statistical Machine Translation using Factored Translation Models, Proceedings of EAMT 2010 Saint-Raphael, 2010

Simov, K., Peev, Z., Kouylekov, M., Simov, A., Dimitrov, M., Kiryakov, A. (2001). CLaRK - an XML-based System for Corpora Development. In: Proc. of the Corpus Linguistics 2001 Conference. Lancaster, UK.

PRESEMT: Pattern Recognition-based Statistically Enhanced MT

George Tambouratzis, Marina Vassiliou, Sokratis Sofianopoulos
Institute for Language and Speech Processing, Athena R.C.
6 Artemidos & Epidavrou Str., Paradissos Amaroussiou, 151 25, Athens, Greece.
{giorg_t; mvas ; s_sofian}@ilsp.gr

Abstract

This document contains a brief presentation of the PRESEMT project that aims in the development of a novel language-independent methodology for the creation of a flexible and adaptable MT system.

1. Introduction

The PRESEMT project constitutes a novel approach to the machine translation task. This approach is characterised by (a) introducing cross-disciplinary techniques, mainly borrowed from the machine learning and computational intelligence domains, in the MT paradigm and (b) using relatively inexpensive language resources. The aim is to develop a language-independent methodology for the creation of a flexible and adaptable MT system, the features of which ensure easy portability to new language pairs or adaptability to particular user requirements and to specialised domains with minimal effort. PRESEMT falls within the Corpus-based MT (CBMT) paradigm, using a small bilingual parallel corpus and a large TL monolingual corpus. Both these resources are collected as far as possible over the web, to simplify the development of resources for new language pairs.

The main aim of PRESEMT has been to alleviate the reliance on specialised resources. In comparison, Statistical MT requires large parallel corpora for the source and target languages. PRESEMT relaxes this requirement by using a small parallel corpus, augmented by a large TL monolingual corpus.

2. PRESEMT system structure

The PRESEMT system is distinguished into three stages, as shown in Figure 1:

1. Pre-processing stage: This is the stage where the essential resources for the MT system are compiled. It consists of four discrete modules: (a) the **Corpus creation & annotation module**, being responsible for the compilation of monolingual and bilingual corpora over the web and their annotation; (b) the **Phrase aligner module**, which processes a bilingual corpus to perform phrasal level alignment within a language pair; (c) the **Phrasing model generator** that elicits an SL phrasing model on the basis of the aforementioned alignment and employs it as a parsing tool during the translation process; (d) the **Corpus modelling module**, which creates semantics-based TL models used for disambiguation purposes during the translation process.

2. Main translation engine: The translation in PRESEMT is a top-down two-phase process, distinguished into the **Structure selection module**, where the constituent phrases of an SL sentence are reordered according to the TL, and the **Translation equivalent selection module** where translation disambiguation is resolved and word order within phrases is established. Closely integrated to the translation engine, but not part of the main translation process, is the Optimisation module, which is responsible for automatically improving the performance of the two translation phases by fine-tuning the values of the various system parameters.

3. Post-processing stage: The third stage is user-oriented and comprises (i) the Post-processing and (ii) the User Adaptation modules. The first module allows the user to modify the system-generated translations towards their requirements. The second module enables PRESEMT to adapt to this input so that it learns to generate translations closer to the users' requirements. The post-processing stage represents work in progress to be reported in future publications, the present article focussing on the actual strategy for generating the translation.

Proceedings of the 13th Conference of the European Chapter of the Association for Computational Linguistics, pages 65–68,
Avignon, France, April 23 - 27 2012. ©2012 Association for Computational Linguistics

3. Processing of the bilingual corpus

The bilingual corpus contains literal translations, to allow the extrapolation of mapping information from SL to TL, though this may affect the translation quality. The Phrase aligner module (PAM) performs offline SL – TL word and phrase alignment within this corpus. PAM serves as a language-independent method for mapping corresponding terms within a language pair, by circumventing the problem of achieving compatibility between the outputs of two different parsers, one for the SL and one for the TL. PAM relies on a single parser for the one language and generates an appropriate phrasing model for the other language in an automated manner.

The phrases are assumed to be flat and linguistically valid. As a parser, any available tool may be used (the TreeTagger (Schmid, 1994) is used in the present implementation for English). PAM processes a bilingual corpus of SL – TL sentence pairs, taking into account the parsing information in one language (in the current implementation the TL side) and making use of a bilingual lexicon and information on potential phrase heads; the output being the bilingual corpus aligned at word, phrase and clause level. Thus, at a phrasal level, the PAM output indicates how an SL structure is transformed into the TL. For instance, based on a sentence pair from the parallel corpus, the SL sentence with structure A-B-C-D is transformed into A'-C'-D'-B', where X is a phrase in SL and X' is a phrase in TL. Further PAM details are reported in Tambouratzis et al. (2011).

The PAM output in terms of SL phrases is then handed over to the Phrasing model generator (PMG), which is trained to determine the phrasal structure of an input sentence. PMG reads the SL phrasing as defined by PAM and generates an SL phrasing model using a probabilistic methodology. This phrasing model is then applied in segmenting any arbitrary SL text being input to the PRESEMT system for translation. PMG is based on the Conditional Random Fields model (Lafferty et al., 1999) which has been found to provide the highest accuracy. The SL text segmented into phrases by PMG is then input to the 1st translation phase. For a new language pair, the PAM-PMG chain is implemented without any manual correction of outputs.

4. Organising the monolingual corpus

The language models created by the Corpus modelling module can only serve translation disambiguation purposes; thus another form of interfacing with the monolingual corpus is essential for the word reordering task within each phrase. The size of the data accessed is very large. Typically, a monolingual corpus contains 3 billion words, 10^8 sentences and approximately 10^9 phrases. Since the models for the TL phrases need to be accessed in real-time to allow word reordering within each phrase, the module uses the phrase indexed representation of the monolingual corpus. This phrase index is created based on four criteria: (i) phrase type, (ii) phrase head lemma, (iii) phrase head PoS tag and (iv) number of tokens in the phrase.

Indexing is performed by extracting all phrases from the monolingual corpus, each of which is transformed to the java object instance used within the PRESEMT system. The phrases are then organised in a hash map that allows multiple values for each key, using as a key the 4 aforementioned criteria. Statistical information about the number of occurrences of each phrase in the corpus is also included. Finally, each map is serialised and stored in the appropriate file in the PRESEMT path, with each file being given a suitable name for easy retrieval. For example, for the English monolingual corpus, all verb phrases with head lemma "*read*" (verb) and PoS tag "*VV*" containing 2 tokens in total are stored in the file "*Corpora\EN\Phrases\VC\read_VV*". If any of these criteria has a different value, then a separate file is created (for instance for verb phrases with head "*read*" that contain 3 tokens).

5. Main translation engine

The PRESEMT translation process entails first the establishment of the sentence phrasal structure and then the resolution of the intra-phrasal arrangements, i.e. specifying the correct word order and deciding upon the appropriate candidate translation. Both phases involve searching for suitable matching patterns at two different levels of granularity, the first (coarse-grained) aiming at defining a TL-compatible ordering of phrases in the sentence and the second (fine-grained) determining the internal structure of phrases. While the first phase utilises the small bilingual corpus, the second phase makes use of the large monolingual corpus. To reduce the translation time required, both corpora are processed in advance and the processed resources are stored in such a form as be retrieved as rapidly as possible during translation.

5.1 Translation Phase 1: Structure selection module

Each SL sentence input for translation is tagged and lemmatised and then it is segmented into phrases by the Phrasing model generator on the basis of the SL phrasing model previously created. For establishing the correct phrase order according to the TL, the parallel corpus needs to be pre-processed using the Phrase aligner module to identify word and phrase alignments between the equivalent SL and TL sentences.

During structure selection, the SL sentence is aligned to each SL sentence of the parallel corpus, as processed by the PAM and assigned a similarity score using an algorithm from the dynamic programming paradigm. The similarity score is calculated by taking into account edit operations (replacement, insertion or removal) needed to be performed in the input sentence in order to transform it to the corpus SL sentence. Each of these operations has an associated cost, considered as a system parameter. The aligned corpus sentence that achieves the highest similarity score is the most similar one to the input source sentence. This comparison process relies on a set of similarity parameters (e.g. phrase type, phrase head etc.), the values of which are optimised by employing the optimisation module.

The implementation is based on the Smith-Waterman algorithm (Smith and Waterman, 1981), initially proposed for determining similar regions between two protein or DNA sequences. The algorithm is guaranteed to find the optimal local alignment between the two input sequences at clause level.

5.2 Translation Phase 2: Translation equivalent selection module

After establishing the order of phrases within each sentence, the second phase of the translation process is initiated, comprising two distinct tasks. The first task is to resolve the lexical ambiguity, by picking one lemma from each set of possible translations (as provided by a bilingual dictionary). In doing so, this module makes use of the semantic similarities between words which have been determined by the Corpus Modelling module through a co-occurrence analysis on the monolingual TL corpus. That way, the best combination of lemmas from the sets of candidate translations is determined for a given context.

In the second task, the most similar phrases to the TL structure phrases are retrieved from the monolingual corpus to provide local structural information such as word-reordering. A matching algorithm selects the most similar from the set of the retrieved TL phrases through a comparison process, which is viewed as an assignment problem, using the Gale-Shapley algorithm (Gale and Shapley, 1962).

6. Experiments & evaluation results

To date MT systems based on the PRESEMT methodology have been created for a total of 8 languages, indicating the flexibility of the proposed approach. Table 1 illustrates an indicative set of results obtained by running automatic evaluation metrics on test data translated by the 1st PRESEMT prototype for a selection of language pairs, due to space restrictions.

In the case of the language pair English-to-German, these results are contrasted to the ones obtained when translating the same test set with Moses (Koehn et al., 2007).It is observed that for the English-to-German language pair, PRESEMT achieved approximately 50% of the MOSES BLEU score and 80% of the MOSES with respect to the Meteor and TER scores. These are reasonably competitive results compared to an established system such as Moses. Furthermore, it should taken into consideration that (a) the PRESEMT results were obtained by the 1st system prototype, (b) PRESEMT is still under development and (c) only one reference translation was used per sentence.

Newer versions of the PRESEMT system, incorporating more advanced versions of the different modules are expected to result in substantially improved translation accuracies. In particular, the second translation phase will be further researched. In addition, experiments have indicated that the language modelling module can provide additional improvement in the performance. Finally, refinements in PAM and PMG may lead in increased translation accuracies.

7. Links

Find out more about the project on the **PRESEMT website**: www.presemt.eu. Also, the PRESEMT **prototype** may be tried at: presemt.cslab.ece.ntua.gr:8080/presemt_interface_test

Acknowledgments

The research leading to these results has received funding from the European Community's Seventh Framework Programme (FP7/2007-2013) under grant agreement n° 248307.

References

Gale D. and L. S. Shapley. 1962. College Admissions and the Stability of Marriage. American Mathematical Monthly, Vol. 69, pp. 9-14.

Koehn P., H. Hoang, A. Birch, C. Callison-Burch, M. Federico, N. Bertoldi, B. Cowan, W. Shen, C. Moran, R. Zens, C. Dyer, O. Bojar, A. Constantin, and E. Herbst. 2007. Moses: Open Source Toolkit for Statistical Machine Translation. In Proceedings of the ACL-2007 Demo and Poster Sessions.

Kuhn H. W. 1955. The Hungarian method for the assignment problem. Naval Research Logistics Quarterly, Vol. 2, pp.83-97.

Lafferty J., A. McCallum, F. Pereira. 2001. Conditional Random Fields: Probabilistic Models for Segmenting and Labelling Sequence Data. Proceedings of ICML Conference, pp.282-289.

Munkres J. 1957. Algorithms for the assignment and transportation problems. Journal of the Society for Industrial and Applied Mathematics, Vol. 5, pp.32-38.

Schmid, H. 1994. Probabilistic Part-of-Speech Tagging Using Decision Trees, Proceedings of International Conference on New Methods in Language Processing, Manchester, UK.

Smith T. F. and M. S. Waterman. 1981. Identification of Common Molecular Subsequences. Journal of Molecular Biology, 147: 195–197.

Tambouratzis G., F. Simistira, S. Sofianopoulos, N. Tsimboukakis and M. Vassiliou 2011. A resource-light phrase scheme for language-portable MT, Proceedings of the 15th International Conference of the European Association for Machine Translation, 30-31 May 2011, Leuven, Belgium, pp. 185-192.

Table 1 – PRESEMT Evaluation results for different language pairs.

Language Pair		Sentence set		Metrics				
SL	TL	Number	Source	BLEU	NIST	Meteor	TER	
English	German	189	web	0.1052	3.8433	0.1939	83.233	
German	English	195	web	0.1305	4.5401	0.2058	74.804	
Greek	English	200	web	0.1011	4.5124	0.2442	79.750	
English	German	189	web	0.2108	5.6517	0.2497	68.190	**Moses**

Figure 1 – PRESEMT system architecture.

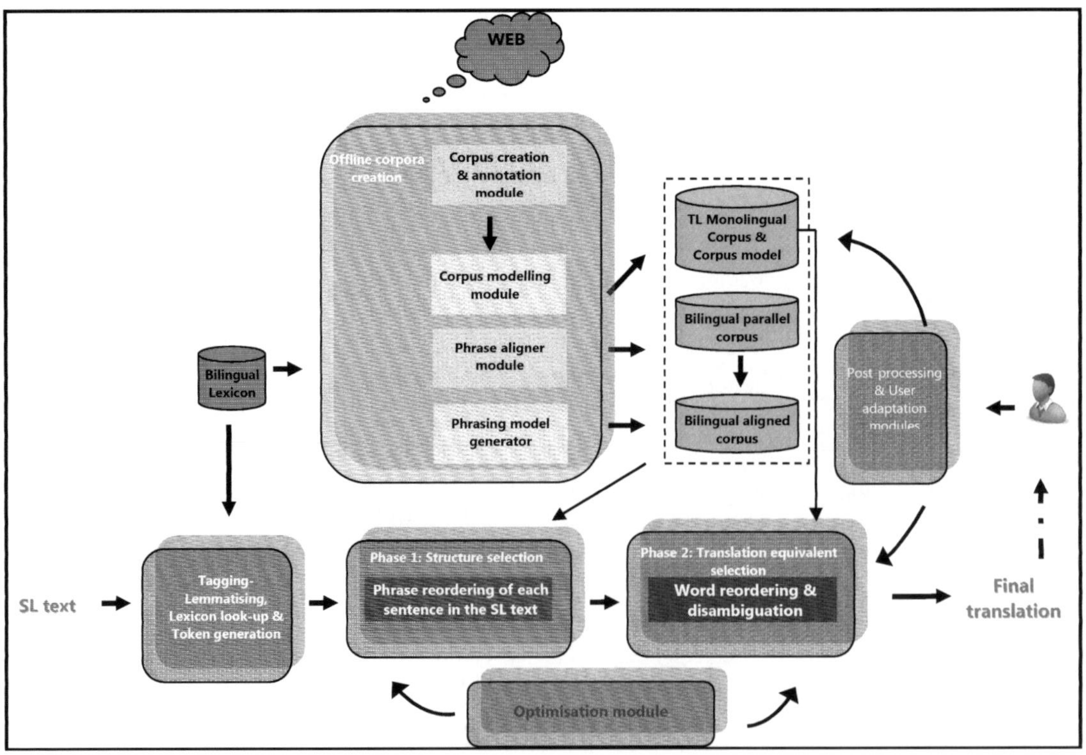

PLUTO: Automated Solutions for Patent Translation[i]

John Tinsley, Alexandru Ceausu, Jian Zhang

Centre for Next Generation Localisation
School of Computing
Dublin City University, Ireland
{jtinsley;aceausu;jzhang}@computing.dcu.ie

1 Introduction

PLUTO is a commercial development project supported by the European Commission as part of the FP7 programme which aims to eliminate the language barriers that exist worldwide in the provision of multilingual access to patent information. The project consortium comprises four partners: the Centre for Next Generation Localisation at Dublin City University,[1] ESTeam AB,[2] CrossLang,[3] and the Dutch Patent Information User Group (WON).[4] Research and development is carried out in close collaboration with user groups and intellectual property (IP) professionals to ensure solutions and software are delivered that meet actual user needs.

1.1 The need for patent translation

The number of patent applications filed worldwide is continually increasing, with over 1.8 million new filings in 2010 alone. Yet Despite the fact that patents are filed in dozens of different languages, language barriers are no excuse in the case of infringement. When carrying our prior-art and other searches IP professionals must ensure they include collections which encompass all potential relevant patents. Such searches will typically return results – a set of patent documents – 30% of which will be in a foreign language.

As professional translation for patents is such a specialist task, translators command a premium fee for this service, often up to €0.50 per word for Asian languages. This often results in high or unworkable translation costs for innovators. While free machine translation (MT) tools such as Google translate have unquestionably been beneficial in helping to reduce the need to resort to expensive human translation, the quality is still often inadequate as the models are too general to cope with the intricacies of patent text.

In what follows, we will provide an overview of some of the technologies being developed in PLUTO to address the need for higher quality MT solutions for patents and how these are deployed for the benefit of IP professionals.

2 Language Technology for Patents

Patent translation is a unique task given the style of language used in patent documents. This language, so-called "patentese", typically comprises a mixture of highly-specific technical terminology and legal jargon and is often written with the express purpose of obfuscating the intended meaning. For example, in 2001 an innovation was granted in Australia for a "Circular Transportation Facilitation Device", i.e. a wheel.[5]

Patents are also characterised by a proliferation of extremely long sentences, complex chemical formula, and other constructs which make the task for MT more difficult.

2.1 Domain-specfic machine translation

The patent translation systems used in PLUTO have been built using the MaTrEx MT framework (Armstrong et al., 2006). The systems are domain specific in that they have been trained exclusively using parallel patent corpora. A number of experiments related to domain adaptation of the language and translation models have been carried out in the context of these systems. The principal findings from this work were that systems combining all available patent data for a given language were preferable (Ceausu et al. 2011).

[1] www.cngl.ie
[2] www.esteam.se
[3] www.crosslang.com
[4] www.won-nl.com

[5] http://pericles.ipaustralia.gov.au/aub/pdf/nps/2002/0808/2001100012A4/2001100012.pdf

Proceedings of the 13th Conference of the European Chapter of the Association for Computational Linguistics, pages 69–71,
Avignon, France, April 23 - 27 2012.

Significant pre-processing techniques are also applied to the input text to account for specific features of patent language. For instance, sentence splitting based on the marker hypothesis (Green, 1979) is used to reduce long sentences to more manageable lengths, while named-entity recognition is applied to isolate certain structures, such as chemical compounds and references to figures, in order to treat them in a specific manner.

Additionally, various language-specific techniques are used for relevant MT systems. For example, a technique called word packing (Ma et al., 2007), is exploited for Chinese—English. This is a bilingually motivated task which improves the precision of word alignment by "packing" several consecutive words together which correspond to a single word in the corresponding language.

Japanese—English is a particularly challenging pair due to the divergent word ordering between the two languages. To overcome this, we employ preordering of the input text (Talbot et al. 2011) in order to harmonise the word ordering between the two languages and reduce the likelihood of ordering errors. This is done using a rule-based technique called head-finalisation (Isozaki et al., 2010) which moves the English syntactic head towards the end of the phrase to emulate the Japanese word order.

Finally, we use compound splitting and true casing modules for our English—German MT systems in order to reduce the occurrence of out-of-vocabulary words.

2.2 Translation memory integration

In order to further improve the translation quality, we are developing an engine to automatically combine the outputs of the MT system and a translation memory (TM).

The engine works by taking a patent document as input and searching for full matches on paragraph, sentence, and segment (sub-sentential) level in the TM. If no full matches are found, fuzzy matches are sought above a predetermined threshold and combined with the output of the MT system using phrase- and word-level alignment information.

For patents, most leverage from the TM is seen at segment level, particularly as the patent claims are often written using quite a rigid structure. This is due to that fact that, as patents typically describe something novel which may never have been written about previously, there is often little repetition of full sentences.

2.3 Evaluation

The performance of the patent MT systems in PLUTO is evaluated using a range of methods aimed not only at gauging general quality, but also identifying areas for improvement and relative performance against similar systems.

In addition to assessing the MT systems using automatic evaluation metrics such as BLEU (Papineni et al., 2002) and METEOR (Banerjee et al. 2005), large-scale human evaluations are also carried out. MT system output is ranked from 1—5 based on the overall quality of translation, and individual translation errors are identified and classified in an error categorisation task.

On top of this standalone evaluation, the PLUTO MT systems are also benchmarked against leading commercial systems across two MT paradigms: Google Translate for statistical MT and Systran (Enterprise) for rule-based MT. A comparative analysis is carried out using both the automatic and human evaluation techniques described above. This comparison is also applied to the output of the PLUTO MT systems and the output of the integrated TM/MT system in order to quantify the improvements achieved using the translation memories.

The main findings from the first round of evaluations for our French—English and Portuguese—English systems showed that our MT systems score relatively high based on human judgments -- 3.8 out of 5 on average -- while being ranked higher than the commercial systems approximately 75% of the time. More details on these experiments can be found in Ceausu et al. (2011).

3 Patent Translation Web Service

The PLUTO MT systems are deployed as a web service (Tinsley et al., 2010). The main entry point for end users is through a web browser plugin which allows them to access translations on-the-fly regardless of the search engine being used to find relevant patents. In addition to the browser plugin, users also have the option to input text directly or upload patent documents in a number of formats including PDF and MS Word.

A number of further natural language processing techniques are exploited to improve the user experience. *N*-gram based language identification is used to send input to the correct MT system; while frequency based keyword extraction provides users with potentially important terms with which to carry out subsequent searches.

Corresponding source and target segments are highlighted on both word and phrase level, while users have the option of post-editing translations which are stored in a personal terminology database and applied to future translations.

The entire framework has been designed to facilitate the patent professional in their daily workflow. It provides them with a consistency of translation quality and features regardless of the search tools being used to locate relevant patents.

This has been validated through extensive user experience testing which included a usability evaluation of the translation output.

4 Looking Forward

The PLUTO project has been running for just over two years and is scheduled to end in March 2013. Our goal by that time is to have established a viable commercial offering to capitalize on the state-of-the-art research and development into automated patent translation.

In the meantime, we will continue to build upon our existing work by building MT systems for additional language pairs and iteratively improving upon our baseline translation performance. Significant effort will also be spent on optimising the integration of translation memories with MT using techniques such as those described in He et al. (2011).

Acknowledgements

The PLuTO project (ICT-PSP-250416) is funded under the European Union's ICT Policy Support Programme as part of the Competitiveness and Innovation Framework Programme

References

Armstrong, S., M. Flanagan, Y. Graham, D. Groves, B. Mellebeek, S. Morrissey, N. Stroppa and A. Way. 2006. *MaTrEx: Machine Translation Using Examples.* TC-STAR OpenLab on Speech Translation. Trento, Italy.

Banerjee, S. and Lavie, A. (2005). *METEOR: An Automatic Metric for MT Evaluation with Improved Correlation with Human Judgments.* In Proceedings of Workshop on Intrinsic and Extrinsic Evaluation Measures for MT and/or Summarization at the 43th Annual Meeting of the Association of Computational Linguistics (ACL-05), Ann Arbor, MI.

Ceausu, Alexandru, John Tinsley, Andrew Way, Jian Zhang, Paraic Sheridan, *Experiments on Domain Adaptation for Patent Machine Translation in the PLuTO project*, The 15th Annual Conference of the European Association for Machine Translation, EAMT-2011, Leuven, Belgium

Green, T., *The necessity of syntax markers. two experiments with artificial languages.* Journal of Verbal Learning and Behavior, 18:481{496}, 1979.

Isozaki, H., Sudoh, K., Tsukada, H., and Duh, K. *Head finalization: A simple reordering rule for SOV languages.* In Proceedings of the 5th Workshop on Machine Translation (WMT), Upsala, Sweden.

Ma, Yanjun, Nicolas Stroppa, and Andy Way. 2007. Boostrapping Word Alignment via Word Packing. In *Proceedings of the 45th Annual Meeting of the Association for Computational Linguistics (ACL 2007)*, Prague, Czech Republic, pp.304—311

Papineni, K., Roukos, S.,Ward, T., and Zhu,W.-J. (2002). *BLEU: a Method for Automatic Evaluationof Machine Translation.* In Proceedings of the 40th Annual Meeting of the Association for Computational Linguistics (ACL-02), pages 311–318, Philadelphia, PA.

Talbot, David, Hideto Kazawa, Hiroshi Ichikwa, Jason Katz-Brown, Masakazu Seno, Franz Och *A Lightweight Evaluation Framework for Machine Translation Reordering,* In Proceedings of the Sixth Workshop on Statistical Machine Translation (July 2011), Edinburgh, Scotland.pp. 12-21

Tinsley, J., A. Way and P. Sheridan 2010. *PLuTO: MT for Online Patent Translation* In Proceedings of the 9th Conferences of the Association for Machine Translation in the Americas. Denver, CO, USA.

[i] This paper is an extended abstract intended to accompany an oral presentation. It is not intended to be a standalone scientific article.

ATLAS - Human Language Technologies integrated within a Multilingual Web Content Management System

Svetla Koeva
Department of Computational Linguistics, Institute for Bulgarian
Bulgarian Academy of Sciences
svetla@dcl.bas.bg

Abstract

The main purpose of the project ATLAS (Applied Technology for Language-Aided CMS) is to facilitate multilingual web content development and management. Its main innovation is the integration of language technologies within a web content management system. The language processing framework, integrated with web content management, provides automatic annotation of important words, phrases and named entities, suggestions for categorisation of documents, automatic summary generation, and machine translation of summaries of documents. A machine translation approach, as well as methods for obtaining and constructing training data for machine translation are under development.

1 Introduction

The main purpose of the European project ATLAS (Applied Technology for Language-Aided CMS)[1] is to facilitate multilingual web content development and management. Its main innovation is the integration of language technologies within a web content management system. ATLAS combines a language processing framework with a content management component (i-Publisher)[2] used for creating, running and managing dynamic content-driven websites. Examples of such sites are i-Librarian,[3] a free online library of digital documents that may be personalised according to the user's needs and requirements; and EUDocLib,[4] a free online library of European legal documents. The language processing framework of these websites provides automatic annotation of important words, phrases and named entities, suggestions for categorisation of documents, automatic summary generation, and machine translation of a summary of a document (Karagyozov et al. 2012). Six European Union languages – Bulgarian, German, Greek, English, Polish, and Romanian are supported.

2. Brief overview of existing content management systems

The most frequently used open-source multilingual web content management systems (WordPress, Joomla, Joom!Fish, TYPO3, Drupal)[5] offer a relatively low level of multilingual content management. None of the platforms supports multiple languages in their

[1] http://www.atlasproject.eu

[2] http://i-publisher.atlasproject.eu/

[3] http://www.i-librarian.eu/

[4] http://eudoclib.atlasproject.eu/

[5] http://wordpress.com/, http://www.joomla.org/, http://www.joomfish.net/, http://typo3.org/, http://drupal.org/

native states. Instead, they rely on plugins to handle this: WordPress uses the WordPress Multilingual Plugin, Drupal needs a module called Locale, and Joomla needs a module called Joomfish. There are modules, like those provided by ICanLocalize[6], than can facilitate selection within Drupal and WordPress of the material to be translated, but the actual translation is done by human translators. To the best of our knowledge, none of the existing content management systems exploits language technologies to provide more sophisticated text content management. This is proved by the data published at the CMS Critic[7] - an online media providing news, reviews, articles and interviews for about 60 content management systems. Taking into account that the online data are in many cases multilingual and documents stored in a content management system are usually related by means of sharing similar topics or domains it can be claimed that the web content management systems need the power of modern language technologies. In comparison ATLAS offers the advantage of integration of natural language processing in the multilingual content management.

3 Selection of "core" words

ATLAS suggests "core" words (plus phrases and named entities), i.e., the most essential words that capture the main topic of a given document. Currently the selection of core words is carried out in a two-stage process: identification of candidates and ranking. For the identification stage a language processing chain is applied that consists of the following tools: sentence splitter, tokenizer, PoS tagger, lemmatizer, word sense disambiguator (assigns a unique sense to a word), NP extractor (marks up noun phrases in the text) and NE extractor (marks up named entities in the text). After this stage, the target core words are ranked according to their importance scores, which are estimated by features such as frequency, linguistic correlation, phrase length, etc., combined by heuristics to obtain the final ranking strategy. The core words are displayed in several groups: named entities (locations, names, etc.) - both single words and phrases, and noun phrases - terms, multiword expressions or noun phrases with a hight frequency. For example among the "core" noun phrases extracted from Cocoa Fundamentals Guide[8] are the following phrases: *Object-Oriented Programming, Objective-C language, Cocoa application, Cocoa program*, etc. Even though the language processing chains that are applied differ from language to language, this approach offers a common ground for language processing and its results can be comfortably used by advanced language components such as document classification, clause-based summarisation, and statistical machine translation. Content navigation (such as lists of similar documents) based on interlinked text annotations is also provided.

4 Automatic categorisation

Automatic document classification (assigning a document to one or more domains or categories from a set of labels) is of great importance to a modern multilingual web content management system. ATLAS provides automatic multi-label categorisation of documents into one or more predefined categories. This starts with a training phase, in which a statistical model is created based on a set of features from already labelled documents. There are currently four classifiers, two of which exploit the Naïve Bayesian algorithm, the two others Relative entropy and Class-featured centroid, respectively. In the classifying phase, the model is used to assign one or more labels to unlabelled documents. The results from the different classifiers are combined and the final classification result is determined by a majority voting system. The automatic text categorisation is at the present stage able to handle documents in Bulgarian and English. For example, the Cocoa Fundamentals Guide is automatically categorised under the domain *Computer science*, and unter the Topics *Computer science, Graphics and Design, Database Management*, and *Programming*.

5 Text summarization

Two different strategies for obtaining summaries are used in ATLAS. The strategy for short texts is based on identification of the discourse structure and produces a summary that can be classified as a type of excerpt, thus it is possible to indicate the length of the summary as a percentage of the original text. Summarisation of short texts in ATLAS draws on the whole language processing chain and also adds a couple of other modules to

[6] http://www.icanlocalize.com/

[7] http://www.cmscritic.com/

[8] https://developer.apple.com/library/mac/documentation/Cocoa/Conceptual/CocoaFundamentals/CocoaFundamentals.pdf

the chain: clause splitting, anaphora resolution, discourse parsing and summarization. The method used for short texts (Cristea et al. 2005) exploits cohesion and coherence properties of the text to build intermediate structures. Currently, the short text summarisation modules are implemented for English and Romanian.

The strategy for long texts assembles a template summary based on extraction of relevant information specific to different genres and is for the time being still under development.

6 Machine translation

For i-Publisher, machine translation serves as a translation aid for publishing multilingual content. The ability to display content in multiple languages is combined with a computer-aided localization of the templates. Text for a localization is submitted to the translation engine and the output is subject to human post-processing.

For i-Librarian and EuDocLib, and for any website developed with i-Publisher, the machine translation engine provides a translation of the document summary provided earlier in the chain. This will give the user rough clues about documents in different languages, and a basis to decide whether they are to be stored.

6.1 Obtaining training corpora

The development of a translation engine is particularly challenging, as the translation should be able to be used in different domains and within different text genres. In addition, most of the language pairs in question belong to the less resourced group for which bilingual training and test material is available in limited amounts (Gavrila and Vertan 2011). For instance, parallel corpora incorporating Bulgarian are relatively small and usually domain-specific, with mostly literary or administrative texts. ATLAS' administrative subcorpus contains texts from EU legislation created between the years 1958 and 2011, available as an online repositories, i.e., the EuroParl Corpus (Koehn 2005); the JRC-Acquis (Steinberger 2006), and includes all the accessible texts in the target languages. The scientific / administrative subcorpus consists of administrative texts published by the European Medicines Evaluation Agency (EMEA) in the years between 1978 and 2009. It is part of the OPUS collection (Tiedemann 2009). The mass media subcorpus contains news reports as well as some other journalistic texts published in nine Balkan languages and English from October 2002 until the present day on the East Europe information website[9]. The fiction subcorpus was compiled manually by harvesting freely available texts on the Internet, scanning, and from donations by authors. So far, it consists of texts in Bulgarian, English, and German. The subcorpus of informal texts consists of subtitles of films: feature films, documentaries, and animations, all part of the OPUS collection (Tiedemann 2009). Automatic collection of corpora is preferred to manual, and for that purpose a set of simple crawlers was designed. They are modified for each source to ensure efficiency. Figure 1 presents some statistical data for the Bulgarian-English parallel corpus, the largest in the collection (the vertical axis shows the number of words, while the horizontal - the domain distribution).

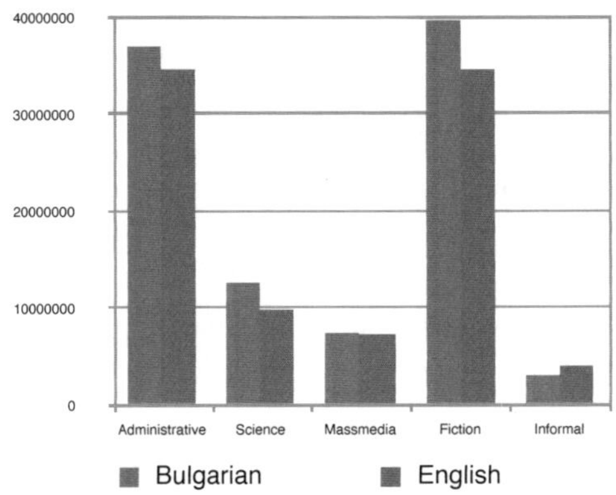

Figure 1 Bulgarian-English parallel corpus

Two basic methods are used to enlarge the existing parallel corpora. In the first, the available training data for statistical machine translation are extended by means of generating paraphrases (e.g. compound nouns are paraphrased into (semi-) equivalent phrases with a preposition, and vice versa). The paraphrases can be classified as morphological (where the difference is between the forms of the phrase constituents), lexical (based on semantic similarity between constituents) and phrasal (based on syntactic transformations). Paraphrase generation methods that operate both on a single monolingual corpus or on parallel corpus are discussed by Madnani and Dorr 2010. For instance, one of the methods for paraphrase generation from a monolingual corpus considers as paraphrases all words and phrases that are distributionally similar, that is, occurring with the

[9] http://setimes.com/

same sets of anchors (Paşca and Dienes 2005). An approach using phrase-based alignment techniques shows how paraphrases in one language can be identified using a phrase in a second language as a pivot (Bannard and Callison-Burch 2005).

The second method performs automatic generation of parallel corpora (Xu and Sun 2011) by means of automatic translation. This method can be applied for language pairs for which parallel corpora are still limited in quantity. If, say, a Bulgarian-English parallel corpus exists, a Bulgarian Polish parallel corpus can be constructed by means of automatic translation from English to Polish. To control the quality of the automatically generated data, multiple translation systems can be used, and the compatibility of the translated outputs can be calculated. Thus, both methods can fill gaps in the available data, the first method by extending existing parallel corpora and the second by automatic construction of parallel corpora.

6.2 Accepted approach

Given that the ATLAS platform deals with languages from different language families and that the engine should support several domains, an interlingua approach is not suitable. Building transfer systems for all language pairs is also time-consuming and does not make the platform easily portable to other languages. When all requirements and limitations are taken into account, corpus-based machine translation paradigms are the best option that can be considered (Karagyozov et al. 2012). For the ATLAS translation engine it was decided to use a hybrid architecture combining example-based and statistical machine translation at the word-based level (i.e., no syntactic trees will be used). The ATLAS translation engine interacts with other modules of the system. For example, the document categorisation module assigns one or more domains to each document, and if no specific trained translation model for the respective domain exists, the user gets a warning that the translation may be inadequate with respect to lexical coverage. Each input item to the translation engine is then processed by the example-based machine translation component.

If the input as a whole or important chunks of it are found in the translation database, the translation equivalents are used and, if necessary, combined (Gavrila 2011). In all other cases the input is sent further to the Moses-based machine translation component which uses a part-of-speech and domain-factored model (Niehues and Waibel 2010).

Like the architecture of the categorization engine, the translation system in ATLAS is able to accommodate and use different third-party translations engines, such as those of Google, Bing, and Yahoo.

The ATLAS machine translation module is still under development. Some experiments in translation between English, German, and Romanian have been performed in order to define: what parameter settings are suitable for language pairs with a rich morphology, what tuning steps lead to significant improvements, wheather the PoS-factored models improve significantly the quality of results (Karagyozov et al. 2012).

7 Conclusion

To conclude, ATLAS enables users to create, organise and publish various types of multilingual documents. ATLAS reduces the manual work by using automatic classification of documents and helps users to decide about a document by providing summaries of documents and their translations. Moreover, the user can easily find the most relevant texts within large document collections and get a brief overview of their content. A modern web content management systems should help users come to grips with the growing complexity of today's multilingual websites. ATLAS answers to this task.

Acknowledgments

ATLAS (Applied Technology for Language-Aided CMS) is a European project funded under the CIP ICT Policy Support Programme, Grant Agreement 250467.

References

Bannard and Callison-Burch 2005: Bannard, Colin and Chris Callison-Burch. Paraphrasing with bilingual parallel corpora. In *Proceedings of ACL,* pages 597–604, Ann Arbor, MI.

Cristea et al. 2005: Cristea, D., Postolache, O., Pistol, I. (2005). Summarisation through Discourse Structure. *Computational Linguistics and Intelligent Text Processing, 6th International Conference CICLing 2005* (pp. 632-644). Mexico City, Mexico: Springer LNSC, vol. 3406.

Gavrila 2011: Gavrila, M. Constrained recombination in an example-based machine translation system. In M. L. Vincent Vondeghinste (Ed.), *15th Annual Conference of the European Association for Machine Translation*, Leuven, Belgium, pp. 193-200.

Gavrila and Vertan 2011: Gavrila Monica and Cristina Vertan. Training data in statistical machine translation – the more, the better? In *Proceedings of the RANLP-2011 Conference*, September 2011, Hissar, Bulgaria, pp. 551-556.

Karagyozov et al. 2012: Diman Karagiozov, Anelia Belogay, Dan Cristea, Svetla Koeva, Maciej Ogrodniczuk, Polivios Raxis, Emil Stoyanov and Cristina Vertan. i-Librarian – Free online library for European citizens, In *Infotheca*, Belgrade, to appear.

Koehn 2005: Koehn, Ph. Europarl: A Parallel Corpus for Statistical Machine Translation, *Proceedings of MT Summit*, pp. 79–86.

Madnani and Dorr 2010: Nitin Madnani and Bonnie Dorr. 2010. Generat- ing phrasal and sentential paraphrases: A survey of data-driven methods. *Computational Linguistics,* 36(3), pp. 341–388.

Niehues and Waibel 2010: Niehues Jan and Alex Waibel, *Domain Adaptation in Statistical Machine Translation using Factored Translation Models*, Proceedings of EAMT 2010 Saint-Raphael.

Paşca and Dienes 2005: Paşca, Marius and Péter Dienes. 2005. Aligning needles in a haystack: Paraphrase acquisition across the Web. In *Proceedings of IJCNLP*, Jeju Island, pp. 119-130.

Steinberger et al. 2006: Steinberger, R., Pouliquen, B., Widiger, A., Ignat, C., Erjavec, T., Tufiş, D., Varga, D. (2006). The JRC-Acquis: A multilingual aligned parallel corpus with 20+ languages. *Proceedings of LREC 2006*. Genoa, Italy.

Tiedemann 2009: Tiedemann, J. News from OPUS - A Collection of Multilingual Parallel Corpora with Tools and Interfaces. In: N. Nicolov, K. Bontcheva, G. Angelova, R. Mitkov (eds.) *Recent Advances in Natural Language Processing* (vol. V), John Benjamins, Amsterdam/Philadelphia, pp. 237–248.

Xu and Sun 2011: Jia Xu and Weiwei Sun. Generating virtual parallel corpus: A compatibility centric method. In Proceedings of the Machine Translation Summit XIII.

Tree-based Hybrid Machine Translation

Andreas Kirkedal
Centre for Computational Modelling of language
Institute for International Language Studies and Computational Linguistics
Copenhagen Business School
ask.isv@cbs.dk

Abstract

I present an automatic post-editing approach that combines translation systems which produce syntactic trees as output. The nodes in the generation tree and target-side SCFG tree are aligned and form the basis for computing structural similarity. Structural similarity computation aligns subtrees and based on this alignment, subtrees are substituted to create more accurate translations. Two different techniques have been implemented to compute structural similarity: *leaves* and *tree-edit distance*. I report on the translation quality of a machine translation (MT) system where both techniques are implemented. The approach shows significant improvement over the baseline for MT systems with limited training data and structural improvement for MT systems trained on Europarl.

1 Introduction

Statistical MT (SMT) and rule-based MT (RBMT) have complimentary strengths and combining their output can improve translation quality. The underlying models in SMT lack linguistic sophistication when compared to RBMT systems and there is a trend towards incorporating more linguistic knowledge by creating hybrid systems that can exploit the linguistic knowledge contained in hand-crafted rules and the knowledge extracted from large amounts of text.

Hierarchical phrases (Chiang, 2005) are encoded in a tree structure just as linguistic trees. Most RBMT systems also encode the analysis of a sentence in a tree. The rules generating hierarchical trees are inferred from unlabeled corpora and RBMT systems use hand-crafted rules based in linguistic knowledge. While the trees are generated differently, alignments between nodes and subtrees in the generation phase can be computed. Based on the computed alignments, substitution can be performed between the trees.

The automatic post-editing approach proposed in this paper is based on *structural similarity*. The tree structures are aligned and subtree substitution based on the similarity of subtrees performed. This knowledge-poor approach is compatible with the surface-near nature of SMT systems, does not require other information than what is available in the output, and ensures that the approach is generic so it can, in principle, be applied to any language pair.

2 Hybrid Machine Translation

Hybrid machine translation (HMT) is a paradigm that seeks to combine the strengths of SMT and RBMT. The different approaches have complementary strengths and weaknesses (Thurmair, 2009) which have led to the emergence of HMT as a subfield in machine translation research.

The strength of SMT is robustness - i.e. it will always produce an output - and fluency due to the use of language models. A weakness of SMT is the lack of explicit linguistic knowledge, which make translation phenomena requiring such information, e.g. long-distance dependencies, difficult to handle.

RBMT systems translate more accurately in cases without parse failure, since they can take more information into account e.g. morphological, syntactic or semantic information, where SMT only uses surface forms. RBMT often suffer from lack of robustness when parsing fails and

Proceedings of the 13th Conference of the European Chapter of the Association for Computational Linguistics, pages 77–86,
Avignon, France, April 23 - 27 2012. ©2012 Association for Computational Linguistics

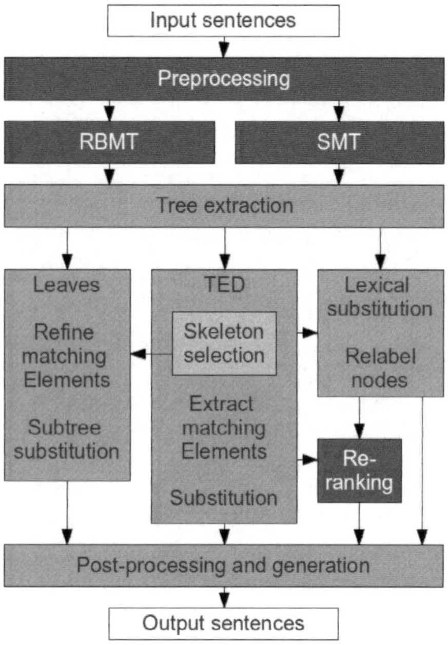

Figure 1: Hybrid system architecture.

in lexical selection in transfer. RBMT systems are also very costly to build, and maintenance and development can be very complex e.g. due to the interdependency of rules.

The post-editing approach attempts to incorporate the linguistic knowledge encoded in target-side dependency trees into hierarchical trees produced by an SMT system.

2.1 Related work

System combinations by coupling MT systems serially or in parallel have been attempted before e.g. via hypothesis selection (Hildebrand and Vogel, 2008), by combining translation hypotheses locally using POS tags (Federmann et al., 2010) or by statistical post-editing (SPE) (Simard et al., 2007). In hypothesis selection approaches, a number of MT systems produce translations for an n-best list and use a re-ranking module to rescore the translations. Using this approach, the best improvements are achieved with a large number of systems running in parallel and this is not feasible in a practical application, mostly due to the computational resources required by the component systems. The translations will also not be better than the one produced by the best component system. Tighter integration of rule-based and statistical approaches have also been proposed: Adding probabilities to parse trees, pre-translation word reordering, enriching the phrase table with output phrases from a rule-based system (Eisele et al., 2008), creating training data from RBMT systems etc. The factored translation models also present a way to integrate rule-based parsing systems.

```
Jeg [jeg] 1S NOM @SUBJ #1->2
arbejder [arbejde] <mv> V PR AKT @FS-STA #2->0
hjemme [hjemme] <aloc> ADV LOC @<ADVL #3->2
. [.] PU @PU #4->0
```

Figure 2: Disambiguated CG representation for *I work at home*. Dependency annotation is indicated by the #-character.

The automatic post-editing approach proposed here does not exactly fit the classification of parallel coupling approaches in Thurmair (2009). Other coupling architectures with post-editing work on words or phrases and generate confusion networks or add more information to identify substitution candidates, while the units focused on here are graphs and no additional information is added to the MT output. This approach does select a skeleton upon which transformations are conducted as in Rosti et al. (2007) and requires the RBMT system to generate a target side language analysis which must be available to the post-editing systems, but does not require a new syntactic analysis of noisy MT output. The architecture of the hybrid system used in this paper is parallel coupling with post-editing. A diagram of the implemented systems can be seen in Figure 1. The dark grey boxes represent pre-existing modules and open source software and the light grey boxes represent the additional modules developed to implement the post-editing approach.

2.2 RBMT Component

The Danish to English translation engine in GramTrans (Bick, 2007) is called through an API. The output is a constraint grammar (CG) analysis on the target language side after all transfer and target side transformation rules have been applied. Example output is shown in Figure 2. In the analysis, dependency information is provided and they form the basis for creating the tree used for structural similarity computation. Part-of-speech tags, source and target surface structure, sentence position and dependency information are extracted from the CG analysis.

GramTrans is created to be robust and produce as many dependency markings as possible to be used in later translation stages. Errors in the assignment of functional tags propagate to the dependency level and can result in markings that will produce a dependency tree and a number of unconnected subgraphs with circularities. This presents a problem if the dependency markings are the basis for creating a dependency tree because it is not straight-forward to reattach a subgraph correctly, when the grammatical tags cannot be relied upon.

2.3 SMT Component

A CKY+ algorithm for chart decoding is implemented in Moses (Koehn et al., 2007) for tree-based models and is used as the SMT component system in this paper.

Hierarchical phrases are phrases that can contain subphrases, i.e. a hierarchical phrase contains non-terminal symbols. An example rule from Danish to English:

$$X_1 \text{ i øvrigt } X_2 \longrightarrow \text{moreover, } X_1 \; X_2$$

X_n is a nonterminal and the subscript identifies how the nonterminals are aligned. The hierarchical phrases are learned from bitext with unannotated data and are formally productions from a synchronous context-free grammar (SCFG) and can be viewed as a move towards syntax-based SMT (Chiang, 2005). Since hierarchical phrases are not linguistic, Chiang makes a distinction between *linguistically* syntax-based MT and *formally* syntax-based MT where hierarchical models fall in the latter category because the structures they are defined over are not linguistically informed, i.e. unannotated bitexts.

A hierarchical model is based on a SCFG and the elementary structures are rewrite rules:

$$X \longrightarrow \langle \gamma, \alpha, \sim \rangle$$

As above, X is a nonterminal, γ and α are both strings of terminals and nonterminals and $\sim$ is a 1-to-1 correspondence between nonterminals in γ and α. As in shown previously, the convention is to use subscripts to represent $\sim$.

To maintain the advantage of the phrase-based approach, *glue rules* are added to the rules that are otherwise learned from raw data:

$$S \longrightarrow \langle S_1 X_2, S_1 X_2 \rangle$$
$$S \longrightarrow \langle X_1, X_1 \rangle$$

Only these rewrite rules contain the nonterminal S. These rules are added to give the model

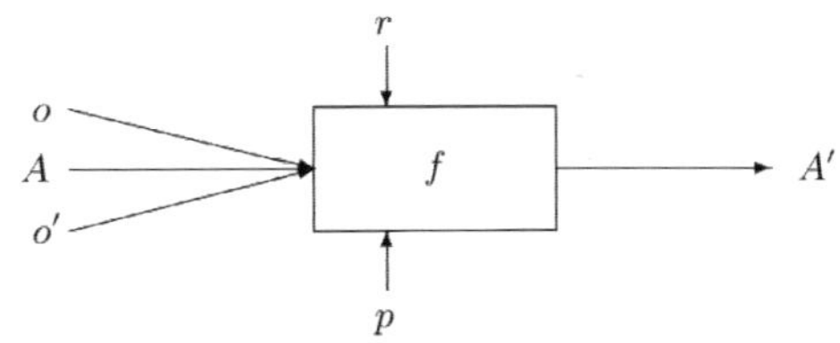

Figure 3: The matching process.

the option of combining partial hypotheses serially and they make the hierarchical model as robust as the traditional phrase-based approaches.

The Moses chart decoder was modified to output trace information from which the n-best hierarchical trees can be reconstructed. The trace information contains the derivations which produce the translation hypotheses.

The sentence–aligned Danish-English part of Europarl (Koehn, 2005) was used for training, and to tune parameters with MERT, the test set from the NAACL WMT 2006 was used (Koehn and Monz, 2006). GIZA++ aligns hierarchical phrases which were extracted by Moses to train a translation model and a language model was trained with SRILM (Stolcke, 2002). Moses was trained using the Experimental Management System (EMS) (Koehn, 2010) and the configuration followed the standard guidelines in the syntax tutorial.[1] To train SRILM, the English side of Europarl was used.

3 Matching Approach

The post-editing approach relies on structures output by the component systems. It is necessary to find similar structures to perform subtree substitution. Matching structures is a problem in several application areas such as semantic web, schema and ontology integration, query mediation etc. Structures include database schemas, directories, diagrams and graphs. Shvaiko and Euzenat (2005) provide a comprehensive survey of matching techniques.

The *matching operation* determines an alignment between two structures and an alignment is a set of *matching elements*. A matching element is a quintuple: $\langle id, e, e', n, R \rangle$:

id Unique id.

e, e' Elements from different structures.

n Confidence measure.

[1] http://www.statmt.org/moses/?n=Moses.SyntaxTutorial

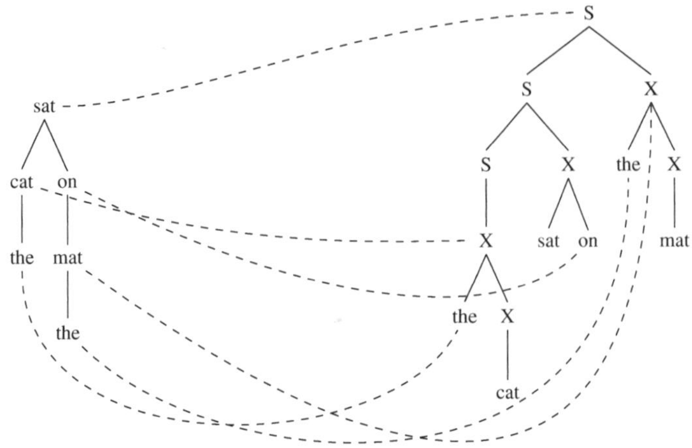

Figure 4: The refined alignment from dependency tree to hierarchical tree.

R The relation holding between the elements.

The resources that can be used in the matching process are shown in Figure 3. o and o' are the structures to be matched, A is an optional existing alignment, r is external resources, p is parameters, weights and thresholds and A' is the set of matching elements created by the process. In this paper, only matching elements with an equivalence relation ($=$) are used.

The returned alignment can be a new alignment or a refinement of A. o will be a dependency tree and o' the hierachical trees from the SMT component system. To compute the initial alignment A between hierarchical and dependency trees, the source to target language phrase alignment output by the component systems is used. So the initial alignment between leaf nodes in target-side trees are computed over the alignment to the source language.

An important decision regarding this hybrid approach is how to compute the alignment and the size of the substituted subtrees. Irrespective of which technique is chosen to compute structural similarity, the resulting alignment should be refined to contain matching elements between internal nodes as shown in Figure 4.

3.1 Alignment Challenges

The change made to the chart decoder to output the n-best trace information is simple and does not output the alignment information. Currently, the tree extraction module computes an alignment between the source and target language phrases.

The segmentation of words into phrases done by Moses does not always correspond to the word-based segmentation required by the CG parser; phrases recognised by the CG parser rarely correspond to phrases in Moses and the hierarchical phrase alignment is not easy to handle.

Aligning hierarchical phrases like **(a)** in Figure 5 is not complicated. The ordering is identical and the Danish word *offentliggøres* is aligned to *will be published*. The numbers `1-3` refer to the alignment of non-terminal nodes based on phrase positions.

It is more complicated to align **(b)** in Figure 5. There are two methods of handling this type of alignment appropriate for the component systems. Because there are an equal number of tokens in the English phrase and Danish phrase, aligning the tokens 1-1 monotonically would be a solution that, in this case, results in a correct alignment.

Another approach relies on weak word reordering between Danish and English and would align *findes* with *there are*. This reduces the alignment problem to aligning *vi der* with *we*. In this case, the alignment is noisy, but usable for creating matching elements. Both approaches are implemented in the hybrid system and the first approach supercedes the second due to the advantage of correlating with the CG approach.

An initial element-level alignment between nodes in a dependency tree and a hierarchical tree is computed over the source language and creates a set of *matching elements* containing aligned nodes.

3.2 Alignment Refinement

Between a dependency and an hierarchical tree, an element-level alignment needs to be refined to

```
(a)    offentliggøres X : X -> will be published X : 1-3
(b)    vi X der X findes : X -> X, we X there are : 1-3 3-0
```

Figure 5: Simplified example of a simple alignment.

a structure-level alignment similar to the one in Figure 4.

Not all matching elements in an initial alignment should be refined e.g. if both nodes in a matching element are leaf nodes, no refinement is needed. Criteria for selecting initial matching elements for refinement are needed.

In the RBMT output, there are no indications of where the parser encountered problems. If a surface form is an out-of-vocabulary (OOV) word, the morphological analyser is used to assign a lexical category based on the word form, hypothesise additional tags based on the analysis and proceed with parsing. In the SMT output, an OOV marker is appended to a surface form to indicate that the word has not been translated. The marker gives an indication of where enriching a hierarchical tree with RBMT output can result in improvement of translation quality.

Based on these observations, hierarchical trees are chosen to function as skeletons. Substituting dependency subtrees into a hierarchical tree is more straightforward than using dependency trees as skeletons. It was not possible to identify head-dependent relations based solely on the information contained in hierarchical subtrees while removing subtrees from hierarchical trees and inserting dependency subtrees does not destroy linguistic information in the tree and dependency subtrees can easily be transformed into a hierarchical-style subtree.

Leaves Based on the OOV marker, a matching technique based on leaf nodes is implemented to refine matching elements and based on this alignment, substitute hierarchical subtrees with dependency subtrees.

The dependency subtree is identified by collecting all descendants of a node. The descendants are handled as leaf nodes because both leaf and nonterminal nodes contain surface forms in a dependecy tree.

The dependency trees provided by GramTrans are not always projective. Subtrees may not represent a continuous surface structure and a continuous subtree must be isolated before an alignment between subtrees can be found because the hierarchical trees resemble phrase structure trees and discontinuous phrases are handled using glue rules.

To identify the corresponding subtree in the hierarchical tree, the matching elements that contain the nodes in the dependency subtree are collected and a path from each leaf node to the root node is computed. The intersection of nodes is retrieved and the root node of the subtree identified as the lowest node present in all paths. It is not always possible to find a common root node besides the root node of the entire tree. To prevent the loss of a high amount of structural information, the root node cannot be replaced or deleted.

3.3 Substitution based on an edit script

An algorithm for computing structural similarity is the *Tree Edit Distance* (TED) algorithm, which computes how many operations are necessary for transforming one tree into another tree. Following Zhang and Shasha (1989) and Bille (2005), the operations are defined on nodes and the trees are ordered, labelled trees. There are 3 different edit operations:

rename Change the label of a node in a tree.

delete Remove a node n from a tree. Insert the children of n as children of the parent of n so the sequence of children are preserved. The deleted node may not be the root node.

insert Insert a node as the child of a node n in a tree. A subsequence of children of n are inserted as children of the new node so the sequence of children are preserved. An insertion is the inverse operation of a deletion.

A cost function is defined for each operation. The goal is to find the sequence of edit operations that turns a tree T_1 into another tree T_2 with minimum cost. The sequence of edit operations is called an *edit script* and the cost of the optimal edit script is the tree edit distance.

The cost functions should return a distance metric and satisfy the following conditions:

1. $\gamma(i \rightarrow j) \geq 0$ and $\gamma(i \rightarrow i) = 0$

2. $\gamma(i \to j) = \gamma(j \to i)$

3. $\gamma(i \to k) \leq \gamma(i \to j) + \gamma(j \to k)$

γ is the cost of an edit operation.

The *edit distance mapping* is a representation of an edit script. A rename operation is represented as $(i_1 \to j_2)$ where the subscript denotes that the nodes i and j belong to different trees. $(i_1 \to \epsilon)$ represents a deletion and $(\epsilon \to j_2)$ an insertion.

The cost of an edit distance mapping is given by:

$$\gamma(M) = \sum_{(i,j)\in M} \gamma(i \to j) + \sum_{i \in T_1} \gamma(i \to \epsilon) + \sum_{j \in T_2} \gamma(\epsilon \to j)$$

$j \in T_2$ means j is in the set of nodes in T_2.

It is important to note that the trees are ordered trees. The unordered version of the tree edit distance problem is NP-hard, while polynomial algorithms based on dynamic programming exist for ordered trees.

The algorithm does not require an input alignment or external resources. The cost functions for deletion, insertion and renaming must be defined on the information present in the nodes and a unique id must be assigned to the nodes. This id is assigned by traversing the tree depth-first and assigning an integer as id. The algorithm visits each node in the trees in post order and determines based on the cost assigned by the cost functions, which edit operation should be performed.

To generate matching elements that align dependency nodes to nonterminal hierarchical nodes, cost functions for edit operations are modified to assign a lower cost to rename operations where one of the nodes is a hierarchical nonterminal node. If two nodes have the same target and source phrase, a rename operation does not incur any cost and neither does the renaming of untranslated phrases. This ensures that matching elements from the initial alignment that does not require refinement are not altered. Also, if the source is the same and the difference in sentence position is no more than five, the renaming cost is reduced. Experiments showed that a window of five words was necessary to account for differences in sentence position and prevent alignment to nodes later in the sentence with the same source phrase.

This technique is independent of the OOV marker and creates a structure-level alignment. The substitutions performed can be of very high quality but some untranslated words might not be handled. If the system finds any OOV words in the hierachical tree after substitution, a rename operation is carried out on the node.

The extracted matching elements are noisy because they rely on the noisy source to target language alignment and the RBMT engine can also produce an inaccurate translation making the substitution counter-productive. Further limitations on the cost functions become too restrictive and produce too few matching elements. To avoid some of the noise, all permutations of applying substitutions based on the edit script are generated, re-ranked and the highest scoring hypothesis chosen as the translation.

3.4 Generation

To ensure that the surface string generated from the newly created tree will have the correct word ordering, the dependency subtree is transformed before being inserted into the hierarchical tree. To create the insertion tree, the dependency nodes are inserted as leaf nodes of a dummy node. The dummy node is inserted before the root node of the aligned hierarchical subtree and the information on the root node copied to the new node. Subsequently, the hierarchical nodes are removed from the tree. If both nodes in a matching element are leaf nodes, the hierarchical node is relabeled with information from the dependency node.

4 Experiments

The experiments have been conducted between Danish and English. The language model trained with EMS is used to re-rank translation alternatives. BLEU (Papineni et al., 2002), TER (Snover et al., 2006) and METEOR (Banerjee and Lavie, 2005) scores will be reported.

4.1 Experimental Setup

Two sets of five experiments have been conducted. The first set of experiments use the initial 100,000 lines from Europarl for training Moses and the second set of experiments use the full Europarl corpus of ca. 1.8 mio sentences. The SMT baseline is the hierarchical version of Moses.

TED Skeleton Selection The impact of choosing the translation hypothesis with a minimal edit

Metrics:	BLEU	TER	METEOR
RBMT baseline	19.35	64.54	53.19
SMT baseline	30.16 (22.63)	57.16 (63.10)	59.51 (50.72)
Lexical substitution	**30.53** (**25.28**)	**56.40** (60.56)	**61.22** (57.24)
Leaves technique	29.06 (21.96)	57.96 (64.80)	60.09 (54.32)
TED skeleton(any bias)	30.16 (22.63)	57.08 (62.98)	59.46 (50.75)
TED-R 1-best	29.78 (25.16)	57.25 (60.51)	59.87 (57.31)
TED-R skeleton(any bias)	29.99 (25.18)	56.72 (**60.44**)	60.79 (**57.34**)

Table 1: Automatic evaluation. 100k experiments in parentheses

distance to the dependency tree from the rule-based system is investigated. In one setting, the cost functions adhere to the constrictions of computing a distance metric. Two settings test the impact of biasing the insertion and deletion cost functions to assign a lower cost to inserting/deleting nonterminals, i.e. turning the dependency tree into the hierarchical tree and vice versa.

TED is computed for 20 translation hypotheses and the best performing setting reported.

Leaves An experiment using the leaves technique has been conducted. The experiment is performed using the best hypothesis from Moses and also using TED to chose the most structurally similar skeleton. The best setting will be reported.

Lexical substitution To be able to compare a more naive approach, subtree substitution based on the initial element-level alignment between leaf nodes is used. In this approach, a subtree is one node. The technique is identical to using the RBMT lexicon to lookup untranslated words and inserting them in the translation.

TED-R An experiment where the mappings that represent a rename operation, which are produced during TED computation, are extracted and used as matching elements is conducted. Mapping elements containing only punctuation or the root node of either tree are discarded. All combinations of substitutions based on the extracted matching elements are performed and the highest ranking hypothesis according to a language model is chosen as the final translation.

The extracted matching elements may not incorporate all the untranslated nodes. All untranslated nodes are subsequently translated using lexical substitution as mentioned above. The subtrees inserted into the hierarchical tree will undergo the same transformation as the subtrees inserted using the leaves technique.

This experiment is evaluated using both the 1-best hierarchical tree as skeleton and choosing the skeleton using TED. All three settings are tested and the best performing experiment reported.

4.2 Evaluation

The results of the automatic evaluation can be seen in Table 1. *Skeleton* indicates that TED was used to pick the hierarchical tree. The best evaluations are in bold.

100k The RBMT baseline is outperformed by all hybrid configurations, though it does have a higher METEOR score than the SMT baseline and skeleton selection. Lexical substitution and TED-R obtains an increase of ca. 2.5 BLEU, 4 TER and 4 METEOR points over the best baseline scores. The leaves technique decreases the metrics except for METEOR and the skeleton selection only shows an insignificant improvement.

Europarl Only lexical substitution improve all metrics over the baseline. Using the leaves technique again results in a decrease in BLEU and TER, but improves METEOR. The impact of skeleton selection is similar to previous experiments, but the use of skeleton selection in TED-R has become larger.

Manual Evaluation The evaluators rank 20 sentences randomly extracted from the test set on a scale from 1-5 with 5 being the best and it is possible to assign the same score to multiple translation alternatives. This evaluation was inspired by the sentence ranking evaluation in Callison-Burch et al. (2007). The five sentences to be evaluated will come from the RBMT and SMT baselines, lexical substitution, leaves technique and TED-R skeleton and the evaluators are 5 Danes who have studied translation with English as second language and 3 native English speakers.

The baseline systems make up 85% of the lowest ranking. The distribution between systems is more even for the second lowest ranking with the baselines only accounting for 52.6%. In the middle ranking, the top scorer is lexical substitution

System	1	2	3	4	5	Avg. rank
SMT	**53**	**64**	30	12	1	2.025
RBMT	14	48	61	29	8	2.806
Lex. sub.	3	33	**63**	**58**	3	3.156
Leaves	6	33	61	55	5	3.125
TED-R	3	35	46	55	**21**	3.35

Table 2: Rankings from the manual evaluation of the second set of experiments.

SMT baseline	(COM (1999) 493 - C5-0320 / 1999 - 1999 / 2208 (COS))
Leaves	(came (1999) 493 - C5-0320/1999-1999/2208 (COM COS)) - C5-0320 / 1999 - 1999 / 2208 (
TED-R	(COM (1999) 493 - C5-0320/1999-1999/2208 / 1999 - 1999 / 2208 (COS))

Table 3: Substitution of numbers.

with a small margin to the RBMT baseline and the leaves technique. The many assignments of rank *3* could indicate that many of the translations produced can be used for gisting, i.e. get an impression of what information the source text conveys, but not enough to give a complete understanding, but can also be a result of being the middle value and chosen when the evaluators are in doubt. Lexical substitution is also the top scorer in the second-best ranking, followed closely by the other hybrid configurations and the hybrid systems account for 80.3% of the second-best rankings. TED-R recieves more top rankings than the other systems combined (55.3%). The RBMT baseline achieves second-most top-rankings. This can be attributed to the cases where the rules did not encounter unknown words and created very accurate translations, as is the hallmark of RBMT.

5 Discussion

It is not surprising that lexical substitution achieves a significant increase in all metrics. The approach only translates untranslated words using the RBMT lexicon. This can improve the translation or, because of noisy matching elements, introduce wrong words but the penalty incurred for untranslated words and wrongly translated words is the same if the number of tokens is similar. Further, lexical substitution does not rely on structural similarity and can avoid the potential sources of errors encountered at a later processing stage.

Skeleton selection has little impact on the metrics and distinct derivations can result in the same surface structure, giving the same scores, but it is evident that finding the most similar tree improves substitution.

The improvements observed in the 100k experiments are not evident in the metrics when the full Europarl data is used. The more powerful SMT system is able to handle more translations but manual evaluation reveals a distribution where the majority of rankings for the baseline systems are in the lower half and rankings for the hybrid systems tend more towards the mid-to-upper rankings, with TED-R having more distribution around the second-best and highest score. This indicates that the approach creates more accurate translations.

The leaves technique consistently underperforms lexical substitution, but manual evaluation shows a high correlation between the two methods and their average ranks are similar. TED-R is ranked higher than the leaves technique in the metrics and manual evaluation also ranks TED-R higher than lexical substitution. This suggests that the extra surface structure removed is not present in the reference translation and that TED-R is a better implementation of the post-editing approach.

Subtree substitution, whether using leaves or TED, does not handle parentheses, hyphens and numbers well. The structure severely degrades when performing substitution near these environments. The example in Table 3 shows the errors made by the substitution algorithm. An entire subphrase is duplicated using the leaves technique which introduces an opening parenthesis with no closing counterpart and includes the erroneous translation *came*, while TED-R duplicates */ 1999 - 1999 / 2208*.

The reason for these wayward substitutions can be found in the dependency tree. The matching parentheses are not part of the same subtree and this is the root cause of the problem. The leaves technique is very sensitive to these errors and there is no easy way to prevent spurious parentheses from being introduced. Re-ranking in TED-R could filter these hypotheses out, but because the re-ranking module cannot model this dependency, the sentences with these errors are not always discarded. In the manual evaluation campaign, the sentence from Table 3 was included in the sample sentences. It would seem that the many evaluators did not view this error as important or it was ignored. It would be impossible to find the referenced Council decision based on the translations and dates or monetary amounts might change drastically, which would not be acceptable if the translated text should be ready for publishing after translation. For gisting, where the user knows that the translation is not perfect, this may constitute less of a problem.

6 Future work

The initial alignment is based on the source to target language alignment. In the RBMT module, it is mostly word-based while in Moses, the alignment must be recomputed due to the simplicity of the modification and that the Moses chart decoder cannot output word alignment. The modelling only handles alignment crossing one non-terminal and reduces alignment problems to these cases by assuming a weak reordering.

Future work should include extracting the word alignment from the SMT system to improve source to target language alignment. The MT decoder Joshua can output complete derivations including word-based alignment which would eliminate the need to recompute source to target language alignment which currently produces noisy matching elements. Experiments using a different RBMT engine should also be conducted. The RBMT module does not always produce one complete tree structure for a sentence and the reattachment algorithm handles this by adding any additional graphs to the root node of the tree structure. A RBMT engine that produces complete derivations is likely to improve the translation quality. This will require different tree extraction modules for Joshua and the RBMT engine, but otherwise the system can be reused as is.

6.1 Languages and formalisms

The chosen languages are closely related Germanic languages. While the results seem promising, the applicability of the approach should be tested on a more distant language pair, e.g. Chinese-English or Russian-English if you wish to preserve the possibility of using METEOR for evaluation, but any distant pair for which an RBMT system exists can be used — provided a tree output is available.

The implementation substitutes dependency subtrees into a hierarchical CFG-style tree. A second test of the hybridisation approach is to combine systems where the structures are not as diverse. Hierarchical systems are derived from a SCFG so a RBMT system based on a CFG formalism such as LUCY, could be used to test the generality of the hybridisation approach.

As the TED-R approach does not rely on markers for OOV words, an implementation where hierarchical subtrees are inserted into the RBMT output should also be conducted. The problem of inserting CFG-style subtrees into a dependency tree and generating the correct surface structure must be resolved or a different RBMT system which produce CFG-style trees implemented.

The implementation of the leaves technique relies on the diversity of the tree structures, i.e. that there are element-level similarities between hierarchical leaf nodes and both terminal and non-terminal dependency nodes and that the subtree rooted in a dependency node can be aligned to a hierarchical subtree. The refinement method would have to be altered. The relations and children techniques (Shvaiko and Euzenat, 2005) are good candidates for similar tree structures.

A change of formalism would not require alterations of the tree edit distance approach, as long as the structures are in fact tree structures.

7 Conclusion

The post-editing approach proposed in this paper combines the strengths of statistical and rule-based machine translation and improve translation quality, especially for the least accurate translations. The structural and knowledge-poor approach is novel and has not been attempted before. It exploits structural output to create hybrid translations and uses the linguistic knowledge encoded in structure and on nodes to improve the translation candidates of hierarchical phrase-based MT systems.

Automatic evaluation shows a significant increase over the baselines when training data is limited and also improvement in TER and METEOR for lexical substitution and TED-R with a SMT system trained on the Europarl corpus.

Manual evaluation on test data shows that hybrid translations were generally ranked higher, indicating that the hybrid approach produces more accurate translations.

References

S. Banerjee and A. Lavie. 2005. METEOR: An automatic metric for MT evaluation with improved correlation with human judgments. *Intrinsic and Extrinsic Evaluation Measures for Machine Translation and/or Summarization*, page 65.

E. Bick. 2007. Dan2eng: Wide-coverage danish-english machine translation. *Proceedings of Machine Translation Summit XI*, pages 37–43.

P. Bille. 2005. A survey on tree edit distance and related problems. *Theoretical computer science*, 337(1-3):217–239.

C. Callison-Burch, C. Fordyce, P. Koehn, C. Monz, and J. Schroeder. 2007. (Meta-) evaluation of machine translation. In *Proceedings of the Second Workshop on Statistical Machine Translation*, pages 136–158. Association for Computational Linguistics.

D. Chiang. 2005. A hierarchical phrase-based model for statistical machine translation. In *Proceedings of the 43rd Annual Meeting on Association for Computational Linguistics*, pages 263–270. Association for Computational Linguistics.

A. Eisele, C. Federmann, H. Uszkoreit, H. Saint-Amand, M. Kay, M. Jellinghaus, S. Hunsicker, T. Herrmann, and Y. Chen. 2008. Hybrid machine translation architectures within and beyond the EuroMatrix project. In *Proceedings of the 12th annual conference of the European Association for Machine Translation (EAMT 2008)*, pages 27–34.

C. Federmann, A. Eisele, H. Uszkoreit, Y. Chen, S. Hunsicker, and J. Xu. 2010. Further experiments with shallow hybrid mt systems. In *Proceedings of the Joint Fifth Workshop on Statistical Machine Translation and MetricsMATR*, pages 77–81. Association for Computational Linguistics.

A.S. Hildebrand and S. Vogel. 2008. Combination of machine translation systems via hypothesis selection from combined n-best lists. In *MT at work: Proceedings of the Eighth Conference of the Association for Machine Translation in the Americas*, pages 254–261. Citeseer.

P. Koehn and C. Monz. 2006. Manual and automatic evaluation of machine translation between european languages. In *Proceedings of the Workshop on Statistical Machine Translation*, pages 102–121. Association for Computational Linguistics.

P. Koehn, H. Hoang, A. Birch, C. Callison-Burch, M. Federico, N. Bertoldi, B. Cowan, W. Shen, C. Moran, R. Zens, et al. 2007. Moses: Open source toolkit for statistical machine translation. In *Proceedings of the 45th Annual Meeting of the ACL on Interactive Poster and Demonstration Sessions*, pages 177–180. Association for Computational Linguistics.

P. Koehn. 2005. Europarl: A parallel corpus for statistical machine translation. In *MT summit*, volume 5. Citeseer.

P. Koehn. 2010. An experimental management system. *The Prague Bulletin of Mathematical Linguistics*, 94(-1):87–96.

K. Papineni, S. Roukos, T. Ward, and W.J. Zhu. 2002. BLEU: a method for automatic evaluation of machine translation. In *Proceedings of the 40th annual meeting on association for computational linguistics*, pages 311–318. Association for Computational Linguistics.

A.V.I. Rosti, N.F. Ayan, B. Xiang, S. Matsoukas, R. Schwartz, and B. Dorr. 2007. Combining outputs from multiple machine translation systems. In *Human Language Technologies 2007: The Conference of the North American Chapter of the Association for Computational Linguistics; Proceedings of the Main Conference*, pages 228–235.

P. Shvaiko and J. Euzenat. 2005. A survey of schema-based matching approaches. *Journal on Data Semantics IV*, pages 146–171.

M. Simard, N. Ueffing, P. Isabelle, R. Kuhn, et al. 2007. Rule-based translation with statistical phrase-based post-editing. In *ACL 2007 Second Workshop on Statistical Machine Translation*.

M. Snover, B. Dorr, R. Schwartz, L. Micciulla, and J. Makhoul. 2006. A study of translation edit rate with targeted human annotation. In *Proceedings of Association for Machine Translation in the Americas*, pages 223–231. Citeseer.

A. Stolcke. 2002. SRILM - an extensible language modeling toolkit. In *Proceedings of the international conference on spoken language processing*, volume 2, pages 901–904. Citeseer.

Gregor Thurmair. 2009. Comparing different architectures of Hybrid Machine Translation systems. In *Proceedings of the MT Summit XII*, pages 340–347.

K. Zhang and D. Shasha. 1989. Simple fast algorithms for the editing distance between trees and related problems. *SIAM J. Comput.*, 18(6):1245–1262.

Were the clocks striking or surprising? Using WSD to improve MT performance

Špela Vintar
University of Ljubljana
Dept. of Translation Studies
SI - 1000 Ljubljana,
Aškerčeva 2
spela.vintar@ff.uni-lj.si

Darja Fišer
University of Ljubljana
Dept. of Translation Studies
SI - 1000 Ljubljana,
Aškerčeva 2
darja.fiser@ff.uni-lj.si

Aljoša Vrščaj
University of Ljubljana
Dept. of Translation Studies
SI - 1000 Ljubljana,
Aškerčeva 2
aljosav@gmail.com

Abstract

We report on a series of experiments aimed at improving the machine translation of ambiguous lexical items by using wordnet-based unsupervised Word Sense Disambiguation (WSD) and comparing its results to three MT systems. Our experiments are performed for the English-Slovene language pair using UKB, a freely available graph-based word sense disambiguation system. Results are evaluated in three ways: a manual evaluation of WSD performance from MT perspective, an analysis of agreement between the WSD-proposed equivalent and those suggested by the three systems, and finally by computing BLEU, NIST and METEOR scores for all translation versions. Our results show that WSD performs with a MT-relevant precision of 71% and that 21% of sense-related MT errors could be prevented by using unsupervised WSD.

1 Introduction

Ambiguity continues to be a tough nut to crack in MT. In most known languages certain lexical items can refer to more than a single concept, meaning that MT systems need to choose between several translation equivalents representing different senses of the source word. Wrong choices often result in grave translation errors, as words often refer to several completely unrelated concepts. The adjective *striking* can mean *beautiful, surprising*; *delivering a hard blow* or *indicating a certain time*, and the noun "course" can be *something we give, take, teach* or *eat*.

Our aim was to assess the performance of three MT systems for the English-Slovene language pair and to see whether wordnet-based Word Sense Disambiguation (WSD) could improve performance and assist in avoiding grave sense-related translation errors.

For WSD we use UKB (Agirre and Soroa 2009), a graph-based algorithm that uses wordnet (Fellbaum 1998) and computes the probability of each sense of a polysemous word by taking into account the senses of context words. In our experiment we use Orwell's notorious novel *1984* as the source and its translation into Slovene by Alenka Puhar as the reference translation. We then disambiguate the English source with UKB, assign each disambiguated English word a Slovene equivalent from sloWNet (Fišer 2009) and compare these with the equivalents proposed by Google, Bing and Presis. Results are evaluated in several ways:

- By manually evaluating WSD performance from the MT perspective,
- By analysing the agreement between each of the MT systems and the UKB/wordnet-derived translation,
- By comparing BLEU, NIST and METEOR scores achieved with each translation version.

Our results show that the ad hoc WSD strategies used by the evaluated MT systems can definitely be improved by a proper WSD algorithm, but also that wordnet is not the ideal semantic resource to help resolve translation dilemmas, mainly due to its fine sense granularity.

2 Word Sense Disambiguation and Machine Translation

Wordnet-based approaches to improving MT have been successfully employed by numerous authors, on the one hand as a semantic resource to help resolve ambiguity, and on the other hand as a rich source of domain-specific translation equivalents. As early as 1993 (Knight 1993), wordnet was used as the lower ontology within

Proceedings of the 13th Conference of the European Chapter of the Association for Computational Linguistics, pages 87–92,
Avignon, France, April 23 - 27 2012.

the PANGLOSS MT system. Yuseop et al. (2002) have employed LSA and the semantic similarity of wordnet literals to translate collocations, while Salam et al. (2009) used wordnet for disambiguation and the choice of the correct translation equivalent in an English to Bengali SMT system.

WSD for machine translation purposes slightly differs from traditional WSD, because distinct source language senses, which share the same translation equivalent, need not be differentiated in WSD (Vickrey et al. 2005). This phenomenon is known as parallel ambiguities and is particularly common among related languages (Resnik and Yarowsky 2000). Although early experiments failed to provide convincing proof that WSD can improve SMT, Carpuat and Wu (2007), Chan et al. (2007) and Ali et al. (2009) clearly demonstrate that incorporating a word sense disambiguation system on the lexical level brings significant improvement according to all common MT evaluation metrics.

Still, using wordnet as the source of sense inventories has been heavily criticized not just in the context of MT (Apidianaki 2009), but also within other language processing tasks. The most notorious arguments against wordnet are its high granularity and - as a consequence - high similarity between some senses, but its global availability and universality seem to be advantages that prevail in many cases (Edmonds and Kilgarriff 2002).

Our experiments lie somewhat in between; on the one hand we demonstrate the potential of WSD in MT, especially for cases where different MT systems disagree, and on the other hand we attribute most WSD errors to the inadequacy of the sense splitting in wordnet (see Discussion).

3 Experimental setup

3.1 Corpus and MT systems

Our corpus consists of George Orwell's novel *1984*, first published in English in 1949, and its translation into Slovene by Alenka Puhar, first published in 1967. While it may seem unusual to be using a work of fiction for the assessment of MT systems, literary language is usually richer in ambiguity and thus provides a more complex semantic space than non-fiction.

We translated the entire novel into Slovene with Google Translate[1], Bing[2] and Presis[3], the first two belonging to the family of freely available statistical systems and the latter being a rule-based MT system developed by the Slovenian company Amebis.

For the purposes of further analysis and comparison with our disambiguated corpus all texts - original and translations - have been PoS-tagged and lemmatized using the JOS web service (Erjavec et al. 2010) for Slovene and ToTaLe (Erjavec et al. 2005) for English. Because we can only disambiguate content words, we retained only nouns, verbs, adjectives and adverbs and discarded the rest. After all these preprocessing steps our texts end up looking as follows:

English:
It was a bright cold day in April and the clocks were striking thirteen.
English-preprocessed:
be bright cold day April clock be strike
Slovene-reference:
Bil je jasen, mrzel aprilski dan in ure so bile trinajst.
Slovene-reference-preprocessed:
biti biti jasen mrzel aprilski dan ura biti biti
Slovene-Google:
Bilo je svetlo mrzel dan v aprilu, in ure so bile trinajst presenetljiv.
Slovene-Google-preprocessed:
biti biti svetlo mrzel dan april ura biti biti presenetljiv
Slovene-Bing:
Je bil svetlo hladne dan aprila in v ure so bili presenetljivo trinajst.
Slovene-Bing-preprocessed:
biti biti svetlo hladen dan april ura biti biti presenetljivo
Slovene-Presis:
Svetal hladen dan v aprilu je bilin so ure udarjale trinajst.
Slovene-Presis-preprocessed:
svetel hladen dan april biti bilin biti ura udarjati

Figure 1. Corpus preprocessing

3.2 Disambiguation with UKB and wordnet

The aim of semantic annotation and disambiguation is to identify polysemous lexical items in the English text and assign them the correct sense in accordance with the context. Once the sense of the word has been determined, we can exploit the cross-language links between wordnets of different languages and propose a Slovene translation equivalent from the Slovene wordnet.

We disambiguated the English corpus with UKB, which utilizes the relations between synsets and constructs semantic graphs for each candidate sense of the word. The algorithm then

[1] http://translate.google.com (translation from and into Slovene has been available as of September 2008)

[2] http://www.microsofttranslator.com/ (available for Slovene since 2010)

[3] http://presis.amebis.si (available for English-Slovene since 2002)

computes the probability of each graph based on the number and weight of edges between the nodes representing semantic concepts. Disambiguation is performed in a monolingual context for single- and multiword nouns, verbs, adjectives and adverbs, provided they are included in the English wordnet.

Figure 2 shows the result of the disambiguation algorithm for the word *face,* which has as many as 13 possible senses in wordnet. We are given the probability of each sense in the given context (eg. *0.173463*) and the ID of the synset (eg. *eng-30-05600637-n*), and for the purposes of clarity we also added the literals (words) associated with this particular synset ID in the English (*face, human face*) and Slovene (*fris, obraz, faca*) wordnet respectively. As can be seen from this example, wordnet is - in most cases - a very fine-grained sense inventory, and looking at the Slovene equivalents clearly shows that many of these senses may partly or entirely overlap, at least in the context of translation.

WSD: ctx_Oen.1.1.2 24 !! face

- *W: 0.173463 ID: eng-30-05600637-n ENGWN: face, human face, (the front of the human head from the forehead to the chin and ear to ear) SLOWN: fris, obraz, faca, človeški obraz, (EMPTYDEF)*
- *W: 0.116604 ID: eng-30-08510666-n ENGWN: side, face, (a surface forming part of the outside of an object) SLOWN: stranica, ploskev, (EMPTYDEF)*
- *W: 0.0956895 ID: eng-30-03313602-n ENGWN: face, (the side upon which the use of a thing depends (usually the most prominent surface of an object)) SLOWN: sprednja stran, prava stran, zgornja stran, lice, (EMPTYDEF)*
- *W: 0.0761554 ID: eng-30-04679738-n ENGWN: expression, look, aspect, facial expression, face, (the feelings expressed on a person's face) SLOWN: izraz, pogled, obraz, izraz na obrazu, (EMPTYDEF)*
- *W: 0.0709513 ID: eng-30-03313456-n ENGWN: face, (a vertical surface of a building or cliff) SLOWN: stena, fasada, (EMPTYDEF)*
- *W: 0.0653514 ID: eng-30-06825399-n ENGWN: font, fount, typeface, face, case, (a specific size and style of type within a type family) SLOWN: font, pisava, črkovna družina, vrsta črk, črkovna podoba, črkovni slog, (EMPTYDEF)*
- *W: 0.0629878 ID: eng-30-04838210-n ENGWN: boldness, nerve, brass, face, cheek, (impudent aggressiveness) SLOWN: predrznost, nesramnost, (EMPTYDEF)*
- *W: 0.0610286 ID: eng-30-06877578-n ENGWN: grimace, face, (a contorted facial expression) SLOWN: spaka, grimasa, (EMPTYDEF)*
- *W: 0.0605221 ID: eng-30-03313873-n ENGWN: face, (the striking or working surface of an implement) SLOWN: čelo, podplat, udarna površina, (EMPTYDEF)*
- *W: 0.0579952 ID: eng-30-05601198-n ENGWN: face, (the part of an animal corresponding to the human face) SLOWN: obraz, (EMPTYDEF)*
- *W: 0.0535548 ID: eng-30-05168795-n ENGWN: face, (status in the eyes of others) SLOWN: ugled, dobro ime, (EMPTYDEF)*
- *W: 0.05303 ID: eng-30-09618957-n ENGWN: face, (a part of a person that is used to refer to a person) SLOWN: obraz, (EMPTYDEF)*
- *W: 0.0526668 ID: eng-30-04679419-n ENGWN: face, (the general outward appearance of something) SLOWN: podoba, (EMPTYDEF)*

Figure 2. Disambiguation result for the word *face* with probabilities for each of the twelve senses

As can be seen in Table 1, almost half of all the tokens in the corpus are considered to be ambiguous according to the English wordnet. Since the Slovene wordnet is considerably smaller than the English one, almost half of the different ambiguous words occurring in our corpus have no equivalent in sloWNet. This could affect the results of our experiment, because we cannot evaluate the potential benefit of WSD if we cannot compare the translation equivalent from sloWNet with the solutions proposed by different MT systems. We therefore restricted ourselves to the words and sentences for which an equivalent exists in sloWNet.

Corpus size in tokens	103,769
Corpus size in types	10,982
Ambiguous tokens	48,632
Ambiguous types	7,627
Synsets with no equivalent in sloWNet	3,192

Table 1. Corpus size and number of ambiguous words

One method of evaluating the performance of WSD in the context of Machine Translation is through metrics for automatic evaluation (BLEU, NIST, METEOR etc.). We thus generated our own translation version, in fact a stripped version similar to those in Figure 1 consisting only of content words in their lemmatized form. We translated the disambiguated words with wordnet, exploiting the cross-language universality of the synset ID. However, since we can only propose translation equivalents for the words which are included in wordnet, we had to come up with a translation solution for those which were not. Such words include proper names (*Winston, Smith, London, Oceania*), hyphenated compounds (*pig-iron, lift-shaft, gorilla-faced*) and Orwellian neologisms (*Minipax, Newspeak, thoughtcrime*). We translated these words with three alternative methods:

- Using a general bilingual dictionary,
- Using the English-Slovene Wikipedia and Wiktionary,

- Using the automatically constructed bilingual lexicon from the English-Slovene parallel Orwell corpus.

The fourth option was to leave them untranslated and simply add them to the generated Slovene version.

4 Evaluation

The number of meanings a word can have, the degree of translation equivalence or the quality of the target text are all extremely disputable and vague notions. For this reason we wished to evaluate our results from as many angles as possible, both manually and automatically.

4.1 Manual evaluation of WSD precision in the context of MT

Firstly, we were interested in the performance of the UKB disambiguation tool in the context of MT. Since UKB uses wordnet as a sense inventory, the algorithm assigns a probability to each sense of a lexical item according to its context in an unsupervised way. The precision of UKB for unsupervised WSD is reported at around 58% for all words and around 72% for nouns, but of course these figures measure the number of cases where the algorithm selected the correct wordnet synset from a relatively fine-grained network of possible senses (Agirre and Soroa 2009).

We adjusted the evaluation task to an MT scenario by manually checking 200 disambiguated words and their suggested translation equivalents, and if the equivalent was acceptable we counted it among the positive instances regardless of the selected sense. For example, the English word *breast* has four senses in wordnet: (1) the upper frontal part of a human chest, (2) one of the two soft milk-secreting glands of a woman, (3) meat carved from the breast of a fowl and (4) the upper front part of an animal corresponding to the human chest. For the English sentence *Winston nuzzled his chin into his breast...* UKB suggested the second sense, which is clearly wrong, but since the ambiguity is preserved in Slovene and the word *prsi* can be used for all of the four meanings, we consider this a case of successful disambiguation for the purposes of MT.

Translation equivalent	correct	incorrect	borderline
Number/ %	142 (71%)	46 (23%)	12 (6%)

Table 2: Manual evaluation of WSD performance for MT

The precision of WSD using this relaxed criterion was 71%, with 6% so-called borderline cases. These include cases where the equivalent was semantically correct but had the wrong part of speech (eg. ***glass*** *door* -> ****steklo*** instead of ***steklen***).

4.2 Agreement between each of the MT systems and the disambiguated equivalent

It is interesting to compare the equivalents we propose through our wordnet-based WSD procedure with those suggested by the three MT systems: Presis, Google and Bing.

Total no. of disambiguated tokens	13,737
WSD = reference	3,933
WSD = Presis	4,290
WSD = Google	4,464
WSD = Bing	4,377
WSD = ref = Presis = Google = Bing	2,681
WSD = ref ≠ Presis ≠ Google ≠ Bing	269

Table 3: Comparison of WSD/wordnet-based equivalent and the translations proposed by Presis, Google, Bing and the reference translation

The comparison was strict in the sense that we only took into account the first Slovene equivalent proposed within the same synset. Of the over 48k ambiguous tokens we obviously considered only those which had an equivalent in sloWNet, otherwise comparison with the MT systems would have been impossible. We can see from Table 2 that the WSD/wordnet-based equivalents most often agree with Google translation, and that for approximately every fifth ambiguous word all systems agree with each other and with the reference translation.

If we also look at the number of cases where our WSD-wordnet-based equivalent is the only one to agree with the reference translation, it is safe to assume that these are the cases where WSD could clearly improve MT. Of all the instances where WSD agrees with the reference translation we can subtract the instances where all systems agree, because these need no improvement. Of the remaining 1,252 ambiguous words, 269 or 20% were such that only the WSD/wordnet equivalent corresponded to the reference translation.

4.3 Evaluation with metrics

Finally, we wanted to see how the WSD/wordnet-based translation compares with the three MT systems using the BLEU, NIST and METEOR scores. For the purposes of this comparison we pre-processed all five versions of our corpus - original, reference translation, Presis, Google and Bing translation - by lemmatization, removal of all function words, removal of sentences where the alignment was not 1:1, and finally by removal of the sentences which contained lexical items for which there was no equivalent in sloWNet.

We then generated the sixth version by translating all ambiguous words with sloWNet (see Section 3), and for the words not included in the English wordnet we used four alternative translation strategies; a general bilingual dictionary (dict), wiktionary (wikt), a word-alignment lexicon (align) and amending untranslated words to the target language version (amend).

	BLEU (n=1)	NIST	METEOR
Bing	0.506	3.594	0.455
Google	0.579	4.230	0.481
Presis	0.485	3.333	0.453
WSD	0.440	3.258	0.429
WSD-amend	0.410	3.308	0.430
WSD-dict	0.405	3.250	0.427
WSD-align	0.448	**3.588**	0.434
WSD-wikt	0.442	3.326	0.429

Table 4: Evaluation with metrics

Table 3 shows the results of automatic evaluation; the corpus consisted of 2,428 segments. We can see that our generated version using disambiguated equivalents does not outperform any of the MT systems on any metric, except once when the WSD-align version outperforms Presis on the NIST score and comes fairly close to the Bing score.

It is possible that the improvement we are trying to achieve is difficult to measure with these metrics because our method operates on the level of single words, while the metrics typically evaluate entire sentences and corpora. We are using a stripped version of the corpus, ie. only content words which can potentially be ambiguous, whereas the metrics are normally used to calculate the similarity between two versions of running text. Finally, the corpus we are using for automatic evaluation is very small.

5 Discussion

Although employing WSD and comparing wordnet-based translation equivalents to those proposed by MT systems scored no significant improvement with standard MT evaluation metrics, we remain convinced that the other two evaluation methods show the potential of using WSD, particularly with truly ambiguous words and not those where sense distinctions are slight or vague. A manual inspection of the examples where MT systems disagreed and our WSD-based equivalent was the only one to agree with the reference translation shows that these are indeed examples of grave MT errors. For example, the word *hand* in the sentence *The clock's hands said six meaning eighteen* can only be translated correctly with a proper WSD strategy and was indeed mistranslated as *roka* (body part) by all three systems. If a relatively simplistic and unsupervised technique such as the one we propose can prevent 20% of these mistakes, it is certainly worth employing at least as a post-processing step.

The fact that we explore the impact of WSD on a work of fiction rather than domain-specific texts may also play a role in the results we obtained, although it is not entirely clear in what way. We believe that in general there is more ambiguity in literary texts meaning that a single word will appear in a wider range of senses in a work of fiction than it would in a domain-specific corpus. This might mean that WSD for literary texts is more difficult, however our own experiments so far show no significant difference in WSD performance.

A look at the cases where WSD goes wrong shows that these are typically words with a high number of senses which are difficult to differentiate even for a human. The question from the title of this paper is actually a translation blunder made by both Google and Bing, since *striking* was interpreted in its more expressive sense and translated into Slovene as *presenetljiv [surprising]*. However, UKB also got it wrong and chose the sense defined as *deliver a sharp blow, as with the hand, fist, or weapon* instead of *indicate a certain time by striking*. While these meanings may seem quite easy to tell apart, especially if the preceding word in a sentence is *clock*, *strike* as a verb has as many as 20 senses in Princeton WordNet, and many of these seem very similar. In this case the Slovene translation we propose is "less wrong" than the *surprising* solution offered by Google or Bing, because *udarjati* may actually be used in the *clock* sense as well.

We might also assume that statistical MT systems will perform worse on fiction; results in Table 3 show that both statistical systems outperform the rule-based Presis. Then again, Orwell's 1984 has been freely available as a parallel corpus for a very long time and it is therefore possible that both Google and Bing have used it as training data for their SMT model.

6 Conclusion

We described an experiment in which we explore the potential of WSD to improve the machine translation of ambiguous words for the English-Slovene language pair. We utilized the output of UKB, a graph-based WSD tool using wordnet, to select the appropriate equivalent from sloWNet. Manual evaluation showed that the correct equivalent was proposed in 71% of the cases. We then compared these equivalents with the output of three MT systems. While the benefit of WSD could not be proven with the BLEU, NIST and METEOR scores, the correspondence of the WSD/wordnet-based equivalent with the reference translation was high. Furthermore it appears that in cases where MT systems disagree WSD can help choose the correct equivalent.

As future work we plan to redesign the experiment so as to directly use WSD as a post-processing step to machine translation instead of generating our own stripped translation version. This would provide better comparison grounds. In order to improve WSD precision we intend to combine two different algorithms and use it only in cases where both agree. Also, we intend to experiment with different text types and context lengths to be able to evaluate WSD performance in the context of MT on a larger scale.

References

Eneko Agirre and Aitor Soroa. 2009. Personalizing PageRank for Word Sense Disambiguation. Proceeding of the European Association of Computational Linguistics conference (EACL09).

Ola Mohammad Ali, Mahmoud Gad Alla and Mohammad Said Abdelwahab. 2009. Improving machine translation using hybrid dictionary-graph based word sense disambiguation with semantic and statistical methods. International Journal of Computer and Electrical Engineering, 1/5.

Marianna Apidianaki. 2009. Data-driven semantic analysis for multilingual WSD and lexical selection in translation. Proceedings of the 12th Conference of the European Chapter of the ACL, pages 77–85, Athens, Greece, Association for Computational Linguistics.

Marine Carpuat and Dekai Wu. 2007. Improving statistical machine translation using word sense disambiguation. Proceedings of Empirical Methods in Natural Language Processing and Computational Natural Language Learning (EMNLP-CoNLL).

Yee Seng Chan, Hwee Tou Ng and David Chiang. 2007. Word Sense Disambiguation Improves Statistical Machine Translation. In Proceedings of the 45th Annual Meeting of the Association of Computational Linguistics (Prague, Czech Republic). 33-40.

Philip Edmonds and Adam Kilgarriff. 2002. Introduction to the Special Issue on Evaluating Word Sense Disambiguation Systems. Natural Language Engineering 8 (4): 279–291.

Tomaž Erjavec, Darja Fišer, Simon Krek and Nina Ledinek. 2010. The JOS Linguistically Tagged Corpus of Slovene. Proceedings of the 7th International Conference on Language Resources and Evaluation (LREC'10), Malta.

Christiane Fellbaum. 1998. WordNet: An Electronic Lexical Database. Cambridge, MA: MIT Press.

Darja Fišer. 2009. Leveraging Parallel Corpora and Existing Wordnets for Automatic Construction of the Slovene Wordnet. Human language technology: challenges of the information society, (LNCS 5603). Berlin; Heidelberg: Springer: 359-368.

Kevin Knight. 1993. Building a large ontology for machine translation. Proceedings of the ARPA Human Language Technology Workshop, Plainsboro, New Jersey.

Philip Resnik and David Yarowsky. 2000. Distinguishing Systems and Distinguishing Senses: New Evaluation Methods for Word Sense Disambiguation. Natural Language Engineering, 5(2): 113-133.

Khan Md. Anwarus Salam, Mumit Khan and Tetsuro Nishino. 2009. Example based English-Bengali machine translation using wordnet. Proceedings of TriSA'09, Japan.

David Vickrey, Luke Biewald, Marc Teyssier in Daphne Koller. 2005. Word-Sense Disambiguation for Machine Translation. Proceedings of the Conference Empirical Methods in Natural Language Processing (EMNLP).

Kim Yuseop, Jeong-Ho Chang in Byoung-Tak Zhang (2002): Target Word Selection Using WordNet and Data-Driven Models in Machine Translation. Proceedings of the Conference PRICAI'02: Trends in Artificial Intelligence.

Bootstrapping Method for Chunk Alignment in Phrase Based SMT

Santanu Pal

Department of Computer Science and Engineering
Jadavpur University
santanu.pal.ju@gmail.com

Sivaji Bandyopadhyay

Department of Computer Science and Engineering
Jadavpur University
sivaji_cse@yahoo.com

Abstract

The processing of parallel corpus plays very crucial role for improving the overall performance in Phrase Based Statistical Machine Translation systems (PB-SMT). In this paper the automatic alignments of different kind of chunks have been studied that boosts up the word alignment as well as the machine translation quality. Single-tokenization of Noun-noun MWEs, phrasal preposition (source side only) and reduplicated phrases (target side only) and the alignment of named entities and complex predicates provide the best SMT model for bootstrapping. Automatic bootstrapping on the alignment of various chunks makes significant gains over the previous best English-Bengali PB-SMT system. The source chunks are translated into the target language using the PB-SMT system and the translated chunks are compared with the original target chunk. The aligned chunks increase the size of the parallel corpus. The processes are run in a bootstrapping manner until all the source chunks have been aligned with the target chunks or no new chunk alignment is identified by the bootstrapping process. The proposed system achieves significant improvements (2.25 BLEU over the best System and 8.63 BLEU points absolute over the baseline system, 98.74% relative improvement over the baseline system) on an English- Bengali translation task.

1 Introduction

The objective of the present research work is to analyze effects of chunk alignment in English – Bengali parallel corpus in a Phrase Based Statistical Machine Translation system. The initial sentence level aligned English-Bengali corpus is cleaned and filtered using a semi-automatic process. More effective chunk level alignments are carried out by bootstrapping on the training corpus to the PB-SMT system.

The objective in the present task is to align the chunks in a bootstrapping manner using a Single tokenized MWE aligned SMT model and then modifying the model by inserting the aligned chunks to the parallel corpus after each iteration of the bootstrapping process, thereby enhancing the performance of the SMT system. In turn, this method deals with the many-to-many word alignments in the parallel corpus. Several types of MWEs like phrasal prepositions and Verb-object combinations are automatically identified on the source side while named-entities and complex predicates are identified on both sides of the parallel corpus. In the target side only, identification of the Noun-noun MWEs and reduplicated phrases are carried out. Simple rule-based and statistical approaches have been used to identify these MWEs. The parallel corpus is modified by considering the MWEs as single tokens. Source and target language NEs are aligned using a statistical transliteration technique. These automatically aligned NEs and Complex predicates are treated as translation examples, i.e., as additional entries in the phrase table (Pal.et al 2010, 2011). Using this augmented phrase table each individual source chunk is translated into the target chunk and then validated with the target chunks on the target side. The validated source-target chunks are con-

Proceedings of the 13th Conference of the European Chapter of the Association for Computational Linguistics, pages 93–100, Avignon, France, April 23 - 27 2012.

sidered as further parallel examples, which in effect are instances of atomic translation pairs to the parallel corpus. This is a well-known practice in domain adaptation in SMT (Eck et al., 2004; Wu et al., 2008). The preprocessing of the parallel corpus results in improved MT quality in terms of automatic MT evaluation metrics.

The remainder of the paper is organized as follows. Section 2 briefly elaborates the related work. The PB-SMT system is described in Section 3. The resources used in the present work are described in Section 4. The various experiments carried out and the corresponding evaluation results have been reported in Section 5. The conclusions are drawn in Section 6 along with future work roadmap.

2 Related work

A multi lingual filtering algorithm generates bilingual chunk alignment from Chinese-English parallel corpus (Zhou.et al, 2004). The algorithm has three steps, first, the most frequent bilingual chunks are extracted from the parallel corpus, second, a clustering algorithm has been used for combining chunks which are participating for alignment and finally one English chunk is generated corresponding to a Chinese chunk by analyzing the highest co-occurrences of English chunks. Bilingual knowledge can be extracted using chunk alignment (Zhou.et al, 2004). The alignment strategies include the comparison of dependency relations between source and target sentences. The dependency related candidates are then compared with the bilingual dictionary and finally the chunk is aligned using the extracted dependency related words. Ma.et al. (2007) simplified the task of automatic word alignment as several consecutive words together correspond to a single word in the opposite language by using the word aligner itself, i.e., by bootstrapping on its output. Zhu and Chang (2008) extracted a dictionary from the aligned corpus, used the dictionary to re-align the corpus and then extracted the new dictionary from the new alignment result. The process goes on until the threshold is reached.

An automatic extraction of bilingual MWEs is carried out by Ren et al. (2009), using a log likelihood ratio based hierarchical reducing algorithm to investigate the usefulness of bilingual MWEs in SMT by integrating bilingual MWEs into the Moses decoder (Koehn et al., 2007). The system has observed the highest improvement with an additional feature that identifies whether or not a bilingual phrase contains bilingual MWEs. This approach was generalized in Carpuat and Diab (2010) where the binary feature is replaced by a count feature which is representing the number of MWEs in the source language phrase.

MWEs on the source and the target sides should be both aligned in the parallel corpus and translated as a whole. However, in the state-of-the-art PB-SMT systems, the constituents of an MWE are marked and aligned as parts of consecutive phrases, since PB-SMT (or any other approaches to SMT) does not generally treat MWEs as special tokens. Another problem with SMT systems is the wrong translation of some phrases. Sometimes some phrases are not found in the output sentence. Moreover, the source and target phrases are mostly many-to-many, particularly so for the English—Bengali language pair. The main objective of the present work is to see whether prior automatic alignment of chunks can bring any improvement in the overall performance of the MT system.

3 PB-SMT System Description

The system follows three steps; the first step is prepared an SMT system with improved word alignment that produces a best SMT model for bootstrapping. And the second step is produced a chunk level parallel corpus by using the best SMT model. These chunk level parallel corpuses are added with the training corpus to generate the new SMT model in first iteration. And finally the whole process repeats to achieve better chunk level alignments as well as the better SMT model.

3.1 SMT System with improved Word Alignment

The initial English-Bengali parallel corpus is cleaned and filtered using a semi-automatic process. Complex predicates are first extracted on both sides of the parallel corpus. The analysis and identification of various complex predicates like, compound verbs (*Verb + Verb*), conjunct verbs (*Noun /Adjective/Adverb + Verb*) and serial verbs (*Verb + Verb + Verb*) in Bengali are done following the strategy in Das.et al. (2010).

Named-Entities and complex predicates are aligned following a similar technique as reported in Pal.et al (2011). Reduplicated phrases do not occur very frequently in the English corpus; some of them (like correlatives, semantic reduplications) are not found in English (Chakraborty and Bandyopadhyay, 2010). But reduplication plays a crucial role on the target Bengali side as they occur with high frequency. These reduplicated phrases are considered as a single-token so that they may map to a single word on the source side. Phrasal prepositions and verb object combinations are also treated as single tokens. Once the compound verbs and the NEs are identified on both sides of the parallel corpus, they are assembled into single tokens. When converting these MWEs into single tokens, the spaces are replaced with underscores ('_'). Since there are already some hyphenated words in the corpus, hyphenation is not used for this purpose. Besides, the use of a special word separator (underscore in this case) facilitates the job of deciding which single-token MWEs to be de-tokenized into its constituent words, before evaluation.

3.1.1 MWE Identification on Source Side

The UCREL1 Semantic analysis System (USAS) developed by Lancaster University (Rayson.et al, 2004) has been adopted for MWE identification. The USAS is a software tool for the automatic semantic analysis of English spoken and written data. Various types of Multi-Word Units (MWU) that are identified by the USAS software include: verb-object combinations (e.g. stubbed out), noun phrases (e.g. riding boots), proper names (e.g. United States of America), true idioms (e.g. living the life of Riley) etc. In English, Noun-Noun (NN) compounds, i.e., noun phrases occur with high frequency and high lexical and semantic variability (Tanaka.et al, 2003). The USAS software has a reported precision value of 91%.

3.1.2 MWE Identification on Target Side

Compound nouns are identified on the target side. Compound nouns are nominal compounds where two or more nouns are combined to form a single phrase such as *'golf club'* or *'computer science department'* (Baldwin.et al, 2010). Each element in a compound noun can function as a lexeme in independent of the other lexemes in different context. The system uses Point-wise Mutual Information (PMI), Log-likelihood Ratio (LLR) and Phi-coefficient, Co-occurrence measurement and Significance function (Agarwal.et al, 2004) measures for identification of compound nouns. Final evaluation has been carried out by combining the results of all the methods. A predefined cut-off score has been considered and the candidates having scores above the threshold value have been considered as MWEs.

The repetition of noun, pronoun, adjective and verb are generally classified as two categories: repetition at the (a) expression level and at the (b) contents or semantic level. In case of Bengali, The expression-level reduplication are classified into five fine-grained subcategories: (i) Onomatopoeic expressions (***khat khat***, knock knock), (ii) Complete Reduplication (***bara-bara***, big big), (iii) Partial Reduplication (***thakur-thukur***, God), (iv) Semantic Reduplication (***matha-mundu***, head) and (v) Correlative Reduplication (***maramari***, fighting).

For identifying reduplications, simple rules and morphological properties at lexical level have been used (Chakraborty and Bandyopadhyay, 2010). The Bengali monolingual dictionary has been used for identification of semantic reduplications.

An NE and Complex Predicates parallel corpus is created by extracting the source and the target (single token) NEs from the NE-tagged parallel corpus and aligning the NEs using the strategies as applied in (Pal.et al, 2010, 2011).

3.1.3 Verb Chunk / Complex Predicate Alignment

Initially, it is assumed that all the members of the English verb chunk in an aligned sentence pair are aligned with the members of the Bengali complex predicates. Verb chunks are aligned using a statistical aligner. A pattern generator extracts patterns from the source and the target side based on the correct alignment list. The root form of the main verb, auxiliary verb present in the verb chunk and the associated tense, aspect and modality information are extracted for the source side token. Similarly, root form of the Bengali verb and the associated vibhakti (inflection) are identified on the target side token. Similar patterns are extracted for each alignment in the doubtful alignment list.

Each pattern alignment for the entries in the doubtful alignment list is checked with the patterns identified in the correct alignment list. If both the source and the target side patterns for a doubtful alignment match with the source and the target side patterns of a correct alignment, then the doubtful alignment is considered as a correct one.

The doubtful alignment list is checked again to look for a single doubtful alignment for a sentence pair. Such doubtful alignments are considered as correct alignment.

[1] http://www.comp.lancs.ac.uk/ucrel

The above alignment list as well as NE aligned lists are added with the parallel corpus for creating the SMT model for chunk alignment. The system has reported 15.12 BLEU score for test corpus and 6.38 (73% relative) point improvement over the baseline system (Pal.et al, 2011).

3.2 Automatic chunk alignment

3.2.1 Source chunk extraction

The source corpus is preprocessed after identifying the MWEs using the UCREL tool and single tokenizing the extracted MWEs. The source sentences of the parallel corpus have been parsed using Stanford POS tagger and then the chunks of the sentences are extracted using CRF chunker[2] The CRF chunker detects the chunk boundaries of noun, verb, adjective, adverb and prepositional chunks from the sentences. After detection of the individual chunks by the CRF chunker, the boundary of the prepositional phrase chunks are expanded by examining the series of noun chunks separated by conjunctions such as *'comma', 'and'* etc. or a single noun chunk followed by a preposition. For each individual chunk, the head words are identified. A synonymous bag of words is generated for each head word. These bags of words produce more alternative chunks which are decoded using the best SMT based system (Section 3.1). Additional translated target chunks for a single source chunk are generated.

CRF Chunker output

bodies/NNS/B-NP of/IN/B-PP all/DT/B-NP ages/NNS/I-NP ,/,/O colors/NNS/I-NP and/CC/O sizes/NNS/I-NP don/VB/B-VP the/DT/B-NP very/JJ/I-NP minimum/NN/I-NP in/IN/B-PP beachwear/NN/B-NP and/CC/O idle/VB/B-VP away/RP/B-PRT the/DT/B-NP days/NNS/I-NP on/IN/B-PP the/DT/B-NP sun/NN/I-NP kissed/VBN/I-NP copacabana/NN/I-NP and/CC/O ipanema/NN/I-NP beaches/NNS/I-NP ./././O

Noun chunk Expansion and boundary detection

(bodies/NNS/B-NP) (of/IN/B-PP) (all/DT/B-NP ages/NNS/I-NP ,/,/I-NP colors/NNS/I-NP and/CC/I-NP sizes/NNS/I-NP) (don/VB/B-VP) (the/DT/B-NP very/JJ/I-NP minimum/NN/I-NP) (in/IN/B-PP) (beachwear/NN/B-NP) (and/CC/B-O) (idle/VB/B-VP) (away/RP/B-PRT) (the/DT/B-NP days/NNS/I-NP) (on/IN/B-PP) (the/DT/B-NP sun/NN/I-NP kissed/VBN/I-NP copacabana/NN/I-NP and/CC/I-NP ipanema/NN/I-NP beaches/NNS/I-NP) (./././B-O)

Prepositional phrase expansion and extraction

bodies
of all ages , colors and sizes
don
the very minimum
in beachwear
and
idle
away
the days
on the sun kissed copacabana and ipanema beaches

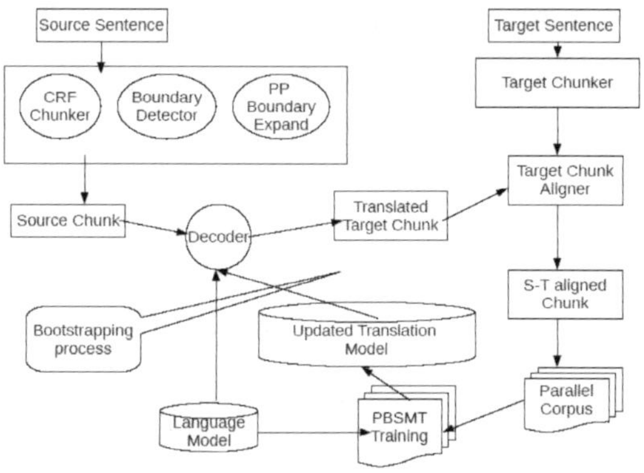

Figure 1.System architecture of the Automatic chunk alignment model

3.2.2 Target chunk extraction

The target side of the parallel corpus is cleaned and parsed using the shallow parser developed by the consortia mode project "Development of Indian Language to Indian Language Machine Translation (IL-ILMT) System Phase II" funded by Department of Information Technology, Government of India. The individual chunks are extracted from the parsed output. The individual chunk boundary is expanded if any noun chunk contains only single word and several noun chunks occur consecutively. The content of the individual chunks are examined by checking their POS categories. At the time of boundary expansion, if the system detects other POS category words except noun or conjunction then the expansion process stops immediately and new chunk boundary beginning is identified. The IL-ILMT system generates the head word for each individual chunk. The chunks for each sentence are stored in a separate list. This list is used as a

[2] http://crfchunker.sourceforge.net/

validation resource for validate the output of the statistical chunk aligner.

3.2.3 Source-Target chunk Alignment

The extracted source chunks are translated using the generated SMT model. The translated chunks as well as their alternatives are validated with the original target chunk. During validation checking, if any match is found between the translated chunk and the target chunk then the source chunk is directly aligned with the original target chunk. Otherwise, the source chunk is ignored in the current iteration for any possible alignment. The source chunk will be considered in the next alignment. After the current iteration is completed, two lists are produced: a chunk level alignment list and an unaligned source chunk list. The produced alignment lists are added with the parallel corpus as the additional training corpus to produce new SMT model for the next iteration process. The next iteration process translates the source chunks that are in the unaligned list produced by the previous iteration. This process continues until the unaligned source chunk list is empty or no further alignment is identified.

3.2.4 Source-Target chunk Validation

The translated target chunks are validated with the original target list of the same sentence. The extracted noun, verb, adjective, adverb and prepositional chunks of the source side may not have a one to one correspondence with the target side except for the verb chunk. There is no concept of prepositional chunks on the target side. Some time adjective or adverb chunks may be treated as noun chunk on the target side. So, chunk level validation for individual categories of chunks is not possible. Source side verb chunks are compared with the target side verb chunks while all the other chunks on the source side are compared with all the other chunks on the target side. Head words are extracted for each source chunk and the translated head words are actually compared on the target side taking into the consideration the synonymous target words. When the validation system returns positive, the source chunk is aligned with the identified original target chunk.

4 Tools and Resources used

A sentence-aligned English-Bengali parallel corpus containing 14,187 parallel sentences from the travel and tourism domain has been used in the present work. The corpus has been collected from the consortium-mode project "Development of English to Indian Languages Machine Translation (EILMT) System Phase II[3]". The Stanford Parser[4], Stanford NER, CRF chunker[5] and the Wordnet 3.0[6] have been used for identifying complex predicates in the source English side of the parallel corpus.

The sentences on the target side (Bengali) are parsed and POS-tagged by using the tools obtained from the consortium mode project "Development of Indian Language to Indian Language Machine Translation (IL-ILMT) System Phase II". NEs in Bengali are identified using the NER system of Ekbal and Bandyopadhyay (2008).

The effectiveness of the MWE-aligned and chunk aligned parallel corpus is demonstrated by using the standard log-linear PB-SMT model as our baseline system: GIZA++ implementation of IBM word alignment model 4, phrase-extraction heuristics described in (Koehn et al., 2003), minimum-error-rate training (Och, 2003) on a held-out development set, target language model trained using SRILM toolkit (Stolcke, 2002) with Kneser-Ney smoothing (Kneser and Ney, 1995) and the Moses decoder (Koehn et al., 2007).

5 Experiments and Evaluation Results

We have randomly identified 500 sentences each for the development set and the test set from the initial parallel corpus. The rest are considered as the training corpus. The training corpus was filtered with the maximum allowable sentence length of 100 words and sentence length ratio of 1:2 (either way). Finally the training corpus contains 13,176 sentences. In addition to the target side of the parallel corpus, a monolingual Bengali corpus containing 293,207 words from the tourism domain was used for the target language model. The experiments have been carried out with different n-gram settings for the language model and the maximum phrase length and found that a 4-gram language model and a maximum phrase length of 4 produce the optimum baseline result. The rest of the experiments have been carried out using these settings.

---

[3] The EILMT and ILILMT projects are funded by the Department of Information Technology (DIT), Ministry of Communications and Information Technology (MCIT), Government of India.

[4] http://nlp.stanford.edu/software/lex-parser.shtml

[5] http://crfchunker.sourceforge.net/

[6] http://wordnet.princeton.edu/

The system continues with the various preprocessing of the corpus. The hypothesis is that as more and more MWEs and chunks are identified and aligned properly, the system shows the improvement in the translation procedure. Table 1 shows the MWE statistics of the parallel training corpus. It is observed from Table 1 that NEs occur with high frequency in both sides compared to other types of MWEs. It suggests that prior alignment of the NEs and complex predicates plays a role in improving the system performance.

Training set	English		Bengali	
	T	U	T	U
CPs	4874	2289	14174	7154
reduplicated word	-	-	85	50
Noun-noun compound	892	711	489	300
Phrasal preposition	982	779	-	-
Phrasal verb	549	532	-	-
Total NE words	22931	8273	17107	9106

Table 1. MWE Statistics. (T - Total occurrence, U – Unique, CP – complex predicates, NE – Named Entities)

Single tokenization of NEs and MWEs of any length on both the sides followed by GIZA++ alignment has given a huge impetus to system performance (6.38 BLEU points absolute, 73% relative improvement over the baseline). In the source side, the system treats the phrasal prepositions, verb-object combinations and noun-noun compounds as a single token. In the target side, single tokenization of reduplicated phrases and noun-noun compounds has been done followed by alignments using the GIZA++ tool. From the observation of Table 2, during first iteration there are 81821 chunks are identified from the source corpus and 14534 has been aligned by the system. For iteration 2, there are 67287 source chunks are remaining to align. At the final iteration almost 65% of the source chunks have been aligned.

Training set	English		Bengali	
Iteration	T	U	T	U
1	81821	70321	65429	59627
2	67287	62575	50895	47139
final	32325	31409	15933	15654

Table 2. Chunk Statistics. (T - Total occurrence, U – Unique)

The system performance improves when the alignment list of NEs and complex predicates as well as sentence level aligned chunk are incorporated in the baseline best system. It achieves the BLEU score of 17.37 after the final iteration. This is the best result obtained so far with respect to the baseline system (8.63 BLEU points absolute, 98.74% relative improvement in Table 3). It may be observed from Table 3 that baseline Moses without any preprocessing of the dataset produces a BLEU score of 8.74.

Experiments		Exp	BLEU	NIST
Baseline		1	8.74	3.98
Best System (Alignment of NEs and Complex Predicates and Single Tokenization of various MWEs)		2	15.12	4.48
Baseline Best System + Chunk Alignment	Iteration 1	3	15.87	4.49
	Iteration 2	4	16.28	4.51
	Iteration 3	5	16.40	4.51
	Iteration 4	6	16.68	4.52
	Final Iteration†	**7**	**17.37**	**4.55**

Table 3. Evaluation results for different experimental setups. (The '†' marked systems produce statistically significant improvements on BLEU over the baseline system)

Intrinsic evaluation of the chunk alignment could not be performed as gold-standard word alignment was not available. Thus, extrinsic evaluation was carried out on the MT quality using the well known automatic MT evaluation metrics: BLEU (Papineni et al., 2002) and NIST (Doddington, 2002). Bengali is a morphologically rich language and has relatively free phrase order. Proper evaluation of the English-Bengali

MT evaluation ideally requires multiple set of reference translations. Moreover, the training set was smaller in size.

6. Conclusions and Future work

A methodology has been presented in this paper to show how the simple yet effective preprocessing of various types of MWEs and alignment of NEs, complex predicates and chunks can boost the performance of PB-SMT system on an English—Bengali translation task. The best system yields 8.63 BLEU points improvement over the baseline, a 98.74% relative increase. A subset of the output from the best system has been compared with that of the baseline system, and the output of the best system almost always looks better in terms of either lexical choice or word ordering. It is observed that only 28.5% of the test set NEs appear in the training set, yet prior automatic alignment of the NEs complex predicates and chunk improves the translation quality. This suggests that not only the NE alignment quality in the phrase table but also the word alignment and phrase alignment quality improves significantly. At the same time, single-tokenization of MWEs makes the dataset sparser, but improves the quality of MT output to some extent. Data-driven approaches to MT, specifically for scarce-resource language pairs for which very little parallel texts are available, should benefit from these preprocessing methods. Data sparseness is perhaps the reason why single-tokenization of NEs and compound verbs, both individually and in collaboration, did not add significantly to the scores. However, a significantly large parallel corpus can take care of the data sparseness problem introduced by the single-tokenization of MWEs.

Acknowledgement

The work has been carried out with support from the consortium-mode project "Development of English to Indian Languages Machine Translation (EILMT) System funded by Department of Information Technology, Government of India.

References

Agarwal, Aswini, Biswajit Ray, Monojit Choudhury, Sudeshna Sarkar and Anupam Basu. Automatic Extraction of Multiword Expressions in Bengali: An Approach for Miserly Resource Scenario. In Proc. of International Conference on Natural Language Processing (ICON), pp. 165-174.(2004)

Baldwin, Timothy and Su Nam Kim Multiword Expressions, in Nitin Indurkhya and Fred J. Damerau (eds.) Handbook of Natural Language Processing, Second Edition, CRC Press, Boca Raton, USA, pp. 267—292 (2010)

Banerjee, Satanjeev, and Alon Lavie.. An Automatic Metric for MT Evaluation with Improved Correlation with Human Judgments. In proceedings of the ACL-2005 Workshop on Intrinsic and Extrinsic Evaluation Measures for MT and/or Summarization, pp. 65-72. Ann Arbor, Michigan., pp. 65-72. (2005)

Carpuat, Marine, and Mona Diab. Task-based Evaluation of Multiword Expressions: a Pilot Study in Statistical Machine Translation. In Proc. of Human Language Technology conference and the North American Chapter of the Association for Computational Linguistics conference (HLT-NAACL 2010), Los Angeles, CA (2010)

Chakraborty, Tanmoy and Sivaji Bandyopadhyay. Identification of Reduplication in Bengali Corpus and their Semantic Analysis: A Rule Based Approach. In proc. of the 23rd International Conference on Computational Linguistics (COLING 2010), Workshop on Multiword Expressions: from Theory to Applications (MWE 2010). Beijing, China. (2010)

Das, Dipankar, Santanu Pal, Tapabrata Mondal, Tanmoy Chakraborty, Sivaji Bandyopadhyay. Automatic Extraction of Complex Predicates in Bengali In proc. of the workshop on Multiword expression: from theory to application (MWE-2010), The 23rd International conference of computational linguistics (Coling 2010),Beijing, Chaina, pp. 37-46.(2010)

Doddington, George. Automatic evaluation of machine translation quality using n-gram cooccurrence statistics. In Proc. of the Second International Conference on Human Language Technology Research (HLT-2002), San Diego, CA, pp. 128-132(2002)

Eck, Matthias, Stephan Vogel, and Alex Waibel. Improving statistical machine translation in the medical domain using the Unified Medical Language System. In Proc. of the 20th International Conference on Computational Linguistics (COLING 2004), Geneva, Switzerland, pp. 792-798 (2004)

Ekbal, Asif, and Sivaji Bandyopadhyay. Voted NER system using appropriate unlabeled data. In proc. of the ACL-IJCNLP-2009 Named Entities Workshop (NEWS 2009), Suntec, Singapore, pp.202-210 (2009).

Huang, Young-Sook, Kyonghee Paik, Yutaka Sasaki, "Bilingual Knowledge Extraction Using Chunk Alignment", PACLIC 18, Tokiyo, pp. 127-138, (2004).

Kneser, Reinhard, and Hermann Ney. Improved backing-off for m-gram language modeling. In Proc. of the IEEE Internation Conference on Acoustics, Speech, and Signal Processing (ICASSP), vol. 1, pp. 181–184. Detroit, MI. (1995)

Koehn, Philipp, Franz Josef Och, and Daniel Marcu. Statistical phrase-based translation. In Proc. of HLT-NAACL 2003: conference combining Human Language Technology conference series and the North American Chapter of the Association for Computational Linguistics conference series, Edmonton, Canada, pp. 48-54. (2003)

Koehn, Philipp, Hieu Hoang, Alexandra Birch, Chris Callison-Burch, Marcello Federico, Nicola Bertoldi, Brooke Cowan, Wade Shen, Christine Moran, Richard Zens, Chris Dyer, Ondřej Bojar, Alexandra Constantin, and Evan Herbst. Moses: open source toolkit for statistical machine translation. In Proc. of the 45th Annual meeting of the Association for Computational Linguistics (ACL 2007): Proc. of demo and poster sessions, Prague, Czech Republic, pp. 177-180. (2007)

Koehn, Philipp. Statistical significance tests for machine translation evaluation. In EMNLP-2004: Proc. of the 2004 Conference on Empirical Methods in Natural Language Processing, 25-26 July 2004, Barcelona, Spain, pp 388-395. (2004)

Ma, Yanjun, Nicolas Stroppa, AndyWay. Proceedings of the 45th Annual Meeting of the Association of Computational Linguistics, ,Prague, Czech Republic, June 2007, pp. 304–311 (2007).

Moore, Robert C. Learning translations of named-entity phrases from parallel corpora. In Proc. of 10th Conference of the European Chapter of the Association for Computational Linguistics (EACL 2003), Budapest, Hungary; pp. 259-266. (2003)

Och, Franz J. Minimum error rate training in statistical machine translation. In Proc. of the 41st Annual Meeting of the Association for Computational Linguistics (ACL-2003), Sapporo, Japan, pp. 160-167. (2003)

Pal Santanu, Sudip Kumar Naskar, Pavel Pecina, Sivaji Bandyopadhyay and Andy Way. Handling Named Entities and Compound Verbs in Phrase-Based Statistical Machine Translation, In proc. of the workshop on Multiword expression: from theory to application (MWE-2010), The 23rd International conference of computational linguistics (Coling 2010),Beijing, Chaina, pp. 46-54 (2010)

Pal, Santanu Tanmoy Chakraborty , Sivaji Bandyopadhyay, "Handling Multiword Expressions in Phrase-Based Statistical Machine Translation", Machine Translation Summit XIII(2011),Xiamen, China, pp. 215-224 (2011)

Papineni, Kishore, Salim Roukos, Todd Ward, and Wei-Jing Zhu. BLEU: a method for automatic evaluation of machine translation. In Proc. of the 40th Annual Meeting of the Association for Computational Linguistics (ACL-2002), Philadelphia, PA, pp. 311-318 (2002)

Rayson, Paul, Dawn Archer, Scott Piao, and Tony McEnery. The UCREL Semantic Analysis System. In proc. Of LREC-04 Workshop: Beyond Named Entity Recognition Semantic Labeling for NLP Tasks, pages 7-12, Lisbon, Porugal (2004)

Ren, Zhixiang, Yajuan Lü, Jie Cao, Qun Liu, and Yun Huang. Improving statistical machine translation using domain bilingual multiword expressions. In Proc. of the 2009 Workshop on Multiword Expressions, ACL-IJCNLP 2009, Suntec, Singapore, pp. 47-54 (2009).

Stolcke, A. SRILM—An Extensible Language Modeling Toolkit. Proc. Intl. Conf. on Spoken Language Processing, vol. 2, pp. 901–904, Denver (2002).

Tanaka, Takaaki and Timothy Baldwin. Noun- Noun Compound Machine Translation: A Feasibility Study on Shallow Processing. In Proc. of the Association for Computational Linguistics- 2003, Workshop on Multiword Expressions: Analysis, Acquisition and Treatment, Sapporo, Japan, pp. 17–24 (2003)

Wu, Hua Haifeng Wang, and Chengqing Zong. Domain adaptation for statistical machine translation with domain dictionary and monolingual corpora. In Proc. of the 22nd International Conference on Computational Linguistics (COLING 2008), Manchester, UK, pp. 993-1000 (2008)

Xuan-Hieu Phan, "CRFChunker: CRF English Phrase Chunker", http://crfchunker.sourceforge.net/, (2006)

Zhou, Yu, chengquing Zong, Bo Xu, "Bilingual Chunk Aliment in Statistical Machine Translation", IEEE International Conference on Systems, Man and Cybernetics, pp. 1401-1406, (2004)

Design of a hybrid high quality machine translation system

Kurt Eberle
Johanna Geiß
Mireia Ginestí-Rosell
Lingenio GmbH
Karlsruher Straße 10
69 126 Heidelberg, Germany

[k.eberle,j.geiss,m.ginesti-rosell]
@lingenio.de

Bogdan Babych
Anthony Hartley
Reinhard Rapp
Serge Sharoff
Martin Thomas
Centre for Translation Studies
University of Leeds
Leeds, LS2 9JT, UK

[B.Babych,A.Hartley,R.Rapp,
S.Sharoff,M.Thomas]@leeds.ac.uk

Abstract

This paper gives an overview of the ongoing FP7 project HyghTra (2010 – 2014). The HyghTra project is conducted in a partnership between academia and industry involving the University of Leeds and Lingenio GmbH (company). It adopts a hybrid and bootstrapping approach to the enhancement of MT quality by applying rule-based analysis and statistical evaluation techniques to both parallel and comparable corpora in order to extract linguistic information and enrich the lexical and syntactic resources of the underlying (rule-based) MT system that is used for analysing the corpora. The project places special emphasis on the extension of systems to new language pairs and corresponding rapid, automated creation of high quality resources. The techniques are fielded and evaluated within an existing commercial MT environment.

1 Motivation

Statistical Machine Translation (SMT) has been around for about 20 years, and for roughly half of this time SMT and the 'traditional' *Rule-based Machine Translation* (RBMT) have been seen as competing paradigms. During the last decade however, there is a trend and growing interest in combining the two methodologies. In our approach these two approaches are viewed as complementary.

Advantages of SMT are low cost and robustness, but definite disadvantages of (pure) SMT are that it needs huge amounts of data, which for many language pairs are not available and are unlikely to become available in the future. Also, SMT tends to disregard important classificatory knowledge (such as morphosyntactic, categorical and lexical class features), which can be provided and used relatively easily within non-statistical representations.

On the other hand, advantages of RBMT are that its (grammar and lexical) rules and information are understandable by humans and can be exploited for a lot of applications outside of translation (dictionaries, text understanding, dialogue systems, etc.).

The slot grammar approach used in Lingenio systems (cf. McCord 1989, Eberle 2001) is a prime example of such linguistically rich representations that can be used for a number of different applications. Fig.1 shows this by a visualization of (an excerpt of) the entry for the ambiguous German verb *einstellen* in the database that underlies (a) the Lingenio translation products, where it links up with corresponding set of the transfer rules, and (b) Lingenio's dictionary product *TranslateDict*, which is primarily intended for human translators.

Proceedings of the 13th Conference of the European Chapter of the Association for Computational Linguistics, pages 101–112,
Avignon, France, April 23 - 27 2012.

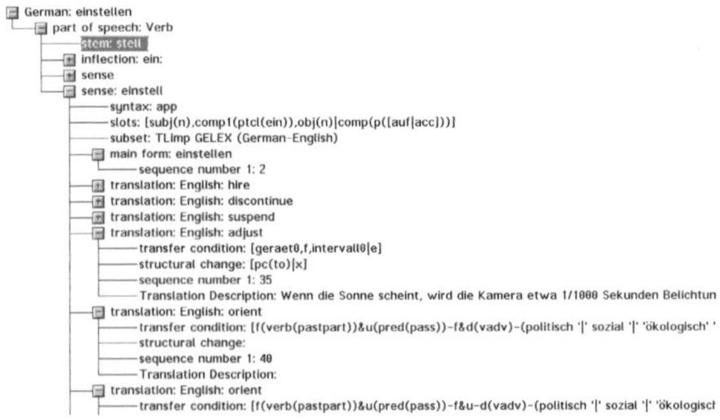

Fig 1 a) data base entry *einstellen*
('translation' represents links between SL and T entries)

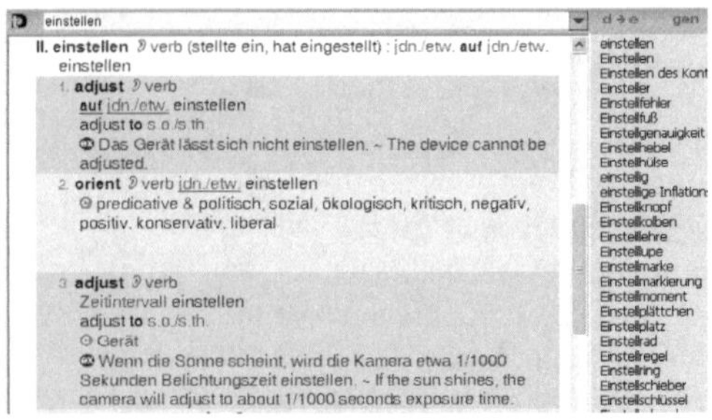

Fig 1 b) product entry *einstellen*

The obvious disadvantages of RBMT are high cost, weaknesses in dealing with incorrect input and in making correct choices with respect to ambiguous words, structures, and transfer equivalents.
SMT output is often surprisingly good with respect to short distance collocations, but often misses correct choices are missed in cases where selectional restrictions take effect on distant words. RBMT output is generally good if the parser assigns the correct analysis to a sentence and if the target words can be correctly chosen from the set of alternatives. However, in the presence of ambiguous words and structures, and where linguistic information is lacking, the decisions may be wrong.
Given the complementarity of SMT and RBMT and their very different strengths and weaknesses, we take a view that an optimized MT architecture must comprise elements of both paradigms. The key issue therefore lies in the identification of such elements and how to connect them to each other. We propose a specific type of hybrid translation – *hy*brid hi*gh* quality *tra*nslation (HyghTra), where core RBMT systems are created and enhanced by a range of reliable statistical techniques.

2 Development Methodology

Many hybrid systems described in the literature have attempted to put some analytical abstraction on top of an SMT kernel.[1] In our view this is not the best option because, according to the underlying philosophy, SMT is linguistically ignorant at the beginning and learns all linguistic rules automatically from corpora. However, the extracted information is typically represented in huge data sets which are not readable by humans in a natural way. This means that this type of architecture does not easily provide interfaces for incorporating linguistic knowledge in a canonical and simple way.
Thus we approach the problem from the other end, , integrating information derived from corpora using statistical methods into RBMT systems. Provided the underlying RBMT systems are linguistically sound and sufficiently modular in structure, we believe this to have greater potential for generating high quality output.
We currently use and carry out the following work plan:

(I) Creation of MT systems
(with rule-based core MT information and statistical extension and training):
(a) We start out with declarative analysis and generation components of the considered languages, and with basic *bilingual dictionaries* connecting to one another the entries of relatively small vocabularies comprising the most frequent words of each language in a given translation pair (cf. Fig 1 a).
(b) Having completed this phase, we extend the dictionaries and train the analysis-, transfer- and generation-components of the rule-based core systems using monolingual and bilingual corpora.

[1] A prominent early example is Frederking and colleagues (Frederking & Nirenburg, 1994). For an overview of hybrid MT till the late nineties see Streiter et al. (1999). More recent approaches include Groves & Way (2006a, 2006b). Commercial implementations include *AppTek* (http://www.apptek.com) and *Language Weaver* (http://www.languageweaver.com). An ongoing MT important project investigating hybrid methods is EuroMatrixPlus (http://www.euromatrixplus.net/)

(II) Error detection and improvement cycle:
(a) We automatically discover the most frequent problematic *grammatical constructions* and multiword expressions for commercial RBMT and SMT systems using automatic construction-based evaluation as proposed in (Babych and Hartley, 2009) and develop a framework for fixing corresponding grammar rules and extending grammatical coverage of the systems in a semi-automatic way. This shortens development time for commercial MT and contributes to yielding significantly higher translation quality.

(III) Extension to other languages:
Structural similarity and translation by pivot languages is used to obtain extension to further languages:
High-quality translation between closely related languages (e.g., Russian and Ukrainian or Portuguese and Spanish) can be achieved with relatively simple resources (using linguistic similarity, but also homomorphism assumptions with respect to parallel text, if available), while greater efforts are put into ensuring better-quality translation between more distant languages (e.g. German and Russian). According to our prior research (Babych et al., 2007b) the pipeline between languages of different similarity results in improved translation quality for a larger number of language pairs (e.g., MT from Portuguese or Ukrainian into German is easier if there are high-quality analysis and transfer modules for Spanish and Russian into German (respectively). Of course, (III) draws heavily on the detailed analysis and MT systems that the industrial partner in HyghTra provides for a number of languages.

In the following sections we give more details of the work currently done with regard to (I) and with regard to parts of (II): the creation of a new MT system following the strategy sketched. We cannot go further into detail with (II) and (III) here, which will become a priority for future research.

3 Creation of a new system

Early pilot studies covering some aspects of the strategy described here (using information from pivot languages and similarity) showed promising results (Rapp, 1999; Rapp & Martín Vide, 2007; see also Koehn & Knight, 2002).

We expect that the proposed semi-automatic creation of a new MT system as sketched above will work best if one of the two languages involved is already 'known' by modules to which the system has access. Against the background of the pipeline approach mentioned above in (III), this means that we assume an analysis and translation system that continuously grows by 'learning' new languages where 'learning' is facilitated by information about the languages already 'known' and by exploiting similarity assumptions – and, of course, by being fed with information prepared and provided by the human 'companion' of the system.
From this perspective, we assume the following steps of extending the system (with work done by the 'companion' and work done by the system)

1. Acquire parallel and comparable corpora.
2. Define a core of the morphology of the new language and compile a basic dictionary for the most frequent words and translations. Morphological representations and features for new languages are derived both manually and automatically, as proposed in (Babych et al., 2012 (in preparation)).
3. Using established alignment technology (e.g. Giza++) and parallel corpora, generate a first extension of this dictionary.
4. Expand the dictionary of step 3 using comparable corpora as proposed in a study by Rapp (1999). This is applicable mainly to single word units.
5. Expand coverage of multiword-units using novel technology.
6. Cross-validate the new dictionary with respect to available ones by transitivity.
7. Integrate the new dictionary into the new MT system as developing from reusing components and adding new components as in 8.
8. Complete morphology and spell out declarative analysis and generation grammar for the new language.
9. Automatically evaluate the translations of the most frequent grammatical constructions and multiword expressions in a machine-translated corpus, prioritising support for these constructions with a type of risk-assessment framework proposed in Babych and Hartley (2008).
10. Extend support for high-priority constructions semi-automatically by mining correct

translations from parallel corpora.

11. Train and evaluate the new grammar and transfer of the new MT system using the new dictionary on the basis of available parallel corpora.

The following sections give an overview of the different steps.

Step 1: Acquire parallel and comparable corpora

As our parallel corpus, we use the Europarl. The size of the current version is up to 40 million words per language, and several of the languages we are currently considering are covered. Also, we make use of other parallel corpora such as the Canadian Hansards (Proceedings of the Canadian Parliament) for the English–French language pair. For non-EU Languages (mainly Russian), we intend to conduct a pilot study to establish the feasibility of retrieving parallel corpora from the web, a problem for which various approaches have been proposed (Resnik, 1999; Munteanu & Marcu, 2005; Wu & Fung, 2005).

In addition to the parallel corpora, we will need large monolingual corpora in the future (at least 200 million words) for each of the six languages. Here, we intend to use newspaper corpora supplemented with text collections downloadable from the web.

The corpora are stored in a database that allows for assigning analyses of different depth and nature to the sentences and for alignment between the sentences and their analyses. The architecture of this database and the corresponding analysis and evaluation frontend is described in (Eberle et al 2010, 2012). Section *Results* contains examples of such representations.

Step 2: Compile a basic dictionary for the most frequent words

A prerequisite of the suggested hybrid approach with rule-based kernel is to define morphological classifications for the new language(s). This is done exploiting similarities to the classifications as available for the existing languages. Currently, this has been carried out for Dutch (on the basis of German) and for Spanish (on the basis of French/other Romance languages). The most frequent words (the basic vocabulary of a language) are typically also the most ambiguous ones. Since the Lingenio systems are lexically driven transfer systems (cf. Eberle 2001), we define (a) structural conditions, which inform the choice of the possible target words (single words or multiword expressions) and (b)restructuring conditions, as necessary (cf. Fig 1 a: attributes *'transfer conditions'* and *'structural change'*). In order to ensure quality this must be done by human lexicographers and therefore costly for a large dictionary. However, we manually create only very small basic dictionaries and extend these (semi-automatically) step 3 and those which follow.
Some important morphosyntactic features of the language are derived from a monolingual corpus annotated with publicly available part-of-speech taggers and lemmatisers. However, these tools often do not explicitly represent linguistic features needed for the generation stage in RBMT. In (Babych et al., 2012) we propose a systematic approach to recovering such missing generation-oriented representations from grammar models and statistical combinatorial properties of annotated features.

Step 3: Generating dictionary extensions from parallel corpora

Based on parallel corpora, dictionaries can be derived using established techniques of automatic sentence alignment and word alignment. For sentence alignment, the length-based Gale & Church aligner (1993) can be used, or – alternatively – Dan Melamed's GSA-algorithm (Geometric Sentence Alignment; Melamed, 1999). For segmentation of text we use corresponding Lingenio-tools (unpublished).[2]
For word alignment Giza++ (Och & Ney, 2003) is the standard tool. Given a word alignment, the extraction of a (SMT) dictionary is relatively straightforward. With the exception of sentence segmentation, these algorithms are largely language independent and can be used for all of the languages that we consider. We did this for a number of language pairs on the basis of the

[2] If these cannot be applied because of lack of information about a language, we intend to use the algorithm by Kiss & Strunk (2006). An open-source implementation of parts of the Kiss & Strunk algorithm is available from Patrick Tschorn at http://www.denkselbst.de/sentrick/index.html.

Europarl-texts considered (as stored in our database). In order to optimize the results we use the dictionaries of step 1 as set of *cognates* (cf. Simard at al 1992, Gough & Way 2004), as well as other words easily obtainable from the internet that can be used for this purpose (like company names and other named entities with cross-language identity and terminology translations). Using the morphology component of the new language and the categorial information from the transfer relation, we compute the basic forms of the inflected words found. Later, we intend to further improve the accuracy of word alignment by exploiting chunk type syntactic information of the narrow context of the words (cf. Eberle & Rapp 2008). An early stage variant of this is already used in Lingenio products. The corresponding function AutoLearn<word> extracts new word relations on the basis of existing dictionaries and (partial) syntactic analyses. (Fig 2 gives an example).

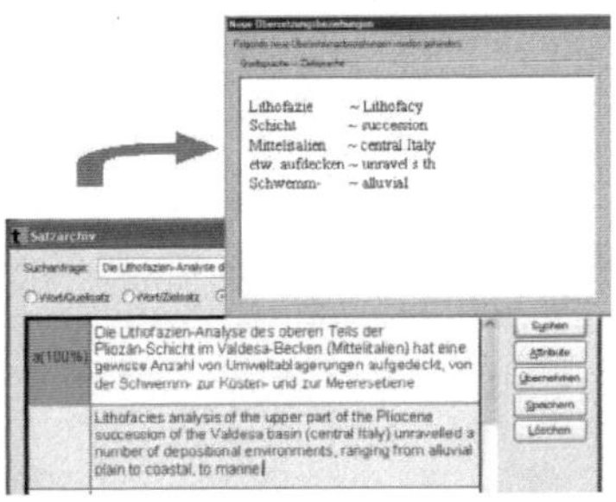

Fig 2 AutoLearn<word>: new entries using transfer links and syntactic analysis

Given the relatively small size of the available parallel corpora, we expect that the automatically generated dictionaries will comprise about 20,000 entries each (This corresponds to first results on the basis of German↔English). This is far too small for a serious general purpose MT system. Note that, in comparison, the English↔German dictionary used in the current Lingenio MT product comprises more than 480,000 keywords and phrases.

Step 4: Expanding dictionaries using comparable corpora (word equations)

In order to expand the dictionaries using a set of monolingual comparable corpora, the basic approach pioneered by Fung & McKeown (1997) and Rapp (1995, 1999) is to be further developed and refined in the second phase of the project as to obtain a practical tool that can be used in an industrial context.

The basic assumption underlying the approach is that across languages there is a correlation between the co-occurrences of words that are translations of each other. If – for example – in a text of one language two words *A* and *B* co-occur more often than expected by chance, then in a text of another language those words that are translations of *A* and *B* should also co-occur more frequently than expected. It is further assumed that a small dictionary (as generated in step 2) is available at the beginning, and that the aim is to expand this basic lexicon. Using a corpus of the target language, first a co-occurrence matrix is computed whose rows are all word types occurring in the corpus and whose columns are all target words appearing in the basic lexicon. Next a word of the source language is considered whose translation is to be determined. Using the source-language corpus, a co-occurrence vector for this word is computed. Then all known words in this vector are translated to the target language. As the basic lexicon is small, only some of the translations are known. All unknown words are discarded from the vector and the vector positions are sorted in order to match the vectors of the target-language matrix. Using standard measures for vector similarity, the resulting vector is compared to all vectors in the co-occurrence matrix of the target language. The vector with the highest similarity is considered to be the translation of our source-language word.

From a previous pilot study (Rapp, 1999) it can be expected that this methodology achieves an accuracy in the order of 70%, which means that only a relatively modest amount of manual post-editing is required.

The automatically generated results are improved and the amount of post-editing is reduced by exploiting sense (disambiguation) information as available from the analysis component for the 'known' language of the new language pair.. Also we try to exploit categorial and underspecified syntactic information of the contexts of the words similar to what has been suggested for improving word alignment in the previous step (see also Fig.2). Also, as the frequent words are already covered by the basic lexicon (whose production from parallel corpora on the basis of a manually compiled kernel does not show an ambiguity problem of similar significance), and as experience shows that most low frequency words in a full-size lexicon tend to be unambiguous, the ambiguity problem is reduced further for the words investigated and extracted by this comparison method.

Step 5: Expanding dictionaries using comparable corpora (multiword units)

In order to account for technical terms, idioms, collocations, and typical short phrases, an important feature of an MT lexicon is a high coverage of multiword units. Very recent work conducted at the University of Leeds (Sharoff et al., 2006) shows that dictionary entries for such multiword units can be derived from comparable corpora if a dictionary of single words is available. It could even be shown that this methodology can be superior to deriving multiword-units from parallel corpora (Babych et al., 2007). This is a major breakthrough as comparable corpora are far easier to acquire than parallel corpora. It even opens up the possibility of building domain-specific dictionaries by using texts from different domains.

The outline of the algorithm is as follows:

- Extract collocations from a corpus of the source language (Smadja, 1993)
- To translate a collocation, look up all its words using any dictionary
- Generate all possible permutations (sequences) of the word translations
- Count the occurrence frequencies of these sequences in a corpus of the target language and test for significance
- Consider the most significant sequence to be the translation of the source language collocation

Of course, in later steps of the project, we will experiment on filtering these sequences by exploiting structural knowledge similarly to what was described in the two previous steps. This can be obtained on the basis of the declarative analysis component of the new language which is developed in parallel.

Step 6: Cross-validate dictionaries

The combination of the corpus-based methods for automatic dictionary generation as described in steps 3 to 5 will lead to high coverage dictionaries as the availability of very large monolingual corpora is no major problem for our languages. However, as all steps are error prone, it can be expected that a considerable number of dictionary entries (e.g. 50%) are not correct. To facilitate (but not eliminate) the manual verification of the dictionary, we will perform an automatic cross-check which utilizes the dictionaries' property of *transitivity*. What we mean by this is that if we have two dictionaries, one translating from language A to language B, the other from language B to language C, then we can also translate from language A to C by use of the intermediate language (or interlingua) B. That is, the property of transitivity, although having some limitations due to ambiguity problems, can be exploited to automatically generate a raw dictionary for A to C. Lingenio has some experience with this method having exploited it for extending and improving its English ↔ French dictionaries using French ↔ German and German ↔ English.

As the corpus-based approach (steps 3 to 5) allows us to also generate this type of dictionary via comparable corpora, we have two different ways to generate a dictionary for a particular language pair. This means that we can validate one with the other. Furthermore, with increasing number of language pairs created, there are more and more languages that can serve as interlingua or 'pivot': This, step by step, gives an increasing potential for mutual cross-validation.

Specific attention will be paid to automating as far as possible the creation of selectional restrictions to be assigned to the transfer relations of the new dictionaries in all steps of dictionary creation (2–6). We will try to do this on the basis of the analysis components as available for the languages considered: These are: a completely worked out analysis component for the 'old' language, a declarative (chunk parsing) component for the new one (compare the two following steps for this).

Step 7: Integrate dictionaries in existing machine translation systems

Lingenio has a relatively rich infrastructure for automatic importation of various kinds of lexical information into the database used by the analyses and translation systems. If necessary the information on hand (for instance from conventional dictionaries of publishing houses) is completed and normalized during or before importation. This may be executed completely automatically – by using the existing analyses components and resources respectively as databases – or interactively – by asking the lexicographer for additional information, if needed.

For example, there may be a list of multiword expressions to be imported into the database. In order to have available correct syntactic and semantic information for these expressions, they are analysed by the parser of the corresponding language. From the analysis found, the information necessary to describe the new lemma in the lexicon with respect to semantic type and syntactic structure is obtained. The same information is used to automatically create correct restructuring constraints for translation relations which use the new lemma as target. If the parser does not find a sound syntactic description, for example because some basic information or the expression is missing in the lexical database, the lexicographer is asked for the missing information or is handed over the expression to code it manually.

Using these tools importation of new lexical information, as provided in the previous steps, is considerably accelerated.

Step 8: Compile rule bases for new language pairs

Although experience clearly shows that construction and maintenance of the dictionaries is by far the most expensive task in (rule-based) Machine Translation, the grammars (analysis and generation) must of course be developed and maintained also. Lingenio has longstanding experience with the development of grammars, dictionaries and all other components of RBMT.

The used grammar formalism (*slot grammar*, cf. McCord 1991) is unification based and its structuring focuses on dependency, where phrases are analysed into heads and grammatical roles – so called (complement and adjunct) *slots*.

The grammar formalism and basic rule types are designed in a very general way in order to allow good portability from one language to another such that spelling out the declarative part of a grammar does not take very much time (2-4 person months approx. for relatively similar languages like Romance languages according to our experience). The portation of linguistic rules to new languages is also facilitated by the modular design with clearly defined interfaces that make it relatively straightforward to integrate information from corpora.

Given a parallel corpus as acquired in step 1, the following procedure defines grammar development:

1. Define a declarative grammar for the new language and train this grammar on the parallel -corpus according to the following steps:
2. Use a chunk parser for the grammar on the basis of an efficient part-of-speech tagger for the new language.
3. Combine the chunk analyses of the sentence, according to suggestions for packed syntactic structures (cf. Schiehlen 2001 and others) and underspecified representation structures respectively (cf. Eberle, 2004, and others), such that the result represents a disjunction of the possible analyses of the sentence.
4. Filter the alternatives of the representation by using mapping constraints between source and target sentence as can be computed from the lexical transfer relations and the structural analysis of the sentence. For instance, if we know, as in the example of the last section, that in the source sentence there is a relative clause with lexical elements A, B, . . . modifying a head H and that there are translations TH, TA, TB, . . . of H, A, B,. . . , in the target sentence which, among other possibilities, can be supposed to stand in a similar structural relation there, then we prefer this relation to the competing structural possibilities. (Fig. 3 in section *results* shows the corresponding selection for a German-Spanish example in the project database).
5. For each of the remaining structural possibilities of the thus revised underspecified representation, take its lexical material and underspecified structuring as a context for its successful firing. For instance, if the possibility is left that O is the direct object of VP, where VP is an underspecified verbal phrase and O an underspecified nominal phrase (i.e. where details of the substructuring are not spelled out), take the sentence as a reference for direct object complementation and O and VP as contexts which accept this complementation.

6. Develop more abstract conditions from the conditions learned according to (5) and integrate the different cases.
7. Tune the results using standard methods of corpus-based linguistics. Among other things this means: Distinguish between training and test corpora, adjust weights according to the results of test runs, etc.

The basic idea of the proposed learning procedure is similar to that used with respect to learning lexical transfer relations: Do not define the statistical model for the 'ignorant' state, where the surface items of the bilingual corpora are considered. Instead, define it for appropriate maximally abstract analyses of the sentences (which, of course, must be available automatically), because, then, much smaller sets of data will do. Here, the important question is: What is the most abstract level of representation that can be reached automatically and which shows reliable results? We think that it is the level of underspecified syntactic description as used in the procedure above.

The result of training the grammar is a set of rules which assign weights and contexts to each filler rule of the declarative grammar and thus allow to estimate how likely it is that a particular rule is applied in a particular context in comparison with other rules (Fig. 4 and 5 in section *results* give an overview of the relevance of grammar rules and their triggering conditions w.r.t. German).

We mentioned that the task of translating texts into each other does not presuppose that each ambiguity in a source sentence is resolved. On the contrary, translation should be *ambiguity preserving* (cf. Kay, Gawron & Norvig 1994, compare the example above). It is obvious that underspecified syntactic representations as suggested here are also especially suited for preserving ambiguities appropriately.

Step 9: Automatically evaluate translations of the most frequent grammatical constructions and multiword expressions in a machine-translated corpus

In a later work package of the project, we will run a large parallel corpus through available (competitive) MT engines, which will be enhanced by automatic dictionaries developed during the previous stages. On the source-language side of the corpus we will automatically generate lists of frequent multiword expressions (MWEs) and grammatical constructions using the methodology proposed in (Sharoff et al., 2006). For each of the identified MWEs and constructions we will generate a parallel concordance using open-source CSAR architecture developed by the Leeds team (Sharoff, 2006). The concordance will be generated by running queries to the sentence-aligned parallel corpora and will return lists of corresponding sentences from gold-standard human translations and corresponding sentences generated by MT. Each of these concordances will be automatically evaluated using standard MT evaluation metrics, such as BLEU. Under these settings parallel concordances will be used as standard MT evaluation corpora in an automated MT evaluation scenario.

Normally BLEU gives reliable results for MT corpora over 7000 words. However, in (Babych and Hartley, 2009; Babych and Hartley, 2008) we demonstrated that if the corpus is constructed in this controlled way, where evaluated fragments of sentences are selected as local contexts for specific multiword expressions or grammatical constructions, then BLEU scores have another "island of stability" for much smaller corpora, which now may consist of only five or more aligned concordance lines. This concordance-based evaluation scenario gives correct predictions of translation quality for the local context of each of the evaluated expressions.

The scores for the evaluated MWEs and constructions will be put in a risk-assessment framework, where we will balance the frequency of constructions and their translation quality. The top priority receive the most frequent expressions that are the most problematic ones for a particular MT engine, i.e., with queries with lowest BLEU scores for their concordances. This framework will allow MT developers to work down the priority list and correct or extend coverage for those constructions which will have the biggest impact on MT quality.

Step 10: Extend support for high-priority constructions semi-automatically by mining correct translations from parallel corpora

At this stage we will automate the procedure of correcting errors and extending coverage for problematic MWEs and grammatical constructions, identified in Step 9. For this we will exploit alignment between source-language sentences and gold-standard human translations. In the target human translations we will identify linguistically-motivated multiword expressions, e.g., using part-of-speech patterns or tf-idf distribution templates (Babych et al., 2007) and run standard alignment tools (e.g., GIZA++) for finding the most probable candidate MWEs that correspond to the problematic source-language expressions. Source and target MWEs paired in this way will form the basis for automatically-generated grammar rules. The rules will normally generalise several pairs of MWEs, and may be underspecified for certain lexical or morphological features. Later such rules will be manually checked and corrected by language specialists in MT development teams that work on specific translation directions.

This procedure will allow to speed up the grammar development procedure for large-scale MT projects and will focus on grammatical constructions with the highest impact on MT quality, establishing them as a top priority for MT developers. In HyghTra and with respect to the languages considered there, this procedure will be integrated into the grammar development and optimization of step 8, in particular it will be related to step 4 of the procedure sketched there. With regard to integration, we aim at an interleaved architecture in the long run.

Step 11: Bootstrap the system

In Step 11, the new grammar and the transfer of the new MT system and the new dictionary may be mutually trained further using the steps before and applying the system to additional corpora.

4 Results

Declarative slot grammars for Dutch and Spanish have been developed using the patterns of German and French – where *declarative* means that there has been used no relevant semantic or other information in order to spell out weighting or filters for rule application -- the only constraint being morphosyntactic accessibility. The necessary morphological information has been adapted similarly from the corresponding model languages.

The basic dictionaries have been compiled manually (Dutch) or extracted from a conventional electronic dictionary (*translateDict* Spanish).

For a subset of the Spanish corpus (reference sentences of the grammar, parts of the open source Leeds corpus (Sharoff, 2006), and Europarl), syntactic analyses have been computed and stored in the database. As the number of analyses grows extremely with the length of sentences, only relatively short sentences (up to 15 words) have been considered. These analyses are currently compared to the analyses of the German translations of the corresponding sentences (one translation per sentence), which are taken as a kind of 'gold' standard as the German analysis component (as part of the translation products) has proven to be sufficiently reliable. On the basis of the comparison a preference on the competitive analyses of the Spanish sentence is entailed and used for defining a statistical evaluation component for the Spanish grammar. Fig.3 shows the corresponding representations in the database for the sentence *Aumenta la demana de energía eléctrica por la ola de calor*[3] and its translation *die Nachfrage nach Strom steigt wegen der Hitzewelle/the demand for electricity increases because of the heat-wave.*

Fig.3 *Selection of analyses via correspondences (prefer first Spanish analysis because of* subj-*congruity)*

The analyses are associated with the corresponding creation protocols, which are structured lists whose items describe, via the identifiers, which rule has been applied when and to what structures in the process of creating the analysis. From the selection of a best analysis for a sentence, we can entail the circumstances under which the application of particular rules are preferred. This has been carried

[3] Sentence taken from the online newspaper *El Día de Concepción del Uruguay*

out - not yet for the 'new' language Spanish, but for the 'known' language German, in order to obtain a measure about how correctly the existing grammar evaluation component can be replaced by the results of the corresponding statistical study.

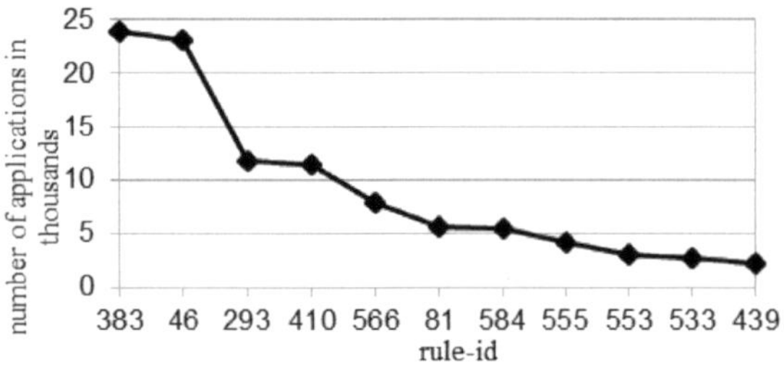

Fig.4 Frequency of applications of rules

cluster applications	similarity	feas mod	feas head
383, 384,..	0,86	sent, ...	emosentaffv,..
557,558,566,..	0,68	denselb,..	gebv, ...

Fig.5 Preliminary constraints related to grammar rule clusters

Fig.4 shows the distribution of rule usages within the training set of analyses (of approx.30.000 sentences). 390 different rules were used with a total of 133708 rule applications. The *subject* rule (383) and the noun determiner rule (46) the most used rules (35% of all applications). Fig 5. illustrates the preliminary results of a clustering algorithm where different rule applications are grouped into clusters and the key features of the head and modifier phrases for each cluster are extracted.

Currently, we try to determine further and tare the linguistic features and the weighting which models best the evaluation for German. (The gold standard that is used in this test is the set of analyses mentioned above). The investigations are not yet completed, but preliminary results on the basis of the morphosyntactic and semantic properties of the neighboring elements are promising. After consolidation, the findings will be transferred to Spanish on the basis of the selection procedure illustrated in Fig. 3. The next step of grammar training in the immediate future will consist of changing the focus to underspecified analyses as described in step 8

5 Conclusions

The project tries to make state-of-the-art statistical methods available for dictionary development and grammar development for a rule-based dominated industrial setting and to exploit such methods there.

With regard to SMT dictionary creation, it goes beyond the current state of the art as it also aims at developing and applying algorithms for the semi-automatic generation of bilingual dictionaries from unrelated monolingual (i.e., comparable) corpora of the source and the target language, instead of using relatively literally translated (i.e., parallel) texts only. Comparable corpora are far easier to obtain than parallel corpora. Therefore the approach offers a solution to the serious data acquisition bottleneck in SMT. This approach is also more cognitively plausible than previous suggestions on this topic, since human bilinguality is normally not based on memorizing parallel texts. Our suggestion models human capacity to translate texts using linguistic knowledge acquired from monolingual data, so it also exemplifies many more features of a truly self-learning MT system (shared also by a human translator).

In addition, the proposal suggests a new method for spelling out grammars and parsers for languages by splitting grammars into declarative kernels and trainable decision algorithms and by exploiting cross-linguistic knowledge for optimizing the results of the corresponding parsers.

For developing different components and dictionaries for the system a bootstrapping architecture is suggested that uses the acquired lexical information for training the grammar of the new language, which in turn uses the (underspecified) parser results for optimizing the lexical information in the corresponding translation dictionaries. We expect that the suggested methods significantly improve translation quality and reduce the costs of creating new language pairs for Machine Translation. The preliminary results obtained so far in the project appear promising.

6 Acknowledgments

This research is supported by a Marie Curie IAPP project taking place within the 7th European Community Framework Programme (Grant agreement no.: 251534)

7 References

Armstrong, S.; Kempen, M.; McKelvie, D.; Petitpierre, D.; Rapp, R.; Thompson, H. (1998). Multilingual Corpora for Cooperation. *Proceedings of the 1st International Conference on Linguistic Resources and Evaluation (LREC)*, Granada, Vol. 2, 975–980.

Babych, B., Hartley, A., Sharoff S.; Mudraya, O. (2007). Assisting Translators in Indirect Lexical Transfer. Proceedings of the 45th Annual Meeting of the ACL.

Babych, B., Anthony Hartley, & Serge Sharoff (2007b) Translating from under-resourced languages: comparing direct transfer against pivot translation. Proceedings of MT Summit XI, 10-14 September 2007, Copenhagen, Denmark, 29-35

Babych, B. & Hartley, A. (2008). Automated MT Evaluation for Error Analysis: Automatic Discovery of Potential Translation Errors for Multiword Expressions. ELRA Workshop on Evaluation "Looking into the Future of Evaluation: When automatic metrics meet task-based and performance-based approaches". Marrakech, Morocco 27 May 2008. *Proceedings of LREC'08.*

Babych, B. and Hartley, A. (2009). Automated error analysis for multiword expressions: using BLEU-type scores for automatic discovery of potential translation errors. Linguistica Antverpiensia, New Series (8/2009): Journal of translation and interpreting studies. Special Issue on Evaluation of Translation Technology.

Babych, B., Babych, S. and Eberle, K. (2012). Deriving generation-oriented MT resources from corpora: case study and evaluation of de/het classification for Dutch Noun (in preparation)

Baroni, M.; Bernardini, S. (2004). BootCaT: Bootstrapping corpora and terms from the web. Proceedings of LREC 2004.

Callison-Burch, C., Miles Osborne, & Philipp Koehn: Re-evaluating the role of BLEU in machine translation research. EACL-2006: 11th Conference of the European Chapter of the Association for Computational Linguistics, Trento, Italy, April 3-7, 2006; pp.249-256

Charniak, E.; Knight, K.; Yamada, K. (2003). Syntax-based language models for statistical machine translation". Proceedings of MT Summit IX.

Eberle, Kurt (2001). FUDR-based MT, head switching and the lexicon. *Proceedings of the the eighth Machine Translation Summit,* Santiage de Compostela.

Eberle, Kurt (2004). *Flat underspecified representation and its meaning for a fragment of German.* Habilitationsschrift, Universität Stuttgart.

Eberle, K.; Rapp, R. (2008). Rapid Construction of Explicative Dictionaries Using Hybrid Machine Translation. *In: Storrer, A.; Geyken, A.; Siebert, A.; Würzner, K._M (eds.) Text Resources and Lexical Knowledge: Selected Papers from the 9th Conference on Natural Language Processing KONVENS 2008. Berlin: Mouton de Gruyter..*

Eckart,K., Eberle, K.; Heid, U. (2010) An infrastructure for more reliable corpus analysis. *Proceedings of the Workshop on Web Services and Processing Pipelines in HLT of LREC-2010* , Valetta.

Eberle, K.; Eckart,K., Heid, U.,Haselbach, B. (2012) A tool/database interface for multi-level analyses. *Proceedings of LREC-2012* , Istanbul.

Frederking, R.; Nirenburg, S.; Farwell, D.; Helmreich, S.; Hovy, E.; Knight, K.; Beale, S.; Domashnev, C.; Attardo, D.; Grannes, D.; Brown, R. (1994). Integrated Translation from Multiple Sources within the Pangloss MARK II Machine Translation System. *Proceedings of Machine Translation of the Americas*, 73–80.

Frederking, Robert and Sergei Nirenburg (1994). Three heads are better than one. In: Proceedings of ANLP-94, Stuttgart, Germany.

Fung, P.; McKeown, K. (1997). Finding terminology translations from non-parallel corpora. *Proceedings of the 5th Annual Workshop on Very Large Corpora,* Hong Kong: August 1997, 192-202.

Gale, W.A.; Church, K.W. (1993). A progrm for aligning sentences in bilingual corpora. *Computational Linguistics,* 19(1), 75–102.

González, J.; Antonio L. Lagarda, José R. Navarro, Laura Eliodoro, Adrià Giménez, Francisco Casacuberta, Joan M. de Val and Ferran Fabregat (2004). SisHiTra: A Spanish-to-Catalan hybrid machine translation system. Berlin: Springer LNCS.

Gough, N., Way, A. (2004). Example-Based Controlled Translation. *Proceedings of the Ninth Workshop of the European Association for Machine Translation*, Valetta, Malta.

Groves, D. & Way, A. (2006b). Hybridity in MT: Experiments on the Europarl Corpus. In *Proceedings of the 11th Conference of the European Association for Machine Translation*, Oslo, Norway, 115–124.

Groves, D.; Way, A. (2006a). Hybrid data-driven models of machine translation. *Machine Translation,* 19(3–4). Special Issue on Example-Based Machine Translation. 301–323.

Habash, N.; Dorr, B. (2002). Handling translation divergences: Combining statistical and symbolic techniques in generation-heavy machine translation. *Proceedings of AMTA-2002,* Tiburon, California, USA.

Kiss, T.; Strunk, J. (2006): Unsupervised multilingual sentence boundary detection. Computational Linguistics 32(4), 485–525.

Koehn, P. (2005). Europarl: *A Parallel Corpus for Statistical Machine Translation.* Proceedings of MT Summit X, Phuket, Thailand

Koehn, P.; Knight, K. (2002). Learning a translation lexicon from monolingual corpora. In: *Proceedings of ACL-02 Workshop on Unsupervised Lexical Acquisition*, Philadelphia PA.

Language Industry Monitor (1992). Statistical methods gaining ground. In: *Language Industry Monitor*, September/October 1992 issue.

McCord, M. (1989). A new version of the machine translation system LMT. *Journal of Literary and Linguistic Computing, 4*, 218–299.

McCord, M. (1991). The slot grammar system. *In: Wedekind, J., Rohrer, C.(eds): Unification in Grammar,* MIT-Press.

Melamed, I. Dan (1999). Bitext maps and aligment via pattern recognition. *Computational Linguistics*, 25(1), 107–130.

Munteanu, D.S.; Marcu, D. (2005). Improving machine translation performance by exploiting non-parallel corpora. *Computational Linguistics*, 31(4), 477–504.

Och, F.J.; Ney, H. (2002). Discriminative trainig and maximum entropy models for statistical machine translation. Proceedings *of the Annual Meeting of the Association for Computational Linguistics*, Philadelphia, PA, 295–302.

Och, F.J.; Ney, H. (2003). A systematic comparison of various statistical alignment models. *Computational Linguistics,* 29(1), 19–51.

Papineni, K.; Roukos, S.; Ward, T.; Zhu, W. (2002). BLEU: A method for automatic evaluation of machine translation. In: *Proceedings of the 40th Annual Meeting of the ACL*, Philadelphia, PA, 311–318.

Rapp, R. (1995). Identifying word translations in non-parallel texts. In: *Proceedings of the 33rd Meeting of the Association for Computational Linguistics.* Cambridge, MA, 1995, 320–322

Rapp, R. (1999). Automatic identification of word translations from unrelated English and German corpora. In: *Proceedings of the 37th Annual Meeting of the Association for Computational Linguistics 1999, College Park, Maryland. 519–526.*

Rapp, R. (2004). A freely available automatically generated thesaurus of related words. In: *Proceedings of the Fourth International Conference on Language Resources and Evaluation (LREC)*, Lisbon, Vol. II, 395–398.

Rapp, R.; Martin Vide, C. (2007). Statistical machine translation without parallel corpora. In: Georg Rehm, Andreas Witt, Lothar Lemnitzer (eds.): *Data Structures for Linguistic Resources and Applications. Proceedings of the Biennial GLDV Conference 2007.* Tübingen: Gunter Narr. 231–240

Resnik, R. (1999). Mining the web for bilingual text. Proceedings of the 37th Annual Meeting of the Association for Computational Linguistics.

Sato, S.; Nagao, M. (1990). Toward memory-based translation. *Proceedings of COLING 1990*, 247–252.

Schiehlen, M. (2001) Syntactic Underspecification. In: Special Research Area 340 – Final report, University of Stuttgart.

Sharoff, S. (2006) Open-source corpora: using the net to fish for linguistic data. In International Journal of Corpus Linguistics 11(4), 435–462.

Sharoff, S.; Babych, B.; Hartley, A. (2006). Using comparable corpora to solve problems difficult for human translators. In: Proceedings of COLING/ACL 2006, 739–746.

Sharoff, S. (2006). A uniform interface to large-scale linguistic resources. In Proceedings of the Fifth Language Resources and Evaluation Conference, LREC-2006, Genoa.

Simard, M., Foster, G., Isabelle, P. (1992). Using Cognates to Align Sentences in Bilingual Corpora. P*roceeedings of the International Conference on Theoretical and Methodological Issues*, Montréal.

Smadja, F. (1993). Retrieving collocations from text: Xtract. *Computational Linguistics*, 19(1), 143–177.

Streiter, O., Carl, M., Haller, J. (eds)(1999). *Hybrid Approaches to Machine Translation.* IAI working papers 36.

Streiter, O.; Carl, M.; Iomdin, L.L.: 2000, A Virtual Translation Machine for Hybrid Machine Translation'. In: *Proceedings of the Dialogue'2000 International Seminar in Computational Linguistics and Applications*. Tarusa, Russia.

Streiter, O.; Iomdin, L.L. (2000). Learning Lessons from Bilingual Corpora: Benefits for Machine Translation. International Journal of Corpus Linguistics, 5(2), 199–230.

Thurmair, G. (2005). Hybrid architectures for machine translation systems. *Language Resources and Evaluation,* 39 (1), 91–108.

Thurmair, G. (2006). Using corpus information to improve MT quality. *Proceedings of the LR4Trans-III Workshop*, LREC, Genova.

Thurmair, G. (2007) Automatic evaluation in MT system production. MT Summit XI Workshop: Automatic procedures in MT evaluation, 11 September 2007, Copenhagen, Denmark,

Veronis, Jean (2006). *Technologies du Langue. Actualités – Comentaires – Réflexions. Translation. Systran or Reverso?* http://aixtal.blogspot.com/2006/01/translation-systran-or-reverso.html

Wu, D., Fung, P. (2005). Inversion transduction grammar constraints for mining parallel sentences from quasi-comparable corpora. *Second International Joint Conference on Natural Language Processing (IJCNLP-2005).* Jeju, Korea.

Can Machine Learning Algorithms Improve Phrase Selection in Hybrid Machine Translation?

Christian Federmann
Language Technology Lab
German Research Center for Artificial Intelligence
Stuhlsatzenhausweg 3, D-66123 Saarbrücken, GERMANY
cfedermann@dfki.de

Abstract

We describe a substitution-based, hybrid machine translation (MT) system that has been extended with a machine learning component controlling its phrase selection. Our approach is based on a rule-based MT (RBMT) system which creates template translations. Based on the generation parse tree of the RBMT system and standard word alignment computation, we identify potential "translation snippets" from one or more translation engines which could be substituted into our translation templates. The substitution process is controlled by a binary classifier trained on feature vectors from the different MT engines. Using a set of manually annotated training data, we are able to observe improvements in terms of BLEU scores over a baseline version of the hybrid system.

1 Introduction

In recent years, the overall quality of machine translation output has improved greatly. Still, each technological paradigm seems to suffer from its own particular kinds of errors: statistical MT (SMT) engines often show poor syntax, while rule-based MT systems suffer from missing data in their vocabularies. Hybrid approaches try to overcome these typical errors by combining techniques from both (or even more) paradigms in an optimal manner.

In this paper we report on experiments with an extended version of the hybrid system we develop in our group (Federmann and Hunsicker, 2011; Federmann et al., 2010). We take the output from an RBMT engine as "translation template" for our hybrid translations and substitute noun phrases[1] by translations from one or several MT engines[2]. Even though a general increase in quality could be observed in previous work, our system introduced errors of its own during the substitution process. In an internal error analysis, these degradations could be classified in the following way:

- external translations were incorrect;
- the structure degraded through substitution;
- phrase substitution failed.

Errors of the first class cannot be corrected, as we do not have an easy way of knowing when the translation obtained from an external MT engine is incorrect. The other classes could, however, be eliminated by introducing additional steps for pre- and post-processing as well as by improving the hybrid substitution algorithm itself. So far, our algorithm relied on many, hand-crafted decision factors; in order to improve translation quality and processing speed, we decided to apply machine learning methods to our training data to train a linear classifier which could be used instead.

This paper is structured in the following way. After having introduced the topics of our work in Section 1, we give a description of our hybrid MT system architecture in Section 2. Afterwards we describe in detail the various decision factors we

[1]We are focusing on noun phrases for the moment as these worked best in previous experiments with substitution-based MT; likely because they usually form consecutive spans in the translation output.

[2]While this could be SMT systems only, our approach supports engines from all MT paradigms. If not all features inside our feature vectors can be filled using the output of some system X, we use defaults as fallback values.

Proceedings of the 13th Conference of the European Chapter of the Association for Computational Linguistics, pages 113–118, Avignon, France, April 23 - 27 2012.

have defined and how these could be used in feature vectors for machine learning methods in Section 3. Our experiments with the classifier-based, hybrid MT system are reported in Section 4. We conclude by giving a summary of our work and then provide an outlook to related future work in Section 5.

2 Architecture

Our hybrid machine translation system combines translation output from:

a) the Lucy RBMT system, described in more detail in (Alonso and Thurmair, 2003), and

b) one or several other MT systems, e.g. Moses (Koehn et al., 2007), or Joshua (Li et al., 2009).

The rule-based component of our hybrid system is described in more detail in section 2.2 while we provide more detailed information on the "other" systems in section 2.3.

2.1 Basic Approach

We first identify noun phrases inside the rule-based translation and compute the most probable correspondences in the translation output from the other systems. For the resulting phrases, we apply a factored substitution method that decides whether the original RBMT phrase should be kept or rather be replaced by one of the candidate phrases. As this shallow substitution process may introduce errors at phrase boundaries, we perform several post-processing steps that clean up and finalise the hybrid translation result. A schematic overview of our hybrid system and its main components is given in figure 1.

2.2 Rule-Based Translation Templates

We obtain the "translation template" as well as any linguistic structures from the RBMT system. Previous work with these structures had shown that they are usually of a high quality, supporting our initial decision to consider the RBMT output as template for our hybrid translation approach. The Lucy translation output can include markup that allows to identify unknown words or other phenomena.

The Lucy system is a transfer-based RBMT system that performs translation in three phases, namely *analysis*, *transfer*, and *generation*. Tree structures for each of the translation phases can be extracted from the Lucy system to guide the hybrid system. Only the 1-best path through the three phases is given, so no alternative translation possibilities can be extracted from the given data; a fact that clearly limits the potential for more deeply integrated hybrid translation approaches. Nonetheless, the availability of these 1-best trees already allowed us to improve the translation quality of the RBMT system as we had shown in previous work.

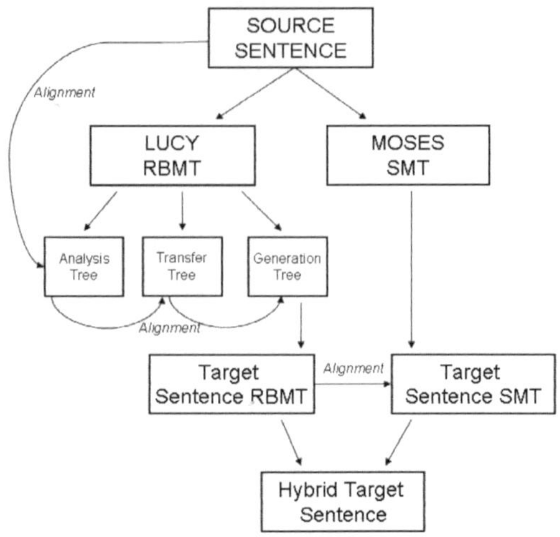

Figure 1: Schematic overview of the architecture of our substitution-based, hybrid MT system.

2.3 Substitution Candidate Translations

We use state-of-the-art SMT systems to create statistical, phrase-based translations of our input text, together with the bidirectional word alignments between the source texts and the translations. Again, we make use of markup which helps to identify unknown words as this will later be useful in the factored substitution method.

Translation models for our SMT systems were trained with lower-cased and tokenised Europarl (Koehn, 2005) training data. We used the LDC Gigaword corpus to train large scale language models and tokenised the source texts using the tokenisers available from the WMT shared task website[3]. All translations are re-cased before they are sent to the hybrid system together with the word alignment information.

[3]Available at `http://www.statmt.org/wmt12/`

The hybrid MT system can easily be adapted to support other translation engines. If there is no alignment information available directly, a word alignment tool is needed as the alignment is a key requirement for the hybrid system. For part-of-speech tagging and lemmatisation we used the TreeTagger (Schmid, 1994).

2.4 Aligning RBMT and SMT Output

We compute alignment in several components of the hybrid system, namely:

source-text-to-tree: we first find an alignment between the source text and the corresponding analysis tree. As Lucy tends to subdivide large sentences into several smaller units, it sometimes becomes necessary to align more than one tree structure to a source sentence.

analysis-transfer-generation: for each of the analysis trees, we re-construct the path from its tree nodes, via the transfer tree, to the corresponding generation tree nodes.

tree-to-target-text: similarly to the first alignment process, we find a connection between generation tree nodes and the corresponding translation output of the RBMT system.

source-text-to-tokenised: as the Lucy RBMT system works on non-tokenised input text and our SMT systems take tokenised input, we need to align the original source text with its tokenised form.

Given the aforementioned alignments, we can then correlate phrases from the rule-based translation with their counterparts from the statistical translations, both on source or target side. As our hybrid approach relies on the identification of such phrase pairs, the computation of the different alignments is critical to achieve a good system combination quality.

All tree-based alignments can be computed with a very high accuracy. However, due to the nature of statistical word alignment, the same does not hold for the alignment obtained from the SMT systems. If the alignment process produces erroneous phrase tables, it is very likely that Lucy phrases and their "aligned" SMT matches simply do not fit the "open slot" inside the translation template. Or put the other way round: the better the underlying SMT word alignment, the greater the potential of the hybrid substitution approach.

2.5 Factored Substitution

Given the results of the alignment process, we can then identify "interesting" phrases for substitution. Following our experimental setup from the WMT10 shared task, we again decided to focus on *noun phrases* as these seem to be best-suited for in-place swapping of phrases.

To avoid errors or problems with non-matching insertions, we want to keep some control on the substitution process. As the substitution process proved to be a very difficult task during previous experiments with the hybrid system, we decided to use machine learning methods instead. For this, we refined our previously defined set of decision factors into values $v \in \mathbb{R}$ which allows to combine them in feature vectors $x_i = v_1 \dots v_p$. We describe the integration of the linear classifier in more detail in Section 3.

2.6 Decision Factors

We used the following factors:

1. **frequency:** frequency of a given candidate phrase compared to total number of candidates for the current phrase;
2. **LM(phrase):** language model (LM) score of the phrase;
3. **LM(phrase)+1:** phrase with right-context;
4. **LM(phrase)-1:** phrase with left-context;
5. **Part-of-speech match?:** checks if the part-of-speech tags of the left/right context match the current candidate phrase's context;
6. **LM(pos)** LM score for part-of-speech (PoS);
7. **LM(pos)+1** PoS with right-context;
8. **LM(pos)-1** PoS with left-context;
9. **Lemma** checks if the lemma of the candidate phrase fits the reference;
10. **LM(lemma)** LM score for the lemma;
11. **LM(lemma)+1** lemma with right-context;
12. **LM(lemma)-1** lemma with left-context.

2.7 Post-processing Steps

After the hybrid translation has been computed, we perform several post-processing steps to clean up and finalise the result:

cleanup first, we perform some basic cleanup such as whitespace normalisation;

multi-words then, we take care of multi-word expressions. Using the tree structures from the RBMT system we remove superfluous whitespace and join multi-words, even if they were separated in the substituted phrase;

prepositions finally, prepositions are checked as experience from previous work had shown that these contributed to a large extent to the amount of avoidable errors.

3 Machine Learning-based Selection

Instead of using hand-crafted decision rules in the substitution process, we aim to train a classifier on a set of annotated training examples which may be better able to extract useful information from the various decision factors.

3.1 Formal Representation

Our training set D can be represented formally as

$$D = \{(x_i, y_i) | x_i \in \mathbb{R}^p, y_i \in \{-1, 1\}\}_{i=1}^{n} \quad (1)$$

where each x_i represents the *feature vector* for sentence i while the y_i value contains the annotated class information. We use a binary classification scheme, simply defining 1 as "good" and -1 as "bad" translations. In order to make use of machine learning methods such as decision trees (Breiman et al., 1984), SVMs (Vapnik, 1995), or the Perceptron (Rosenblatt, 1958) algorithm, we have to prepare our training set with a sufficiently large number of annotated training instances. We give further details on the creation of an annotated training set in section 4.1.

3.2 Creating Hybrid Translations

Using suitable training data, we can train a *binary classifier* (using either a decision tree, an SVM, or the Perceptron algorithm) that can be used in our hybrid combination algorithm.

The *pseudo-code* in Algorithm 1 illustrates how such a classifier can be used in our hybrid MT decoder.

Algorithm 1 Decoding using linear classifier

$good\_candidates \leftarrow []$
for all substitution candidates C_i **do**
    if CLASSIFY(C_i) == "good" **then**
        $good\_candidates \leftarrow C_i$
    end if
end for
$C_{best} \leftarrow$ SELECT-BEST($good\_candidates$)
SUBSTITUTE-IN(C_{best})

We first collect all "good" translations using the `CLASSIFY()` operation, then choose the "best" candidate for substitution with `SELECT-BEST()`, and finally integrate the resulting candidate phrase into the generated translation using `SUBSTITUTE-IN()`. `SELECT-BEST()` could use system-specific confidences obtained during the tuning phase of our hybrid system. We are still experimenting on its exact definition.

4 Experiments

In order to obtain initial experimental results, we created a decision-tree-based variant of our hybrid MT system. We implemented a decision tree learning module following the CART algorithm (Breiman et al., 1984). We opted for this solution as decision trees represent a straightforward first step when it comes to integrating machine learning into our hybrid system.

4.1 Generating Training Data

For this, we first created an annotated data set. In a nutshell, we computed feature vectors and potential substitution candidates for all noun phrases in our training data[4] and then collected data from human annotators which of the substitution candidates were "good" translations and which should rather be considered "bad" examples. We used Appraise (Federmann, 2010) for the annotation, and collected 24,996 labeled training instances with the help of six human annotators. Table 1 gives an overview of the data sets characteristics.

	Translation Candidates		
	Total	"good"	"bad"
Count	24,996	10,666	14,330

Table 1: Training data set characteristics

[4]We used the WMT12 "newstest2011" development set as training data for the annotation task.

	Hybrid Systems		Baseline Systems			
	Baseline	+Decision Tree	Lucy	Linguatec	Moses	Joshua
BLEU	13.9	14.2	14.0	14.7	14.6	15.9
BLEU-cased	13.5	13.8	13.7	14.2	13.5	14.9
TER	0.776	0.773	0.774	0.775	0.772	0.774

Table 2: Experimental results comparing baseline hybrid system using hand-crafted decision rules to a decision-tree-based variant; both applied to the WMT12 "newstest2012" test set data for language pair English→German.

4.2 Experimental Results

Using the annotated data set, we then trained a decision tree and integrated it into our hybrid system. To evaluate translation quality, we created translations of the WMT12 "newstest2012" test set, for the language pair English→German, with a) a baseline hybrid system using hand-crafted decision rules and b) an extended version of our hybrid system using the decision tree.

Both hybrid systems relied on a Lucy translation template and were given additional translation candidates from another rule-based system (Aleksic and Thurmair, 2011), a statistical system based on the Moses decoder, and a statistical system based on Joshua. If more than one "good" translation was found, we used the hand-crafted rules to determine the single, winning translation candidate (implementing SELECT-BEST in the simplest, possible way).

Table 2 shows results for our two hybrid system variants as well as for the individual baseline systems. We report results from automatic BLEU (Papineni et al., 2001) scoring and also from its case-sensitive variant, BLEU-cased.

4.3 Discussion of Results

We can observe improvements in both BLEU and BLEU-cased scores when comparing the decision-tree-based hybrid system to the baseline version relying on hand-crafted decision rules. This shows that the extension of the hybrid system with a learnt classifier can result in improved translation quality.

On the other hand, it is also obvious, that the improved hybrid system was not able to outperform the scores of some of the individual baseline systems; there is additional research required to investigate in more detail how the hybrid approach can be improved further.

5 Conclusion and Outlook

In this paper, we reported on experiments aiming to improve the phrase selection component of a hybrid MT system using machine learning. We described the architecture of our hybrid machine translation system and its main components.

We explained how to train a decision tree based on feature vectors that emulate previously used, hand-crafted decision factors. To obtain training data for the classifier, we manually annotated a set of 24,996 feature vectors and compared the decision-tree-based, hybrid system to a baseline version. We observed improved BLEU scores for the language pair English→German on the WMT12 "newstest2012" test set.

Future work will include experiments with other machine learning classifiers such as SVMs. It will also be interesting to investigate what other features can be useful for training. Also, we intend to experiment with heterogeneous feature sets for the different source systems (resulting in large but sparse feature vectors), adding system-specific annotations from the various systems and will investigate their performance in the context of hybrid MT systems.

Acknowledgments

This work has been funded under the Seventh Framework Programme for Research and Technological Development of the European Commission through the T4ME contract (grant agreement no.: 249119). The author would like to thank Sabine Hunsicker and Yu Chen for their support in creating the WMT12 translations, and is indebted to Hervé Saint-Amand for providing help with the automated metrics scores. Also, we are grateful to the anonymous reviewers for their valuable feedback and comments.

References

Vera Aleksic and Gregor Thurmair. 2011. Personal translator at wmt2011. In *Proceedings of the Sixth Workshop on Statistical Machine Translation*, pages 303–308, Edinburgh, Scotland, July. Association for Computational Linguistics.

Juan A. Alonso and Gregor Thurmair. 2003. The Comprendium Translator system. In *Proceedings of the Ninth Machine Translation Summit*, New Orleans, USA.

L. Breiman, J. Friedman, R. Olshen, and C. Stone. 1984. *Classification and Regression Trees*. Wadsworth and Brooks, Monterey, CA.

Christian Federmann and Sabine Hunsicker. 2011. Stochastic parse tree selection for an existing rbmt system. In *Proceedings of the Sixth Workshop on Statistical Machine Translation*, pages 351–357, Edinburgh, Scotland, July. Association for Computational Linguistics.

Christian Federmann, Andreas Eisele, Yu Chen, Sabine Hunsicker, Jia Xu, and Hans Uszkoreit. 2010. Further experiments with shallow hybrid mt systems. In *Proceedings of the Joint Fifth Workshop on Statistical Machine Translation and MetricsMATR*, pages 77–81, Uppsala, Sweden, July. Association for Computational Linguistics.

Christian Federmann. 2010. Appraise: An open-source toolkit for manual phrase-based evaluation of translations. In Nicoletta Calzolari (Conference Chair), Khalid Choukri, Bente Maegaard, Joseph Mariani, Jan Odijk, Stelios Piperidis, Mike Rosner, and Daniel Tapias, editors, *Proceedings of the Seventh International Conference on Language Resources and Evaluation (LREC'10)*, Valletta, Malta, may. European Language Resources Association (ELRA).

Philipp Koehn, Hieu Hoang, Alexandra Birch, Chris Callison-Burch, Marcello Federico, Nicola Bertoldi, Brooke Cowan, Wade Shen, Christine Moran, Richard Zens, Chris Dyer, Ondrej Bojar, Alexandra Constantin, and Evan Herbst. 2007. Moses: Open source toolkit for statistical machine translation. In *Proc. of ACL Demo and Poster Sessions*, pages 177–180, Jun.

Philipp Koehn. 2005. Europarl: A parallel corpus for statistical machine translation. In *Proceedings of the MT Summit 2005*.

Zhifei Li, Chris Callison-Burch, Chris Dyer, Sanjeev Khudanpur, Lane Schwartz, Wren Thornton, Jonathan Weese, and Omar Zaidan. 2009. Joshua: An open source toolkit for parsing-based machine translation. In *Proceedings of the Fourth Workshop on Statistical Machine Translation*, pages 135–139, Athens, Greece, March. Association for Computational Linguistics.

Kishore Papineni, Salim Roukos, Todd Ward, and Wei-Jing Zhu. 2001. Bleu: a method for automatic evaluation of machine translation. IBM Research Report RC22176(W0109-022), IBM.

F. Rosenblatt. 1958. The Perceptron: A probabilistic model for information storage and organization in the brain. *Psychological Review*, 65:386–408.

Helmut Schmid. 1994. Probabilistic part-of-speech tagging using decision trees. In *Proceedings of the International Conference on New Methods in Language Processing*, Manchester, UK.

Toby Segaran. 2007. *Programming Collective Intelligence: Building Smart Web 2.0 Applications*. O'Reilly, Beijing.

V. N. Vapnik. 1995. *The nature of statistical learning theory*. Springer, New York.

Linguistically-Augmented Bulgarian-to-English Statistical Machine Translation Model

Rui Wang
Language Technology Lab
DFKI GmbH
Saarbrücken, Germany
ruiwang@dfki.de

Petya Osenova and Kiril Simov
Linguistic Modelling Department, IICT
Bulgarian Academy of Sciences
Sofia, Bulgaria
{petya,kivs}@bultreebank.org

Abstract

In this paper, we present our linguistically-augmented statistical machine translation model from Bulgarian to English, which combines a statistical machine translation (SMT) system (as backbone) with deep linguistic features (as factors). The motivation is to take advantages of the robustness of the SMT system and the linguistic knowledge of morphological analysis and the hand-crafted grammar through system combination approach. The preliminary evaluation has shown very promising results in terms of BLEU scores (38.85) and the manual analysis also confirms the high quality of the translation the system delivers.

1 Introduction

In the recent years, machine translation (MT) has achieved significant improvement in terms of translation quality (Koehn, 2010). Both data-driven approaches (e.g., statistical MT (SMT)) and knowledge-based (e.g., rule-based MT (RBMT)) have achieved comparable results shown in the evaluation campaigns (Callison-Burch et al., 2011). However, according to the human evaluation, the final outputs of the MT systems are still far from satisfactory.

Fortunately, recent error analysis shows that the two trends of the MT approaches tend to be complementary to each other, in terms of the types of the errors they made (Thurmair, 2005; Chen et al., 2009). Roughly speaking, RBMT systems often have missing lexicon and thus lack of robustness, while handling linguistic phenomena requiring syntactic information better. SMT systems, on the contrary, are in general more robust, but sometimes output ungrammatical sentences.

In fact, instead of competing with each other, there is also a line of research trying to combine the advantages of the two sides using a hybrid framework. Although many systems can be put under the umbrella of "hybrid" systems, there are various ways to do the combination/integration. Thurmair (2009) summarized several different architectures of hybrid systems using SMT and RBMT systems. Some widely used ones are: 1) using an SMT to post-edit the outputs of an RBMT; 2) selecting the best translations from several hypotheses coming from different SMT/RBMT systems; and 3) selecting the best segments (phrases or words) from different hypotheses.

For the language pair Bulgarian-English, there has not been much study on it, mainly due to the lack of resources, including corpora, preprocessors, etc. There was a system published by Koehn et al. (2009), which was trained and tested on the European Union law data, but not on other domains like news. They reported a very high BLEU score (Papineni et al., 2002) on the Bulgarian-English translation direction (61.3), which inspired us to further investigate this direction.

In this paper, we focus on the Bulgarian-to-English translation and mainly explore the approach of annotating the SMT baseline with linguistic features derived from the preprocessing and hand-crafted grammars. There are three motivations behind our approach: 1) the SMT baseline trained on a decent amount of parallel corpora outputs surprisingly good results, in terms of both statistical evaluation metrics and preliminary manual evaluation; 2) the augmented model gives

Proceedings of the 13th Conference of the European Chapter of the Association for Computational Linguistics, pages 119–128,
Avignon, France, April 23 - 27 2012.

us more space for experimenting with different linguistic features without losing the 'basic' robustness; 3) the MT system can profit from continued advances in the development of the deep grammars thereby opening up further integration possibilities.

The rest of the paper will be organized as follows: Section 2 presents our work on cleaning the corpora and Section 3 briefly describes the preprocessing of the data. Section 4 introduces our factor-based SMT model which allows us to incorporate various linguistic features into an SMT baseline, among which those features coming from the MRS are described in Section 5 in detail. We show our experiments in Section 6 as well as both automatic and manual evaluation of the results. Section 7 briefly mentions some related work and then we summarize this paper in Section 8.

2 Data Preparation

In our experiments we are using the SETIMES parallel corpus, which is part of the OPUS parallel corpus[1]. The data in the corpus was aligned automatically. Thus, we first checked the consistency of the automatic alignments. It turned out that more than 25% of the sentence alignments were not correct. Since SETIMES appeared to be a noisy dataset, our effort was directed into cleaning it as much as possible before the start of the experiments. We first corrected manually more than 25.000 sentence alignments. The the rest of the data set includes around 135,000 sentences. Altogether the data set is about 160,000 sentences, when the manually checked part is added. Thus, two actions were taken:

1. **Improving the tokenization of the Bulgarian part**. The observations from the manual check of the set of 25,000 sentences showed systematic errors in the tokenized text. Hence, these cases have been detected and fixed semi-automatically.

2. **Correcting and removing the suspicious alignments**. Initially, the ratio of the lengths of the English and Bulgarian sentences was calculated in the set of the 25,000 manually annotated sentences. As a rule, the Bulgarian sentences are longer than the English ones. The ratio is 1.34. Then we calculated the ratio for each pair of sentences. After this, the optimal interval was manually determined, such that if the ratio for a given pair of sentences is within the interval, then we assume that the pair is a good one. The interval for these experiments is set to [0.7; 1.8]. All the pairs with ratio outside of the interval have been deleted. Similarly, we have cleaned EMEA dataset.

The size of the resulting datasets are: 151,718 sentence pairs for the SETIMES dataset. Similar approach was undertaken for another dataset from OPUS corpus - EMEA. After the cleaning 704,631 sentence pairs were selected from the EMEA dataset. Thus, the size of the original datasets was decreased by 10%.

3 Linguistic Preprocessing

The data in SETIMES dataset was analysed on the following levels:

- **POS tagging.** POS tagging is performed by a pipe of several modules. First we apply SVM POS tagger which takes as an input a tokenised text and its output is a tagged text. The performance is near 91% accuracy. The SVM POS tagger is implemented using SVMTool (Gimnez and Mrquez, 2004). Then we apply a morphological lexicon and a set of rules. The lexicon add all the possible tags for the known words. The rules reduce the ambiguity for some of the sure cases. The result of this step is a tagged text with some ambiguities unresolved. The third step is application of the GTagger (Georgiev et al., 2012). It is trained on an ambiguous data and select the most appropriate tags from the suggested ones. The accuracy of the whole pipeline is 97.83%. In this pipeline SVM POS Tagger plays the role of guesser for the GTagger.

- **Lemmatization.** The lemmatization module is based on the same morphological lexicon. From the lexicon we extracted functions which convert each wordform into its basic form (as a representative of the lemma). The functions are defined via two operations on

[1] OPUS–an open source parallel corpus, http://opus.lingfil.uu.se/

wordforms: remove and concatenate. The rules have the following form:

if **tag** = **Tag** *then* {*remove* **OldEnd**; *concatenate* **NewEnd**}

where **Tag** is the tag of the wordform, **OldEnd** is the string which has to be removed from the end of the wordform and **NewEnd** is the string which has to be concatenated to the beginning of the word form in order to produce the lemma. The rules are for word forms in the lexicon. Less than 2% of the wordforms are ambiguous in the lexicon (but they are very rare in real texts). Similar rules are defined for unknown words. The accuracy of the lemmatizer is 95.23%.

- **Dependency parsing.** We have trained the MALT Parser on the dependency version of BulTreeBank[2]. We did this work together with Svetoslav Marinov who has experience in using the MALT Parser and Johan Hall who is involved in thedevelopment of Malt Parser. The trained model achieves 85.6% labeled parsing accuracy. It is integrated in a language pipe with the POS tagger and the lemmatizer.

After the application of the language pipeline, the result is represented in a table form following the CoNLL shared task format[3].

4 Factor-based SMT Model

Our approach is built on top of the factor-based SMT model proposed by Koehn and Hoang (2007), as an extension of the traditional phrase-based SMT framework. Instead of using only the word form of the text, it allows the system to take a vector of factors to represent each token, both for the source and target languages. The vector of factors can be used for different levels of linguistic annotations, like lemma, part-of-speech (POS), or other linguistic features. Furthermore, this extension actually allows us to incorporate various kinds of features if they can be (somehow) represented as annotations to the tokens.

The process is quite similar to supertagging (Bangalore and Joshi, 1999), which assigns "rich descriptions (supertags) that impose complex constraints in a local context". In our case, all the linguistic features (factors) associated with each token form a supertag to that token. Singh and Bandyopadhyay (2010) had a similar idea of incorporating linguistic features, while they worked on Manipuri-English bidirectional translation. Our approach is slightly different from (Birch et al., 2007) and (Hassan et al., 2007), who mainly used the supertags on the target language side, English. We primarily experiment with the source language side, Bulgarian. This potentially huge feature space provides us with various possibilities of using our linguistic resources developed in and out of our project.

In particular, we consider the following factors on the source language side (Bulgarian):

- WF - word form is just the original text token.
- LEMMA is the lexical invariant of the original word form. We use the lemmatizer described in Section 3, which operates on the output from the POS tagging. Thus, the 3rd person, plural, imperfect tense verb form 'varvyaha' ('walking-were', They were walking) is lemmatized as the 1st person, present tense verb 'varvya'.
- POS - part-of-speech of the word. We use the positional POS tag set of the BulTreeBank, where the first letter of the tag indicates the POS itself, while the next letters refer to semantic and/or morphosyntactic features, such as: Dm - where 'D' stands for 'adverb', and 'm' stand for 'modal'; Ncmsi - where 'N' stand for 'noun', 'c' means 'common', 'm' is 'masculine', 's' is 'singular',and 'i' is 'indefinite'.
- LING - other linguistic features derived from the POS tag in the BulTreeBank tagset (see above).

In addition to these, we can also incorporate syntactic structure of the sentence by breaking down the tree into dependency relations. For instance, a dependency tree can be represented as a set of triples in the form of <parent, relation, child>. <loves, subject, John> and <loves, object, Mary> will represent the sentence "John loves Mary". Consequently, three additional factors are included for both languages:

[2] http://www.bultreebank.org/dpbtb/

[3] http://ufal.mff.cuni.cz/conll2009-st/task-description.html

- DEPREL - is the dependency relation between the current word and the parent node.

- HLEMMA is the lemma of the current word's parent node.

- HPOS is the POS tag of the current word's parent node.

Here is an example of a processed sentence. The sentence is "spored odita v elektricheskite kompanii politicite zloupotrebyavat s dyrzhavnite predpriyatiya." The glosses for the words in the Bulgarian sentence are: spored (*according*) odita (*audit-the*) v (*in*) elektricheskite (*electrical-the*) kompanii (*companies*) politicite (*politicians-the*) zloupotrebyavat (*abuse*) s (*with*) dyrzhavnite (*state-the*) predpriyatiya (*enterprises*). The translation in the original source is : "electricity audits prove politicians abusing public companies." The result from the linguistic processing and the addition of information about head elements are presented in the first seven columns of Table 1.

We extend the grammatical features to have the same size. All the information is concatenated to the word forms in the text. In the next section we present how we extend this format to incorporate the MRS analysis. In the next section we will extend this example to incorporate the MRS analysis of the sentence.

5 MRS Supertagging

Our work on Minimal Recursion Semantic analysis of Bulgarian text is inspired by the work on MRS and RMRS (Robust Minimal Recursion Semantic) (see (Copestake, 2003) and (Copestake, 2007)) and the previous work on transfer of dependency analyses into RMRS structures described in (Spreyer and Frank, 2005) and (Jakob et al., 2010). In this section we present first a short overview of MRS and RMRS. Then we discuss the new features added on the basis of the RMRS structures.

MRS is introduced as an underspecified semantic formalism (Copestake et al., 2005). It is used to support semantic analyses in the English HPSG grammar ERG (Copestake and Flickinger, 2000), but also in other grammar formalisms like LFG. The main idea is that the formalism avoids spelling out the complete set of readings resulting from the interaction of scope bearing operators and quantifiers, instead providing a single underspecified representation from which the complete set of readings can be constructed. Here we will present only basic definitions from (Copestake et al., 2005). For more details the cited publication should be consulted. An MRS structure is a tuple $\langle\ GT,\ R,\ C\ \rangle$, where GT is the top handle, R is a bag of EPs (elementary predicates) and C is a bag of handle constraints, such that there is no handle h that outscopes GT. Each elementary predication contains exactly four components: (1) a handle which is the label of the EP; (2) a relation; (3) a list of zero or more ordinary variable arguments of the relation; and (4) a list of zero or more handles corresponding to scopal arguments of the relation (i.e., holes). RMRS is introduced as a modification of MRS which to capture the semantics resulting from the shallow analysis. Here the following assumption is taken into account the shallow processor does not have access to a lexicon. Thus it does not have access to arity of the relations in EPs. Therefore, the representation has to be underspecified with respect to the number of arguments of the relations. The names of relations are constructed on the basis of the lemma for each wordform in the text and the main argument for the relation is specified. This main argument could be of two types: *referential index* for nouns and *event* for the other part of speeches.

Because in this work we are using only the RMRS relation and the type of the main argument as features to the translation model, we will skip here the explanation of the full structure of RMRS structures and how they are constructed. Thus, we firstly do a match between the surface tokens and the MRS elementary predicates (EPs) and then extract the following features as extra factors:

- EP - the name of the elementary predicate, which usually indicates an event or an entity semantically.

- EOV indicates the current EP is either an event or a reference variable.

Notice that we do not take all the information provided by the MRS, e.g., we throw away the scopal information and the other arguments of the relations. This kind of information is not straightforward to be represented in such 'tagging'-style models, which will be tackled in the future.

This information for the example sentence is

WF	Lemma	POSex	Ling	DepRel	HLemma	HPOS	EP	EoV
spored	spored	R	_	adjunct	zloupotrebyavam	VP	spored_r	e
odita	odit	Nc	npd	prepcomp	spored	R	odit_n	v
v	v	R	_	mod	odit	Nc	v_r	e
elektricheskite	elektricheski	A	pd	mod	kompaniya	Nc	elekticheski_a	e
kompanii	kompaniya	Nc	fpi	prepcomp	v	R	kompaniya_n	v
politicite	politik	Nc	mpd	subj	zloupotrebyavam	Vp	politik_n	v
zloupotrebyavat	zloupotrebyavam	Vp	tir3p	root	-	-	zloupotrebyavam_v	e
s	s	R	_	indobj	zloupotrebyavam	Vp	s_r	e
dyrzhavnite	dyrzhaven	A	pd	mod	predpriyatie	Nc	dyrzhaven_a	e
predpriyatiya	predpriyatie	Nc	npi	prepcomp	s	R	predpriyatie_n	v

Table 1: The sentence analysis with added head information — HLemma and HPOS.

represented for each word form in the last two columns of Table 1.

All these factors encoded within the corpus provide us with a rich selection of factors for different experiments. Some of them are presented within the next section. The model of encoding MRS information in the corpus as additional features does not depend on the actual semantic analysis — MRS or RMRS, because both of them provide enough semantic information.

6 Experiments

6.1 Experiments with the Bulgarian raw corpus

To run the experiments, we use the phrase-based translation model provided by the open-source statistical machine translation system, Moses[4] (Koehn et al., 2007). For training the translation model, the parallel corpora (mentioned in Section 2) were preprocessed with the tokenizer and lowercase converter provided by Moses. Then the procedure is quite standard:

- We run GIZA++ (Och and Ney, 2003) for bidirectional word alignment, and then obtain the lexical translation table and phrase table.
- A tri-gram language model is estimated using the SRILM toolkit (Stolcke, 2002).
- Minimum error rate training (MERT) (Och, 2003) is applied to tune the weights for the set of feature weights that maximizes the official f-score evaluation metric on the development set.

The rest of the parameters we use the default setting provided by Moses.

We split the corpora into the training set, the development set and the test set. For SETIMES, the split is 100,000/500/1,000 and for EMEA, it is 700,000/500/1,000. For reference, we also run tests on the JRC-Acquis corpus[5]. The final results under the standard evaluation metrics are shown in the following table in terms of BLEU (Papineni et al., 2002):

Corpora	Test	Dev	Final	Drop
SETIMES → SETIMES	34.69	37.82	36.49	/
EMEA → EMEA	51.75	54.77	51.62	/
SETIMES → EMEA	13.37	/	/	61.5%
SETIMES → JRC-Acquis	7.19	/	/	79.3%
EMEA → SETIMES	7.37	/	/	85.8%
EMEA → JRC-Acquis	9.21	/	/	82.2%

Table 2: Results of the baseline SMT system (Bulgarian-English)

As we mentioned before, the EMEA corpus is mainly about the description of medicine usage, and the format is quite fixed. Therefore, it is not surprising to see high performance on the in-domain test (2nd row in Table 2). SETIMES, consisting of news articles, is in a less controlled setting. The BLEU score is lower[6]. The results on the out-of-domain tests are in general much lower with a drop of more than 60% in BLEU score (the last column). For the JRC-Acquis corpus, in contrast to the in-domain scores given by Koehn et al. (2009) (61.3), the low out-of-domain results shows a very similar situation as EMEA. A brief manual check of the results indicate that the out-of-domain tests suffer severely from the missing

[4] `http://www.statmt.org/moses/`

[5] `http://optima.jrc.it/Acquis/`

[6] Actually, the BLEU score itself is higher than for most of the other language pairs `http://matrix.statmt.org/`. As the datasets are different, the results are not directly comparable. Here, we just want to get a rough picture. Achieving better performance for Bulgarian-to-English translation than for other language pairs is not the focus of the paper.

lexicon, while the in-domain test for the news articles contains more interesting issues to look into. The better translation quality also makes the system outputs human readable.

6.2 Experiments with the Linguistically-Augmented Bulgarian Corpus

As we described the factor-based model in Section 4, we also perform experiments to test the effectiveness of different linguistic annotations. The different configurations we considered are shown in the first column of Table 3.

These models can be roughly grouped into five categories: word form with linguistic features; lemma with linguistic features; models with dependency features; MRS elementary predicates (EP) and the type of the main argument of the predicate (EOV); and MRS features without word forms. The setting of the system is mostly the same as the previous experiment, except for 1) increasing the training data from 100,000 to 150,000 sentence pairs; 2) specifying the factors during training and decoding; and 3) without doing MERT[7]. We perform the finer-grained model only on the SETIMES data, as the language is more diverse (compared to the other two corpora). The results are shown in Table 3.

The first model is served as the baseline here. We show all the n-gram scores besides the final BLEU, since the some of the differences are very small. In terms of the numbers, POS seems to be an effective factor, as Model 2 has the highest score. Model 3 indicates that linguistic features also improve the performance. Model 4-6 show the necessity of including the word form as one of the factors, in terms of BLEU scores. Model 10 shows significant decrease after incorporating HLEMMA feature. This may be due to the data sparsity, as we are actually aligning and translating bi-grams instead of tokens. This may also indicate that increasing the number of factors does not guarantee performance enhancement. After replacing the HLEMMA with HPOS, the result is close to the others (Model 8). The experiments with features from the MRS analyses (Model 11-16) show improvements over the baseline consistently and using only the MRS features (Model 17-18) also delivers descent results. In future experiments we will consider to include more feature from the MRS analyses.

So far, incorporating additional linguistic knowledge has not shown huge improvement in terms of statistical evaluation metrics. However, this does not mean that the translations delivered are the same. In order to fully evaluate the system, manual analysis is absolutely necessary. We are still far from drawing a conclusion at this point, but the preliminary scores calculated already indicate that the system can deliver decent translation quality consistently.

6.3 Manual Evaluation

We manually validated the output for all the models mentioned in Table 3. The guideline includes two aspects of the quality of the translation: *Grammaticality* and *Content*. *Grammaticality* can be evaluated solely on the system output and *Content* by comparison with the reference translation. We use a 1-5 score for each aspect as follows:

Grammaticality

1. The translation is not understandable.
2. The evaluator can somehow guess the meaning, but cannot fully understand the whole text.
3. The translation is understandable, but with some efforts.
4. The translation is quite fluent with some minor mistakes or re-ordering of the words.
5. The translation is perfectly readable and grammatical.

Content

1. The translation is totally different from the reference.
2. About 20% of the content is translated, missing the major content/topic.
3. About 50% of the content is translated, with some missing parts.
4. About 80% of the content is translated, missing only minor things.
5. All the content is translated.

For the missing lexicons or not-translated Cyrillic tokens, we ask the evaluators to score 2

[7] This is mainly due to the large amount of computation required. We will perform MERT on the better-performing configurations in the future.

ID	Model	BLEU	1-gram	2-gram	3-gram	4-gram
1	WF	38.61	**69.9**	44.6	31.5	22.7
2	WF, POS	**38.85**	**69.9**	**44.8**	**31.7**	**23.0**
3	WF, LEMMA, POS, LING	38.84	**69.9**	44.7	**31.7**	**23.0**
4	LEMMA	37.22	68.8	43.0	30.1	21.5
5	LEMMA, POS	37.49	68.9	43.2	30.4	21.8
6	LEMMA, POS, LING	38.70	69.7	44.6	31.6	22.8
7	WF, DEPREL	36.87	68.4	42.8	29.9	21.1
8	WF, DEPREL, HPOS	36.21	67.6	42.1	29.3	20.7
9	WF, LEMMA, POS, LING, DEPREL	36.97	68.2	42.9	30.0	21.3
10	WF, LEMMA, POS, LING, DEPREL, HLEMMA	29.57	60.8	34.9	23.0	15.7
11	WF, POS, EP	38.74	69.8	44.6	31.6	22.9
12	WF, POS, LING, EP	38.76	69.8	44.6	**31.7**	22.9
13	WF, EP, EOV	38.74	69.8	44.6	31.6	22.9
14	WF, POS, EP, EOV	38.74	69.8	44.6	31.6	22.9
15	WF, LING, EP, EOV	38.76	69.8	44.6	**31.7**	22.9
16	WF, POS, LING, EP, EOV	38.76	69.8	44.6	**31.7**	22.9
17	EP, EOV	37.22	68.5	42.9	30.2	21.6
18	EP, EOV, LING	38.38	69.3	44.2	31.3	22.7

Table 3: Results of the factor-based model (Bulgarian-English, SETIMES 150,000)

for one Cyrillic token and score 1 for more than one tokens in the output translation.

The results are shown in the following two tables, Table 4 and Table 5, respectively. The current results from the manual validation are on the basis of 150 sentence pairs. The numbers shown in the tables are the number of sentences given the corresponding scores. The 'Total' column sums up the scores of all the output sentences by each model.

The results show that linguistic and semantic analyses definitely improve the quality of the translation. Exploiting the linguistic processing on word level — LEMMA, POS and LING — produces the best result. However, the model with only EP and EOV features also delivers very good results, which indicates the effectiveness of the MRS features from the deep hand-crafted grammars. Including more factors (especially the information from the dependency parsing) drops the results because of the sparseness effect over the dataset, which is consistent with the automatic evaluation BLEU score. The last two rows are shown for reference. 'Google' shows the results of using the online translation service provided by `http://translate.google.com/`. The high score (very close to the reference translation) may be because our test data are not excluded from their training data. In future we plan to do the same evaluation with a larger dataset.

The problem with the untranslated Cyrillic tokens in our view could be solved in most of the cases by providing additional lexical information from a Bulgarian-English lexicon. Thus, we also evaluated the possible impact of such a lexicon if it had been available. In order to do this, we substituted each copied Cyrillic token with its translation when there was only one possible translation. We did such substitutions for 189 sentence pairs. Then we evaluated the result by classifying the translations as acceptable or unacceptable. The number of the acceptable translations are 140 in this case.

The manual evaluation of the translation models on a bigger scale is in progress. The current results are promising. Statistical evaluation metrics can give us a brief overview of the system performance, but the actual translation quality is much more interesting to us, as in many cases, the different surface translations can convey exactly the same meaning in the context.

7 Related Work

Our work is also enlightened by another line of research, transfer-based MT models, which are seemingly different but actually very close. In this section, before we mention some previous work in this research direction, we firstly introduce the background of the development of the deep HPSG grammars.

The MRSes are usually delivered together with the HPSG analyses of the text. There already

ID	Model	1	2	3	4	5	Total
1	WF	20	47	5	32	**46**	487
2	WF, POS	20	48	5	37	40	479
3	WF, LEMMA, POS, LING	20	47	6	34	43	483
4	LEMMA	**15**	34	11	46	44	**520**
5	LEMMA, POS	**15**	38	12	**51**	34	**501**
6	LEMMA, POS, LING	20	48	5	34	43	482
7	WF, DEPREL	32	48	3	29	38	443
8	WF, DEPREL, HPOS	45	41	7	23	34	410
9	WF, LEMMA, POS, LING, DEPREL	34	47	5	30	34	433
10	WF, LEMMA, POS, LING, DEPREL, HLEMMA	101	**32**	0	8	9	242
11	WF, POS, EP	19	49	4	34	44	485
12	WF, POS, LING, EP	19	49	3	39	40	482
13	WF, EP, EOV	20	49	2	41	38	478
14	WF, POS, EP, EOV	19	50	3	31	47	487
15	WF, LING, EP, EOV	19	48	5	37	41	483
16	WF, POS, LING, EP, EOV	19	49	5	37	40	480
17	EP, EOV	**15**	41	10	44	40	**503**
18	EP, EOV, LING	20	49	7	38	36	471
19	GOOGLE	0	2	20	52	76	652
20	REFERENCE	0	0	5	51	94	689

Table 4: Manual evaluation of the grammaticality

exist quite extensive implemented formal HPSG grammars for English (Copestake and Flickinger, 2000), German (Müller and Kasper, 2000), and Japanese (Siegel, 2000; Siegel and Bender, 2002). HPSG is the underlying theory of the international initiative LinGO Grammar Matrix (Bender et al., 2002). At the moment, precise and linguistically motivated grammars, customized on the base of the Grammar Matrix, have been or are being developed for Norwegian, French, Korean, Italian, Modern Greek, Spanish, Portuguese, Chinese, etc. There also exists a first version of the Bulgarian Resource Grammar - BURGER. In the research reported here, we use the linguistic modeled knowledge from the existing English and Bulgarian grammars. Since the Bulgarian grammar has limited coverage on news data, dependency parsing has been performed instead. Then, mapping rules have been defined for the construction of RMRSes.

However, the MRS representation is still quite close to the syntactic level, which is not fully language independent. This requires a *transfer* at the MRS level, if we want to do translation from the source language to the target language. The transfer is usually implemented in the form of rewriting rules. For instance, in the Norwegian LOGON project (Oepen et al., 2004), the transfer rules were hand-written (Bond et al., 2005; Oepen et al., 2007), which included a large amount of manual work. Graham and van Genabith (2008) and Graham et al. (2009) explored the automatic rule induction approach in a transfer-based MT setting involving two lexical functional grammars (LFGs), which was still restricted by the performance of both the parser and the generator. Lack of robustness for target side generation is one of the main issues, when various ill-formed or fragmented structures come out after transfer. Oepen et al. (2007) use their generator to generate text fragments instead of full sentences, in order to increase the robustness. We want to make use of the grammar resources while keeping the robustness, therefore, we experiment with another way of transfer involving information derived from the grammars.

In our approach, we take an SMT system as our 'backbone' which robustly delivers some translation for any given input. Then, we augment SMT with deep linguistic knowledge. In general, what we are doing is still along the lines of previous work utilizing deep grammars, but we build a more 'light-weighted' transfer model.

8 Conclusion and Future Work

In this paper, we report our work on building a linguistically-augmented statistical machine translation model from Bulgarian to English.

ID	Model	1	2	3	4	5	Total
1	WF	20	46	5	23	56	499
2	WF, POS	20	48	5	24	53	492
3	WF, LEMMA, POS, LING	20	47	1	24	58	503
4	LEMMA	15	**32**	5	**33**	**65**	**551**
5	LEMMA, POS	15	35	9	32	59	**535**
6	LEMMA, POS, LING	20	48	5	22	55	494
7	WF, DEPREL	32	49	4	14	51	453
8	WF, DEPREL, HPOS	45	41	2	21	41	422
9	WF, LEMMA, POS, LING, DEPREL	34	48	3	20	45	444
10	WF, LEMMA, POS, LING, DEPREL, HLEMMA	101	**32**	0	6	11	244
11	WF, POS, EP	19	49	3	20	59	501
12	WF, POS, LING, EP	19	50	2	20	59	500
13	WF, EP, EOV	19	50	4	16	61	500
14	WF, POS, EP, EOV	19	50	2	23	56	497
15	WF, LING, EP, EOV	19	48	4	18	61	504
16	WF, POS, LING, EP, EOV	19	50	3	24	54	494
17	EP, EOV	**14**	38	7	31	60	**535**
18	EP, EOV, LING	19	49	7	20	55	493
19	GOOGLE	1	0	9	42	98	686
20	REFERENCE	1	0	5	37	107	699

Table 5: Manual evaluation of the content

Based on our observations of the previous approaches on transfer-based MT models, we decide to build a hybrid system by combining an SMT system with deep linguistic resources. We perform a preliminary evaluation on several configurations of the system (with different linguistic knowledge). The high BLEU score shows the high quality of the translation delivered by the SMT baseline; and manual analysis confirms the consistency of the system.

There are various aspects we can improve the ongoing project: 1) The MRSes are not fully explored yet, since we have only considered the EP and EoV features. 2) We would like to add factors on the target language side (English) as well. 3) The guideline of the manual evaluation needs further refinement for considering the missing lexicons as well as how much of the content is *truly* conveyed (Farreús et al., 2011). 4) We also need more experiments to evaluate the robustness of our approach in terms of out-domain tests.

Acknowledgements

This work was supported by the EuroMatrixPlus project (IST-231720) funded by the European Community under the Seventh Framework Programme for Research and Technological Development. The authors would like to thank Tania Avgustinova for fruitful discussions and her helpful linguistic analysis; and also to Laska Laskova, Stanislava Kancheva and Ivaylo Radev for doing the human evaluation of the data.

References

Srinivas Bangalore and Aravind K. Joshi. 1999. Supertagging: an approach to almost parsing supertagging: an approach to almost parsing supertagging: an approach to almost parsing. *Computational Linguistics*, 25(2), June.

Emily M. Bender, Dan Flickinger, and Stephan Oepen. 2002. The grammar Matrix. An open-source starter-kit for the rapid development of cross-linguistically consistent broad-coverage precision grammar. In *Proceedings of the Workshop on Grammar Engineering and Evaluation at the 19th International Conference on Computational Linguistics*, Taipei, Taiwan.

Alexandra Birch, Miles Osborne, and Philipp Koehn. 2007. Ccg supertags in factored statistical machine translation. In *Proceedings of the Second Workshop on Statistical Machine Translation*, pages 9–16, Prague, Czech Republic, June.

Francis Bond, Stephan Oepen, Melanie Siegel, Ann Copestake, and Dan Flickinger. 2005. Open source machine translation with DELPH-IN. In *Proceedings of the Open-Source Machine Translation Workshop at the 10th Machine Translation Summit*, pages 15 – 22, Phuket, Thailand, September.

Chris Callison-Burch, Philipp Koehn, Christof Monz, and Omar F. Zaidan. 2011. Findings of the 2011 workshop on statistical machine translation. In *Proceedings of the 6th Workshop on SMT*.

Yu Chen, M. Jellinghaus, A. Eisele, Yi Zhang, S. Hunsicker, S. Theison, Ch. Federmann, and H. Uszkoreit. 2009.

Combining multi-engine translations with moses. In *Proceedings of the 4th Workshop on SMT*.

Ann Copestake and Dan Flickinger. 2000. An open source grammar development environment and broad-coverage english grammar using hpsg. In *Proceedings of the 2nd International Conference on Language Resources and Evaluation*, Athens, Greece.

Ann Copestake, Dan Flickinger, Carl Pollard, and Ivan Sag. 2005. Minimal recursion semantics: An introduction. *Research on Language & Computation*, 3(4):281–332.

Ann Copestake. 2003. Robust minimal recursion semantics (working paper).

Ann Copestake. 2007. Applying robust semantics. In *Proceedings of the 10th Conference of the Pacific Assocation for Computational Linguistics (PACLING)*, pages 1–12.

Mireia Farreús, Marta R. Costa-jussà, and Maja Popović Morse. 2011. Study and correlation analysis of linguistic, perceptual and automatic machine translation evaluations. *Journal of the American Society for Information Sciences and Technology*, 63(1):174–184, October.

Georgi Georgiev, Valentin Zhikov, Petya Osenova, Kiril Simov, and Preslav Nakov. 2012. Feature-rich part-of-speech tagging for morphologically complex languages: Application to bulgarian. In *Proceedings of EACL 2012*. MIT Press, Cambridge, MA, USA.

Jess Gimnez and Llus Mrquez. 2004. Svmtool: A general pos tagger generator based on support vector machines. In *Proceedings of the 4th LREC*.

Yvette Graham and Josef van Genabith. 2008. Packed rules for automatic transfer-rule induction. In *Proceedings of the European Association of Machine Translation Conference (EAMT 2008)*, pages 57–65, Hamburg, Germany, September.

Yvette Graham, Anton Bryl, and Josef van Genabith. 2009. F-structure transfer-based statistical machine translation. In *Proceedings of the Lexical Functional Grammar Conference*, pages 317–328, Cambridge, UK. CSLI Publications, Stanford University, USA.

Hany Hassan, Khalil Sima'an, and Andy Way. 2007. Supertagged phrase-based statistical machine translation. In *Proceedings of ACL*, Prague, Czech Republic, June.

Max Jakob, Markéta Lopatková, and Valia Kordoni. 2010. Mapping between dependency structures and compositional semantic representations. In *Proceedings of the 7th International Conference on Language Resources and Evaluation (LREC 2010)*, pages 2491–2497.

Philipp Koehn and Hieu Hoang. 2007. Factored translation models. In *Proceedings of EMNLP*.

Philipp Koehn, Hieu Hoang, Alexandra Birch, Chris Callison-Burch, Marcello Federico, Nicola Bertoldi, Brooke Cowan, Wade Shen, Christine Moran, Richard Zens, Chris Dyer, Ondrej Bojar, Alexandra Constantin, and Evan Herbst. 2007. Moses: Open source toolkit for statistical machine translation. In *Proceedings of ACL (demo session)*.

Philipp Koehn, Alexandra Birch, and Ralf Steinberger. 2009. 462 machine translation systems for europe. In *Proceedings of MT Summit XII*.

Philipp Koehn. 2010. *Statistical Machine Translation*. Cambridge University Press, January.

Stefan Müller and Walter Kasper. 2000. HPSG analysis of German. In Wolfgang Wahlster, editor, *Verbmobil. Foundations of Speech-to-Speech Translation*, pages 238 – 253. Springer, Berlin, Germany, artificial intelligence edition.

Franz Josef Och and Hermann Ney. 2003. A systematic comparison of various statistical alignment models. *Computational Linguistics*, 29(1).

Franz Josef Och. 2003. Minimum error rate training in statistical machine translation. In *Proceedings of ACL*.

Stephan Oepen, Helge Dyvik, Jan Tore Lønning, Erik Velldal, Dorothee Beermann, John Carroll, Dan Flickinger, Lars Hellan, Janne Bondi Johannessen, Paul Meurer, Torbjørn Nordgård, , and Victoria Rosén. 2004. Som å kapp-ete med trollet? towards MRS-based norwegian to english machine translation. In *Proceedings of the 10th International Conference on Theoretical and Methodological Issues in Machine Translation*, Baltimore, MD.

Stephan Oepen, Erik Velldal, Jan Tore Lønning, Paul Meurer, Victoria Rosén, and Dan Flickinger. 2007. Towards hybrid quality-oriented machine translation — on linguistics and probabilities in MT. In *Proceedings of the 11th Conference on Theoretical and Methodological Issues in Machine Translation (TMI-07)*, Skovde, Sweden.

Kishore Papineni, Salim Roukos, Todd Ward, and Wei-Jing Zhu. 2002. Bleu: a method for automatic evaluation of machine translation. In *Proceedings of ACL*.

Melanie Siegel and Emily M. Bender. 2002. Efficient deep processing of japanese. In *Proceedings of the 19th International Conference on Computational Linguistics*, Taipei, Taiwan.

Melanie Siegel. 2000. HPSG analysis of Japanese. In Wolfgang Wahlster, editor, *Verbmobil. Foundations of Speech-to-Speech Translation*, pages 265 – 280. Springer, Berlin, Germany, artificial intelligence edition.

Thoudam Doren Singh and Sivaji Bandyopadhyay. 2010. Manipuri-english bidirectional statistical machine translation systems using morphology and dependency relations. In *Proceedings of the Fourth Workshop on Syntax and Structure in Statistical Translation*, pages 83–91, Beijing, China, August.

Kathrin Spreyer and Anette Frank. 2005. Projecting RMRS from TIGER Dependencies. In *Proceedings of the HPSG 2005 Conference*, pages 354–363, Lisbon, Portugal.

Andreas Stolcke. 2002. Srilm - an extensible language modeling toolkit. In *Proceedings of the International Conference on Spoken Language Processing*, volume 2.

Gregor Thurmair. 2005. Hybrid architectures for machine translation systems. *Language Resources and Evaluation*, 39(1).

Gregor Thurmair. 2009. Comparing different architectures of hybrid machine translation systems. In *Proceedings of MT Summit XII*.

Using Sense-labeled Discourse Connectives for Statistical Machine Translation

Thomas Meyer and **Andrei Popescu-Belis**
Idiap Research Institute
Rue Marconi 19, 1920 Martigny, Switzerland
{thomas.meyer, andrei.popescu-belis}@idiap.ch

Abstract

This article shows how the automatic disambiguation of discourse connectives can improve Statistical Machine Translation (SMT) from English to French. Connectives are firstly disambiguated in terms of the discourse relation they signal between segments. Several classifiers trained using syntactic and semantic features reach state-of-the-art performance, with F1 scores of 0.6 to 0.8 over thirteen ambiguous English connectives. Labeled connectives are then used into SMT systems either by modifying their phrase table, or by training them on labeled corpora. The best modified SMT systems improve the translation of connectives without degrading BLEU scores. A threshold-based SMT system using only high-confidence labels improves BLEU scores by 0.2–0.4 points.

1 Introduction

Current approaches to Statistical Machine Translation (SMT) have difficulties in modeling long-range dependencies between words, including those that are due to discourse-level phenomena. Among these, discourse connectives are words that signal rhetorical relations between clauses or sentences. Their translation often depends on the exact relation signaled in context, a feature that current SMT systems were not designed to capture, hence their frequent mistranslations of connectives (see Section 2 below).

In this paper, we present a series of experiments that aim to use, in SMT systems, data with automatically labeled discourse connectives. Section 3 first presents the data sets used in our experiments. We designed classifiers that attempt to assign sense labels to ambiguous discourse connectives, and their scores compare favorably with the state-of-the-art for this task, as shown in Section 4. In particular, we consider WordNet relations and temporal expressions as well as candidate translations of connectives as additional features (Section 4.2).

However, our main goal is not the disambiguation of connectives *per se*, but the use of the labels assigned to connectives as additional input to an SMT system. To the best of our knowledge, our experiments are the first attempts to combine connective disambiguation and SMT. Three solutions to this combination are compared in Section 5: modifying phrase tables, and training on data labeled manually, or automatically, with senses of connectives. We further show that a modified SMT system is best used when the confidence for a given label is high (Section 6). The paper concludes with a comparison to related work (Section 7) and an outline of future work (Section 8).

2 Discourse Connectives in Translation

Discourse connectives such as *although, however, since* or *while* form a functional category of lexical items that are frequently used to mark coherence or discourse relations such as *explanation*, *synchrony* or *contrast* between units of text or discourse. For example, in the Europarl corpus from years 199x (Koehn, 2005), the following nine lexical items, which are often (though not always) discourse connectives, are among the 400 most frequent tokens over a total of 12,846,003 (in parentheses, rank and number of occurrences): *after* (244th/6485), *although* (375th/4062), *however* (110th/12,857), *indeed* (334th/4486), *rather* (316th/4688),

Proceedings of the 13th Conference of the European Chapter of the Association for Computational Linguistics, pages 129–138, Avignon, France, April 23 - 27 2012.

since (190th/8263), *still* (168th/9195), *while* (390th/3938), *yet* (331st/4532) – see also (Cartoni et al., 2011). Discourse connectives can be difficult to translate, because many of them can signal different relations between clauses in different contexts. Moreover, if a wrong connective is used in translation, then a text becomes incoherent, as in the two examples below, taken from Europarl and translated (EN/FR) with Moses (Koehn et al., 2007) trained on the entire corpus:

1. **EN:** *This tax,* ***though*** [contrast], *does not come without its problems.*

   FR-SMT: **Cette taxe,* ***même si*** [concession], *ne se présente pas sans ses problèmes.*

2. **EN:** *Finally, and in conclusion, Mr President, with the expiry of the ECSC Treaty, the regulations will have to be reviewed* ***since*** [causal] *I think that the aid system will have to continue beyond 2002 ...*

   FR-SMT: **Enfin, et en conclusion, Monsieur le président, à l'expiration du traité CECA, la réglementation devra être revu* ***depuis que*** [temporal] *je pense que le système d'aides devront continuer au-delà de 2002 ...*

In the first example, the connective generated by SMT (*même si*, literally "even if") signals a concession and not a contrast, for which the connective *mais* should have been used (as in the reference). In the second example, the connective *depuis que* (literally "from the time") generated by SMT expresses a temporal relation and not a causal one, which should have been conveyed e.g. by the French *car*.

Such examples suggest that the disambiguation of connectives prior to translation could help SMT systems to generate a correct connective in the target language. Of course, depending on the language pair, some ambiguities can be carried over from the source to the target language, so they need not be solved. Still, improving the overall translation of discourse connectives should increase the overall coherence of MT output, with a potential large impact on perceived quality.

3 Data Used in Our Experiments

For both tasks, the disambiguation of connectives and SMT, different training and testing data sets are available. This section shows how we made use of these resources and how we augmented them by manual and automated annotation of the senses of discourse connectives.

3.1 Data for the Disambiguation of Discourse Connectives

One of the most important resources for discourse connectives in English is the Penn Discourse Treebank (Prasad et al., 2008). The PDTB provides a discourse-layer annotation over the Wall Street Journal Corpus (WSJ) and the Penn Treebank syntactic annotation. The discourse annotation consists of manually annotated senses for about 100 types of explicit connectives, for implicit ones, and their clause spans. For the entire WSJ corpus of about 1,000,000 tokens there are 18,459 instances of annotated explicit connectives. The senses that discourse connectives can signal are organized in a hierarchy with 4 toplevel senses, followed by 16 subtypes on the second level and 23 detailed subsenses on the third level. Studies making use of the PDTB to build classifiers usually split the WSJ corpus into Sections 02–21 for training and Section 23 for testing (as we did for our disambiguation experiments, see Section 4).

From the PDTB, we extracted the 13 most frequent and most ambiguous connectives: *after, although, however, indeed, meanwhile, nevertheless, nonetheless, rather, since, still, then, while*, and *yet*. This set shows in particular that connectives signaling contrastive or temporal senses are the most ambiguous ones, hence they are also potentially difficult to translate, as this ambiguity is often *not* preserved across languages (Danlos and Roze, 2011). We used the senses from the second PDTB hierarchy level (as the third level is too fine-grained for EN/FR translation) and generated the training and testing sets listed with statistics in Table 1 (Section 4).

In principle, classifiers trained on PDTB data can be applied directly to label connectives over the English side of the Europarl corpus (Koehn, 2005) used for training and testing SMT. However, to control the difference in register from newswire texts to formal political speech, and to allow for future studies of other languages, we also performed manual annotation (Cartoni et al., 2011) of five connectives over the Europarl corpus (*although, even though, since, though* and *while*).

The manual annotation was performed on subsets of Europarl v5 (years 199x) for the first few hundred occurrences of each connective. Instead of a potentially difficult and costly annotation of senses, as in the PDTB, we performed translation spotting, asking annotators to highlight the translation of each of the five connectives in the French side of the corpus. From the list of all observed translations one can then cluster the necessary sense labels, as some target language connectives clearly signal only one sense or, in cases where ambiguity is preserved, one can group the equally ambiguous connectives under one composite label. For example, *while* is sometimes translated to the French discourse connectives *tandis que* or *alors que* which both preserve the ambiguity of *while* signaling a temporal or contrastive sense. With this method we built the data sets listed with statistics in Table 2 below (Section 4).

3.2 Data for Statistical Machine Translation

The translation data for our SMT experiments has been often used in other MT research work and is freely distributed for the shared tasks of the Workshop on Machine Translation (WMT)[1].

For training our SMT systems, the EN/FR Europarl corpus v5 was used in three ways to integrate data with labeled discourse connectives into SMT: no changes (for MT phrase table modifications), integration of manually annotated data and integration of automatically labeled data. These methods are described below in Section 5 – here, we gather descriptions of the corresponding data.

a: Modification of the phrase table: Europarl (346,803 sentences), labeling the translation model after training.

b: Integration of manual annotation: Europarl (346,803 sentences), minus all 8,901 sentences containing one of the above 5 connective types, plus 1,147 sentences with manually sense-labeled connectives.

c: Integration of automated annotation: Europarl – years 199x (58,673 sentences), all occurrences of the 13 PDTB subset connective types have been labeled by classifiers (in 6,961 sentences).

For Minimum Error Rate tuning (MERT) (Och, 2003) of the SMT systems, we used the 2009 News Commentary (NC) EN/FR development set with the following modifications:

d: Phrase table: NC 2009 (2,051 sentences), no modifications.

e: Manual annotation: NC 2009 (2,051 sentences), minus all 123 sentences containing one of the above 5 connective types, plus 102 sentences with manually sense-labeled connectives.

f: Automated annotation: NC 2009 (2,051 sentences), all occurrences of the 13 PDTB subset connective types have been labeled by classifiers (in 340 sentences).

For testing our modified SMT systems, three test sets were extracted in the following way:

g: 35 sentences from NC 2007, with 7 occurrences for each of the 5 connective types above, manually labeled.

h: 62 sentences from NC 2007 and 2006 with occurrences for the 13 PDTB connective types, automatically labeled with classifiers.

i: 10,311 sentences from the EN/FR UN corpus, all occurrences of the five Europarl connective types, automatically labeled with classifiers.

These test sets might appear small compared to the amount of data normally used for SMT system testing. In our system evaluation however, apart from automated scoring, we also had to perform manual counts of improved translations, which is why we could not evaluate more than a hundred sentences (Section 5). When counting manually for test set (i), it was downsampled to the same amount of 35 and 62 sentences as for sets (g) and (h), by extracting the first occurrences of each connective.

In all experiments, we use the Moses Phrase-based SMT decoder (Koehn et al., 2007) and a 5-gram language model built over the entire French part of the Europarl corpus v5.

4 Automatically Disambiguating Discourse Connectives

4.1 Classifier PT: Trained on PDTB Data

A first classifier ('PT') for ambiguous discourse connectives and their senses was built by using the PDTB subset of 13 ambiguous connectives as training material. For each connective we built a

[1] `statmt.org/wmt10/translation-task.html`

Connective	Number of occurrences and senses				F1 Scores	
	Training set: total and per sense		Test set: total and per sense		PT	PT+
after	507	456 As, 51 As/Ca	25	22 As, 3 As/Ca	0.66	1.00
although	267	135 Cs, 118 Ct, 14 Cp	16	9 Ct, 7 Cs	0.60	0.66
however	176	121 Ct, 32 Cs, 23 Cp	14	13 Ct, 1 Cs	0.33	1.00
indeed	69	37 Cd, 24 R, 3 Ca, 3 E, 2 I	*2	2 R	*0.50	*0.50
meanwhile	117	66 Cj/S, 16 Cd, 16 S, 14 Ct/S, 5 Ct	10	5 S, 5 Ct/S	0.32	0.53
nevertheless	26	15 Ct, 11 Cs	6	4 Cs, 2 Ct	0.44	0.66
nonetheless	12	7 Cs, 3 Ct, 2 Cp	*1	1 Cs	*1.00	*1.00
rather	10	6 R, 2 Al, 1 Ca, 1 Ct	*1	1 Al	*0.00	*0.00
since	166	75 As, 83 Ca, 8 As/Ca	9	4 As, 3 Ca, 2 As/Ca	0.78	0.78
still	114	56 Cs, 51 Ct, 7 Cp	13	9 Ct, 4 Cs	0.60	0.66
then	145	136 As, 6 Cd, 3 As/Ca	6	5 As, 1 Cd	0.83	1.00
while	631	317 Ct, 140 S, 79 Cs, 41 Ct/S, 36 Cd, 18 Cp	37	19 Ct, 10 S, 4 Cs, 4 Ct/S	0.93	0.96
yet	80	46 Ct, 25 Cs, 9 Cp	*2	2 Ct	*0.5	*1.00
Total	**2,320**	–	**142**	–	**0.57**	**0.75**

Table 1: Performance of MaxEnt connective sense classifiers: *Classifier PT* (initial feature set) and *Classifier PT+* (with candidate translation features) for 13 temporal and contrastive connectives in the PDTB. The sense labels are coded as follows. Al: alternative, As: asynchronous, Ca: cause, Cd: condition, Cj: conjunction, Cp: comparison, Cs: concession, Ct: contrast, E: expansion, I: instantiation, R: restatement, S: synchrony. In some cases marked with '*', the test sets are too small to provide meaningful scores.

specialized classifier, by using the Stanford Maximum Entropy classifier package (Manning and Klein, 2003). Maximum Entropy is known to handle discrete features well and has been applied successfully to connective disambiguation before (see Section 7).

An initial set of features can directly be obtained from the PDTB (and must hence be considered as oracle features): the (capitalized) connective token, its POS tag, first word of clause 1, last word of clause 1, first word of clause 2 (the one containing the explicit connective), last word of clause 2, POS tag of the first word of clause 2, type of first word of clause 2, parent syntactical categories of the connective, punctuation pattern of the sentences. Apart from these standard features in discourse connective disambiguation we used WordNet (Miller, 1995) to compute lexical similarity scores with the `lesk` metric (Banerjee and Pedersen, 2002) for all the possible combinations of nouns, verbs and adjectives in the two clauses, as well as antonyms found for these word groups. In addition, we used features that are likely to help detecting temporal relations and were obtained from the Tarsqi Toolkit (Verhagen and Pustejovsky, 2008), which annotates English sentences automatically with the TimeML annotation language for temporal expressions. For example, in the sentence *The crimes may appear small, but the prices can be huge* (PDTB Section 2, WSJ file 0290), for example, our features would indicate the antonyms *small* vs. *huge* that signal the contrast, along with a temporal ordering of the event *appear* before the event *can*.

We report the classifier performances as F1 scores for each connective (weighting precision and recall equally) in Table 1, testing on Section 23 of the PDTB. This sense classifier will be referred to as *Classifier PT* in the rest of the paper, in particular when used for the SMT experiments.

4.2 Classifier PT+: With Candidate Translations as Features

In an attempt to improve Classifier PT, we added a new type of feature, resulting in *Classifier PT+*. Namely, we used candidate translations of discourse connectives from a baseline SMT system (not adapted to connectives). To find these values, a Moses baseline decoder was used to translate the PDTB data, which was then word-aligned (En-

Connective	Number of occurrences and senses				F1
	Size of training set: total and per sense		Test set: total and per sense		Score
although	173	155 Cs, 18 Ct	10	5 Cs, 5 Ct	0.67
even though	179	165 Cs, 14 Ct	10	5 Cs, 5 Ct	1.00
since	413	274 S, 131 Ca, 8 S/Ca	10	5 Ca, 3 S, 2 S/Ca	0.80
though	150	80 Cs, 70 Ct	10	5 Cs, 5 Ct	1.00
while	280	130 Cs, 41 Ct, 89 S/Ct, 13 S/Ca, 7 S	14	4 Cs, 2 Ct, 2 S/Ct, 2 S/Ca, 4 S	0.64
Total	**1,195**	–	**54**	–	**0.82**

Table 2: Performance of a MaxEnt connective sense classifier (*Classifier EU*) for 5 connectives in the Europarl corpus. The sense labels are coded as follows. Cs: Concession, Ct: Contrast, S: Synchrony, Ca: Cause.

glish source with target French) by using GIZA++ (Och and Ney, 2003). In this alignment, we searched for the translation equivalents of the 13 PDTB connectives by using a hand-crafted dictionary of possible French translations. When the translation candidate is not ambiguous – e.g. *bien que* as a translation for *while* clearly signals a concession – its specific sense label was added as the value of an additional feature. In some cases, however, the values of the features are not determined (and are set to NONE): either when the SMT system or GIZA++ failed in translating or aligning a connective, or when the target connective was just as ambiguous as the source one (e.g. *while* translated as *tandis que*, which can be labeled both *temporal* or *contrast*). Overall, this procedure led to an accuracy gain of Classifier PT+ with respect to Classifier PT of about 0.1 to 0.6 F1 score for some of the connectives, as can be seen in the last column of Table 1.

4.3 Classifier EU: Trained on Europarl Data

As explained in Section 3.1, we performed manual annotation of connective senses in Europarl as well, to provide labeled instances directly in the data used for SMT training and to account for the register change. For the Europarl data sets, we built a new MaxEnt classifier (called *Classifier EU*) using the same feature set as Classifier PT. However, all features were this time extracted automatically (no oracle). In particular, we used Charniak and Johnson's (2005) parser to then extract the syntactic features. In Table 2, we report the results of Classifier EU, again in terms of F1 scores. For all three classifiers, PT, PT+ and EU, the F1 scores are in a range of 0.6 and 0.8, thus comparing favorably to the state-of-the-art for discourse connective disambiguation with detailed senses (Section 7). Classifier EU also compares favorably to PT and PT+, as seen for instance for *since* (0.80 vs. 0.78) or *although* (0.67 vs. 0.60–0.66).

5 Use of Labeled Connectives for SMT

In this section, we report on experiments that study the effect of discourse connective labeling on SMT. The experiments differ with respect to the method used for taking advantage of the labels, but also with respect to the data sets and the sense classifiers that are used.

5.1 Evaluation Metrics for MT

The variation in MT quality can be estimated in several ways. On the one hand, we use the BLEU metric (Papineni et al., 2002) with one reference translation as is most often done in current SMT research[2]. To improve confidence in the BLEU scores, especially when test sets are small, we also compute BLEU scores using bootstrapping of data sets (Zhang and Vogel, 2010); the test sets are re-sampled a thousand times and the average BLEU score is computed from individual sample scores. The BLEU approach is not likely, however, to be sensitive enough to the small differences due to the correction of discourse connectives (less than one word per sentence). We therefore additionally resort to a manual evaluation metric, referred to as $\Delta Connectives$, which counts the occurrences of connectives that are better translated by our modified systems compared to the baseline ones.

[2]The scores are generated by the NIST MTeval script version 11b, available from www.itl.nist.gov/iad/mig/tools/.

MT system	N.	Connectives in MT test data			$\Delta Conn.$ (%)			BLEU scores	
		Occ.	Types	Labeling	+	=	–	Standard	Bootstrap
Modified phrase table	1	35	5	manual	29	51	20	39.92	40.54
	2	10,311	5	Cl. EU	34	46	20	22.13	23.63
Trained on manual annotations	3	35	5	manual	32	57	11	41.58	42.38
	4	10,311	5	Cl. EU	26	66	8	22.43	24.00
Trained on automatic annotations (Cl. PT)	5	62	13	Cl. PT	16	60	24	14.88	15.96
	6	10,311	5	Cl. EU	16	66	18	19.78	21.17
Trained on automatic annotations (Cl. PT+)	7	62	13	Cl. PT+	11	70	19	15.67	16.73
	8	10,311	5	Cl. EU	18	68	14	20.14	21.55

Table 3: MT systems dealing with manually and automatically (PT, PT+, EU) sense-labeled connectives: BLEU scores (including bootstrapped ones) and variation in the translation of individual connectives ($\Delta Connectives$, as a percentage). The description of each condition and the baseline BLEU scores are in the text of the article.

5.2 Phrase Table Modification

A first way of using labeled connectives is to modify the phrase table of an SMT system previously trained/tuned on data sets (a)/(d) from Section 3.2, in order to force it to translate each specific sense of a discourse connective (as indicated by its label) with an acceptable equivalent selected among those learned from the training data. Of course, this only handles cases when connectives are translated by explicit lexical items (typically, target connectives) and not by more complex grammatical constructs.

The phrase table modification is done as follows. Based on a small dictionary of the five connective types of Table 2, their acceptable French equivalents and the possible senses, the initial phrase table is searched for phrases containing a connective and each occurrence is inspected to find out which sense is reflected in the translation. If the sense is non-ambiguous, then the table entry is modified to include the label, and the probability score is set to 1 in order to maximize the chance that the respective translation is found during decoding. For instance, for every phrase table entry where *while* is translated as *alors que*, this corresponds to a contrastive use and *while* is changed into *while*_CONTRAST. Or, for the entries where *while* is translated as *bien que*, the lexical entry is changed into *while*_CONCESSION. However, when the source entry is as ambiguous as the target one, no modification is made. This means that during decoding (testing) with labeled sentences, these entries will never be used.

The results of the SMT system are shown in experiments 1 and 2 in Table 3, respectively testing over data set (g) (7 manually annotated sentences for each of the 5 connectives) and over set (i), in which the 5 connectives were automatically labeled with Classifier EU. In the first test, the translations of 29% of the connectives are improved by the modified system, while 20% are degraded and 51% remain unchanged – thus reflecting an overall 10% improvement in the translations of connectives ($\Delta Connectives$). However, for this test set, the BLEU score is about 3 points below the baseline SMT system that used the same phrase table without modification of labels and scores (not shown in Table 3). In experiment 2, however, the BLEU score of the modified system is in the same range as the baseline one (22.13 vs. 22.76). As for $\Delta Connectives$, as it was not possible to score manually all the 10,311 connectives, we sampled 35 sentences and found that 34% of the connectives are improved, 20% are degraded and 46% remain unchanged, again reflecting an improvement in the translation of connectives. This shows that piping automatic labeling and SMT with a modified phrase table does not degrade the overall BLEU score, while increasing $\Delta Connectives$.

5.3 Training on Tagged Corpora

We explored a more principled way to integrate external labels into SMT, by using labeled data (manually or automatically) for training, so that the system directly learns a modified phrase table which allows the translation of labeled data (automatically) when testing.

5.3.1 Manual Gold Annotation

We report first two experiments using the manual gold annotation for the five connective types over Europarl excerpts, used for training. When used also for testing (experiment 3 in Table 3), this can be seen as an oracle experiment, measuring the translation improvement when connective sense labeling is perfect. However, in experiment 4, the SMT system uses the output of an automatic labeler. For training/tuning we used data sets (b)/(e), Section 3.2.

In experiment 3, for test set (g), 32% of the connectives were translated better by the modified system, 57% remained the same, and 11% were degraded. In experiment 4, over a 35 sentence sample of the bigger test set (i), 26% were improved, 66% remained the same, and only 8% were degraded. The baseline SMT system (not shown in Table 3) was built with the same amounts of unlabeled training and tuning data. Overall, the BLEU scores of our modified systems are similar to the baseline ones, though still lower – 41.58 vs. 42.77 for experiment 3, and 22.43 vs. 22.76 for experiment 4, also confirmed by the bootstrapped scores.

Another comparison shows that the system trained on manual annotations (exp. 4) outperforms the system using a modified phrase table (exp. 2) in terms of BLEU scores (22.43 vs. 22.13) and bootstrapped ones (24.00 vs. 23.63).

5.3.2 Automated Annotation

We evaluated an SMT system trained on data that was automatically labeled using the classifiers in Section 4. This method provides a large amount of imperfect training data, and uses no manual annotations at all, except for the initial training of the classifiers. For these experiments (5 and 6 in Table 3), the BLEU scores as well as the manual counts of improved connectives are lower than in the preceding experiments because, overall, less training/tuning data was used – about 15% of Europarl, data sets (c) and (f) in Section 3.2. The baseline system was built over the same amount of data, with no labels.

Testing here was performed over the slightly bigger test set (h) with 62 sentences (13 connective types). The occurrences were tagged with Classifier PT prior to translation (exp. 5). Compared to the baseline system, the translations of 16% of the connectives were improved, while 60% remained the same and 24% were degraded. In experiment 6, the 10,311 UN occurrences for 5 connective types were first tagged with Classifier EU. Evaluated on a sample of 62 sentences, 16% of the connectives were improved, while 66% remained the same and 18% were degraded. Despite less training data, in terms of BLEU, the difference to the respective baseline system (scores not shown in Table 3) is similar in both experimental settings: 19.78 vs. 20.11 for experiment 6 (automated annotation), compared to 22.43 vs. 22.76 for experiment 4 (manual annotation).

Finally, we carried out two experiments (7 and 8) with Classifier PT+, which uses as additional features the translation candidates and has a higher accuracy than PT (Section 4.2). As a result, the translation of connectives ($\Delta Connectives$) is indeed improved compared (respectively) to experiments 5 and 6, as it appears from lines 7–8 of Table 3. Also, the BLEU scores of the corresponding SMT systems are increased in experiments 7 vs. 5 and in 8 vs. 6, and are now equal to the baseline ones (for experiment 8: 20.14 vs. 20.11, or, bootstrapped, 21.55 vs. 21.55).

The results of experiments 7/8 vs. 5/6 indicate that improved classifiers for connectives also improve SMT output as measured by $\Delta Connectives$, with BLEU remaining fairly constant, and therefore are worth investigating in more depth in the future. When comparing manual (experiments 3/4) vs. automated annotation (experiments 5/6/7/8) and their use in SMT, the differences in the scores (BLEU and $\Delta Connectives$) highlight a trade-off: manually annotated data used for training leads to better scores, but noisier and larger training data that is annotated automatically is an acceptable solution when manual annotations are not available.

6 Classifier Confidence Scores

As shown with the above experiments, the accuracy of the connective classifiers influences SMT quality. We therefore hypothesize that an SMT system dealing with labeled connectives would best be used when the confidence of the classifier is high, while a generic SMT system could be used for lower confidence values.

We experimented with the confidence scores of Classifier EU, which assigns a score between 0 and 1 to each of its decisions on the connectives' labels. (All processing is automatic in these ex-

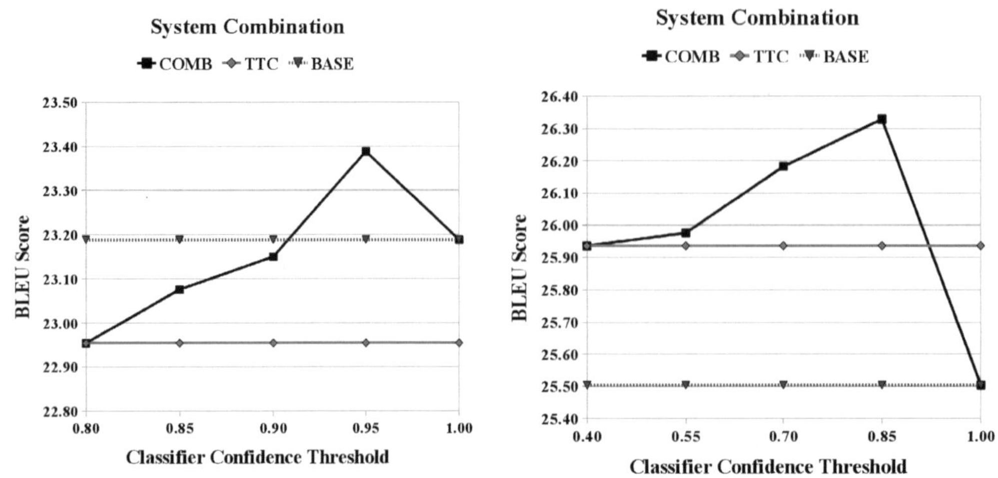

(a) *although* (b) *since*

Figure 1: Use of a combined system (COMB) that directs the input sentences either to a system trained on a sense-labeled corpus (TTC) or to a baseline one (BASE), depending on the confidence of the connective classifier. The x-axis shows the threshold above which TTC is used – BASE being used below it – and the y-axis shows the BLEU scores of COMB with respect to TTC and BASE. Figure (a) is for *although* and (b) for *since*.

periments, and the evaluation is done solely in terms of BLEU). We defined a threshold-based procedure to combine SMT systems: if the confidence for a sense label is above a certain threshold, then the sentence is translated by an SMT system trained on labeled data from experiment 4 (or "tagged corpus", hence noted TTC), and if it is below the threshold, it is sent to a baseline system (noted BASE). The resulting BLEU scores of the combined system (COMB) obtained for various threshold values are shown in Figure 1 for two connectives.

Firstly, we considered all the 1,572 sentences from the UN corpus which contained the connective *although*, labeled either as contrast or concession. We show BLEU scores of the COMB system for several thresholds in the interval of observed confidence scores, along with the scores of BASE and TTC, in Figure 1(a). The results show that the scores of COMB increase with the value of the threshold, and that for at least one value of the threshold (0.95) COMB outperforms both TTC and BASE by 0.20 BLEU points.

To confirm this finding with another connective, we took the first 1,572 sentences containing the connective *since* from the UN corpus. The BLEU scores for COMB are shown for the range of observed confidence values (0.4–1.0) in Figure 1(b). For several values of the threshold, COMB outperforms both BASE and TTC, in particular for 0.85, with a difference of 0.39 BLEU points.

The significance of the observed improvement was tested as follows. For each of the two connectives, we split the test sets of 1,572 sentences each in five folds, and compared for each fold the scores of COMB for the best performing threshold (0.95 or 0.85) with the highest of BASE or TTC (i.e. BASE for *although* and TTC for *since*). We performed a paired t-test to compute the significance of the difference, and found $p = 0.12$ for *although*. This value, although slightly above the conventional boundary of 0.1, shows that the five pairs of scores reflect a significant difference in quality. Similarly, when performing a t-test for *since*, the difference in scores is found significant at the 0.01 level ($p = 0.005$). Of course, COMB is always significantly better than the lower of BASE or TTC ($p < 0.05$). In the future, the system combination will be tested for all connectives, and the respective values of the thresholds will be set on tuning, not on test data.

7 Related Work

Discourse parsing (Marcu, 2000) has proven to be a difficult task, even when complex models (CRFs, SVMs) are used (Wellner, 2009; Hernault et al., 2010). The performance of discourse parsers is in a range of 0.4 to 0.6 F1 score.

With the release of the PDTB, recent research focused on the disambiguation of discourse connectives as a task in its own right. For the disambiguation of explicit connectives, the state-of-the-art performance for labeling all types of connectives in English is quite high. In the PDTB data, the disambiguation of discourse vs. non-discourse uses of connectives reaches 97% accuracy (Lin et al., 2010). The labeling of the four main senses from the PDTB sense hierarchy (temporal, contingency, comparison, expansion) reaches 94% accuracy (Pitler and Nenkova, 2009) – however, the baseline accuracy is already around 85% when using only the connective token as a feature. Various methods for classification and feature analysis have been proposed (Wellner et al., 2006; Elwell and Baldridge, 2008). Other studies have focused on the analysis of highly ambiguous discourse connectives only. Miltsakaki et al. (2005) report classification results for the connectives *since*, *while* and *when*. Using a Maximum Entropy classifier, they reach 75.5% accuracy for *since*, 71.8% for *while* and 61.6% for *when*. As the PDTB was not completed at that time, the data sets and labels are not exactly identical to the ones that we used above (see Section 4).

The disambiguation of senses signaled by discourse connectives can be seen as a word sense disambiguation (WSD) problem for functional words (as opposed to WSD for content words, which is more frequently studied). The integration of WSD into SMT has especially been studied by Carpuat and Wu (2007), who used the translation candidates output by a baseline SMT system as word sense labels. This is similar to our use of translation candidates as an additional feature for classification in Section 4.2. Then, the output of several classifiers based on linguistic features was weighed against the translation candidates output by the baseline SMT system. With this procedure, their WSD+SMT system improved the BLEU scores by 0.4–0.5 for the English/Chinese pair.

Chang et al. (2009) use a LogLinear classifier with linguistic features in order to disambiguate the Chinese particle 'DE' that has five different context-dependent uses (modifier, preposition, relative clause etc.). When the classifier is used to annotate the particle prior to SMT, the output of the translation system improves by up to 1.49 BLEU score for phrase-based Chinese to English translation. Ma et al. (2011) use a Maximum Entropy model to POS tag English collocational particles (e.g. come *down/by*, turn *against*, inform *of*) more specifically than a usual POS tagger does (where only one label is given to all particles). The authors claim the usefulness of such a particle tagger for English/Chinese translation, but do not show its actual integration into an MT system.

These approaches, as well as ours, show that integrating discourse information into SMT is promising and deserves future examination. The disambiguation of word senses, including function words, can improve SMT output when the senses are annotated in a pre-processing step that uses classifiers based on linguistic features at the semantic and discourse levels, which are not available to a state-of-the-art SMT systems.

8 Conclusion and Future Work

This paper has presented methods and results for the disambiguation of temporal and contrastive discourse connectives using MaxEnt classifiers with syntactic and semantic features, in English texts, in terms of senses intended to help SMT. These classifiers have been used to perform experiments with connective-annotated data applied to EN/FR SMT systems. The results have shown an improvement in the translation of connectives for fully automatic systems trained on either hand-labeled or automatically-labeled data. Moreover, BLEU scores were significantly improved by 0.2–0.4 when such systems were only used for connectives that had been disambiguated with high confidence.

In future work we plan to improve the sense classifiers using additional features, to improve their integration with SMT, and to unify our data sets through additional manual annotations over Europarl. The applicability of the method to other languages will also be demonstrated experimentally.

Acknowledgments

We are grateful for the funding of this work to the Swiss National Science Foundation (SNSF), under the COMTIS Sinergia Project n. CRSI22_127510 (see www.idiap.ch/comtis/).

References

Satanjeev Banerjee and Ted Pedersen. 2002. An Adapted Lesk Algorithm for Word Sense Disambiguation Using WordNet. In Alexander Gelbukh, editor, *Computational Linguistics and Intelligent Text Processing*, LNCS 2276, pages 117–171. Springer, Berlin/Heidelberg.

Marine Carpuat and Dekai Wu. 2007. Improving Statistical Machine Translation using Word Sense Disambiguation. *Proc. of EMNLP-CoNLL*, pages 61–72, Prague.

Bruno Cartoni, Sandrine Zufferey, Thomas Meyer, and Andrei Popescu-Belis. 2011. How Comparable are Parallel Corpora? Measuring the Distribution of General Vocabulary and Connectives. *Proc. of the 4th Workshop on Building and Using Comparable Corpora (BUCC)*, pages 78–86, Portland, OR.

Pi-Chuan Chang, Dan Jurafsky, and Christopher D. Manning. 2009. Disambiguating 'DE' for Chinese-English Machine Translation. *Proc. of the Fourth Workshop on Statistical Machine Translation at EACL-2009*, Athens.

Eugene Charniak and Mark Johnson. 2005. Coarse-to-fine n-best Parsing and MaxEnt Discriminative Reranking. *Proc. of the 43rd Annual Meeting of the ACL*, pages 173–180, Ann Arbor, MI.

Laurence Danlos and Charlotte Roze. 2011. Traduction (Automatique) des Connecteurs de Discours. *Actes 18e Conférence sur le Traitement Automatique des Langues Naturelles (TALN)*, Montpellier.

Robert Elwell and Jason Baldridge. 2008. Discourse Connective Argument Identification with Connective Specific Rankers. *Proc. of the 2nd IEEE International Conference on Semantic Computing (ICSC)*, pages 198–205, Santa Clara, CA.

Hugo Hernault, Helmut Prendinger, David A. duVerle, and Mitsuru Ishizuka. 2010. HILDA: A Discourse Parser using Support Vector Machine classification. *Dialogue and Discourse*, 3(1):1–33.

Philipp Koehn, et al. 2007. Moses: Open Source Toolkit for Statistical Machine Translation. *Proc. of 45th Annual Meeting of the ACL, Demonstration Session*, pages 177–180, Prague.

Philipp Koehn. 2005. Europarl: A Parallel Corpus for Statistical Machine Translation. *Proc. of MT Summit X*, pages 79–86, Phuket.

Ziheng Lin, Hwee Tou Ng, and Min-Yen Kan. 2010. A PDTB-styled End-to-end Discourse Parser. Technical Report TRB8/10, School of Computing, National University of Singapore.

Jianjun Ma, Degen Huang, Haixia Liu, and Wenfeng Sheng. 2011. POS Tagging of English Particles for Machine Translation. *Proc. of MT Summit XIII*, pages 57–63, Xiamen.

Christopher Manning and Dan Klein. 2003. Optimization, MaxEnt Models, and Conditional Estimation without Magic. *Tutorial at HLT-NAACL and 41st ACL conferences*, Edmonton, AB and Sapporo.

Daniel Marcu. 2000. *The Theory and Practice of Discourse Parsing and Summarization*. A Bradford Book. The MIT Press, Cambridge, MA.

George A. Miller. 1995. WordNet: A Lexical Database for English. *Communications of the ACM*, 38(11):39–41.

Eleni Miltsakaki, Nikhil Dinesh, Rashmi Prasad, Aravind Joshi, and Bonnie Webber. 2005. Experiments on Sense Annotations and Sense Disambiguation of Discourse Connectives. *Proc. of the 4th Workshop on Treebanks and Linguistic Theories (TLT)*, Barcelona.

Franz Josef Och and Hermann Ney. 2003. A Systematic Comparison of Various Statistical Alignment Models. *Computational Linguistics*, 29(1):19–51.

Franz Josef Och. 2003. Minimum Error Rate Training in Statistical Machine Translation. *Proc. of the 41st Annual Meeting of the ACL*, pages 160–167, Sapporo.

Kishore Papineni, Salim Roukos, Todd Ward, and Wei-Jing Zhu. 2002. BLEU: A method for Automatic Evaluation of Machine Translation. *Proc. of 40th Annual Meeting of the ACL*, pages 311–318, Philadelphia, PA.

Emily Pitler and Ani Nenkova. 2009. Using Syntax to Disambiguate Explicit Discourse Connectives in Text. *Proc. of the 47th Annual Meeting of the ACL and the 4th International Joint Conference of the AFNLP (ACL-IJCNLP), Short Papers*, pages 13–16, Singapore.

Rashmi Prasad, Nikhil Dinesh, Alan Lee, Eleni Miltsakaki, Livio Robaldo, Aravind Joshi, and Bonnie Webber. 2008. The Penn Discourse Treebank 2.0. *Proc. of the 6th International Conference on Language Resources and Evaluation (LREC)*, pages 2961–2968, Marrakech.

Marc Verhagen and James Pustejovsky. 2008. Temporal Processing with the TARSQI Toolkit. *Proc. of the 22nd International Conference on Computational Linguistics (COLING), Demonstrations*, pages 189–192, Manchester, UK.

Ben Wellner, James Pustejovsky, Catherine Havasi, Roser Sauri, and Anna Rumshisky. 2006. Classification of Discourse Coherence Relations: An Exploratory Study using Multiple Knowledge Sources. *Proc. of the 7th SIGdial Meeting on Discourse and Dialog*, pages 117–125, Sydney.

Ben Wellner. 2009. *Sequence Models and Ranking Methods for Discourse Parsing*. PhD thesis, Brandeis University, Waltham, MA.

Ying Zhang and Stefan Vogel. 2010. Significance Tests of Automatic Machine Translation Evaluation Metrics. *Machine Translation*, 24(1):51–65.

Author Index

Association for Computational Linguistics
209 N. Eighth Street
Stroudsburg, Pennsylvania 18360

CURRAN ASSOCIATES INC
proceedings
.com

7th Workshop on Language Technology for Cultural Heritage, Social Sciences, and Humanities

(LaTeCH 2013)

Sofia, Bulgaria
8 August 2013

ISBN: 978-1-62748-998-0